INTEREST AND IDEOLOGY

Interest
and
Ideology

The Foreign Policy Beliefs of American Businessmen

Bruce M. Russett / Elizabeth C. Hanson

YALE UNIVERSITY

W. H. Freeman and Company
San Francisco

Library of Congress Cataloging in Publication Data

Russett, Bruce M.
  Interest and ideology.

  Includes bibliographical references and index.
  1. United States—Foreign relations—1945–   2. United States—Foreign economic relations. 3. Businessmen—United States—Attitudes.
I. Hanson, Elizabeth C., joint author.
II. Title.
JX1417.R88   327.73   75-20030
ISBN 0-7167-0727-6
ISBN 0-7167-0726-8 pbk.

4548639

Printed in the United States of America

10 9 8 7 6 5 4 3 2 1

*To the millions who have died
because someone had a theory*

CONTENTS

PREFACE

In this book we have tried to bring some systematic evidence to bear on a set of questions we believe to have been inadequately investigated in previous research. Moreover, the questions—which concern the roots of foreign policy, and especially the relative importance of ideological and economic influences—seemed sufficiently important both on theoretical and on policy grounds to justify a major research effort. These are extremely difficult questions that have perplexed foreign policy analysts for many years. We do not feel that we have answered all of them definitively, but we do believe that we are closer to obtaining satisfactory answers than when we began. The degree to which we have been successful can be taken as justification of our conviction that modern empirical social science can say something useful if the effort is made, and if it is pursued in a multimethod way. Our effort, incorporating as it does the attempt to state propositions in an empirically testable manner and to devise new ways of bringing evidence to bear, is meant to provide a building block for further scientific work. If it is largely a success, it will lead to the posing of new questions for examination. If it is largely a failure, we hope that we have stated our propositions and described our testing procedures precisely enough to allow others to correct our errors and do a better job. Presumably that is what scientific cumulation is about. The questions are too important to leave in the realm of unsubstantiated theory, and too important to be answered solely by the true believers.

The job was difficult because we were attempting to test a variety of propositions, some of which we regarded as highly plausible and others we regarded as empirically dubious. In one sense, it is often advantageous if a scientist believes passionately in the truth of the theory he is testing. The greater his conviction, the harder he will work to devise ways to demonstrate his theory's correctness, and the more ingenious he will be in devising new ways to find and analyze evidence. Of course, there is a risk that the scientist as true believer will neglect to phrase his propositions in a form that can in principle be refuted, or will ignore evidence that would refute them. To prevent either abuse science establishes the rules for intersubjective verification and demands a series of replications. That too is what scientific cumulation is about.

By some ideals, the scientist should be completely dispassionate, caring nothing for the support or disproof of a particular theory, and seeking only the truth—wherever it leads him. But as we have said, such a dispassionate scientist may easily lack the drive and determination that would lead him to solid results of any sort whatever. Anyway, few social scientists really are so dispassionate. We have lost any former innocence about being "value-free," and recognize that we care, often deeply, about the phenomena we study. We do prefer some theories to others, and we prefer some policy outcomes to others. Other types of scientists—those studying the causes of cancer and heart disease, or seeking to alleviate world hunger—obviously share this kind of passion. Although the rules of scientific procedure provide some very substantial precautions against being misled by an excess of zeal, the scientist himself must be ever-watchful if he is to preserve his intellectual honesty.

In writing this book we certainly have been moved by our own values and preferences. We are not pleased with much of American foreign policy in recent years, least of all the death and injustice that has resulted. Made by fallible human beings, no foreign policy can be perfect, but in our eyes that of the United States has fallen so far short of perfection as to demand a very searching effort to understand what went wrong, why, and how the foreign policy can be improved. Yet we have been unconvinced by any of the various theories that have been offered to explain what went wrong and why. Or rather, to be more precise, we found elements of plausibility and implausibility in all of them, but lacked satisfactory evidence to make a firm choice. Hence this book.

One major difficulty we faced stemmed from the highly controversial nature of theories about the importance of economic interest in determining foreign policy. Such theories, whether concerned with the military-industrial complex, neoimperialism, or other aspects, deserve careful evaluation. We think, in fact, that they deserve more careful scientific evaluation than they have received either from their proponents or from those who would reject them. This is especially true for those varieties derived more or less explicitly from Marxist analyses. Although we found these theories intriguing and overdue for serious attention, we did not become Marxists. Some parts of the theories seemed logical to us, but we were not ready, without much more evidence, to accept the whole system. Could we, given this bias, adequately state economic-determinist, and especially neo-Marxist, theories, in a way that would provide a fair test?

Aristotle advised that an investigator should "lean against" the bias that he knows himself to have, in order to try to be objective. We have tried to do that. But it is easier to do so in evaluating the evidence than it is in stating the hypotheses properly in the first place. In that we were not always helped much by the state of previous literature. Marxists and anti-Marxists alike often fail— as do we all—to state their propositions in a form that can in principle be refuted. As we restated them we must surely have distorted some of them. But though we are non-Marxists, neither are we anti-Marxists, and we hope that we have avoided the worst distortions of the extremes. The judgment finally should be that of other social scientists, whatever theoretical perspective inspires them. Later researchers can restate our hypotheses, and then can subject them—in the original or in revised form—to new tests of the new researchers' devising. Others can correct our errors and move on to further examinations of the topic.*

We have accumulated more than the usual number of debts in the course of this project. Some are to colleagues like Richard Brody, Raymond Duvall, Robert Harlow, and H. Bradford Wester-field who read parts of the manuscript or helped in formulating the research design. Jong Ryool Lee provided invaluable assistance with the computations, and Robert Mandel helped in developing the coding scheme for the content analysis. Mary Carrano did all the things she usually does in coordinating our editorial and re-search activities—in other words, she was indispensable.

Both of us come from dual-career households, and are pain-fully aware of the sacrifices borne by our spouses, Cynthia and Kenneth, so that our careers might be pursued.

Allen Barton and Charles Kadushin of Columbia University made available to us their data on the policy preferences of Amer-ican elites and gave us some valuable advice on procedures and

---

*For those who wish to reanalyze our own data, to confirm or refute our conclusions, all the data are available in machine-readable form from the Inter-University Consortium for Political Research, Ann Arbor, Michigan 48106.

the pitfalls we might encounter in our own data gathering. Similarly, a group at *Fortune* magazine gave us the benefit of their expertise in this kind of survey research. The Richardson Institute for Peace and Conflict Research in London provided the senior author with a congenial year-long escape from his responsibilities in New Haven, making it possible for this book to be written. But the special secret heroes of this book are the more than 1,200 business executives and senior military officers who responded to our survey and interview requests. They gave us, without return, time out of their busy lives; without their generosity there could have been no book.

Empirical research is expensive, requiring funds far beyond the resources of any mere scholar who is not independently wealthy, as we are not. As researchers frequently must do, we accumulated the necessary resources to conduct this study from a number of different sources. The analysis of the stock market responses to international events, and the data gathering phase and some of the analysis of the businessmen's survey, were financed with the funds that remained from a long-term contract held by the senior author for basic quantitative research on international relations, Contract N0014-67-A-0097-0007 with the Advanced Research Projects Agency, Behavioral Sciences, monitored by the Office of Naval Research. Data gathering in the military officers' survey was made possible by a small grant from the Political Science Department of Yale University. The Concilium on International Relations at Yale also provided a grant for travel and for some data analysis. Most of the remaining analysis, and the writing, was supported by a contract from the Advanced Research Program of the Naval War College.

We can almost see the reader's eyebrows rising. We accepted money from agencies of the Department of Defense to do this work, in a controversial and politically sensitive area of foreign policy inquiry. It is customary—and necessary—to note that no person or agency is responsible for what we have written; that responsibility is ours alone. It is also appropriate to say that we are not responsible for other actions of persons or agencies that supported the research, nor do we necessarily approve of those actions. Nevertheless, the reader may still ask, did those who paid the piper call the tune?

We feel satisfied about our answer to that question. From the beginning we realized this would be an expensive and difficult project, and that we might have to try rather hard to find adequate support. But from the beginning, it was a project of our own devising. We identified the questions, built the research design—and then sought financial support. We did not answer anyone's prespecified "request for proposal." At no point whatever did those in the Defense Department who ultimately supported us require any modifications in the research design, and at no stage did they provide any supervision of our operations beyond normal accounting oversight to be sure we did not abscond with the funds. We could not have hoped for more freedom in conducting our research. In fact, we were less hampered by external conditions and supervision than the typical research group funded by other federal research-supporting agencies or private foundations. It was notable too that two foundations turned down our requests before we went to the Navy Department. Perhaps they felt that they would have to compromise themselves were they to support a project that might be politically sensitive. One foundation demanded a much more detailed research design, with an explanation of hypotheses, tests, and so on, than we were able to provide at that initial stage. The naval agency, on the other hand, was prepared to trust us, as scientists, to refine our project properly as it got under way. We think that kind of confidence in a scientist's skill and integrity is to be much appreciated.

In the end, readers will have to decide for themselves whether we trimmed our sails to the naval wind. Our data are available to all, and our procedures are specified as clearly as we could do so. Nothing is secret, and we will sink or swim with scientific replication. Meanwhile, *honi soit qui mal y pense.*

We wish to acknowledge one other debt. The research of this book, especially the survey and interviewing of senior corporate executives and military officers, could have been done only in an open political system. Neither the acquisition nor the dissemination of our findings could have occured without this openness. Often social science researchers take for granted the openness of milieu that is required for their work. For the chance to do social research in a democratic country we are indebted to the lives and deaths of many generations of men and women, prominent and forgotten, in many lands. On their shoulders the modern social scientist stands, or sometimes sits complacently.

Chapters 1–4 and 8 were written by Bruce Russett, and Chapters 6 and 7 were written principally by Elizabeth Hanson; the two authors contributed equally to Chapter 5. Each author, of course, worked over the chapters written initially by the other. Elizabeth

Hanson also gathered the data for Chapter 5 and made a major contribution to the gathering of data for Chapters 3 and 4. The research design evolved from extensive discussions between the authors, and regardless of which of us did the initial draft of a passage, we both accept full responsibility for the result.

An earlier version of Chapter 1 appeared as Bruce M. Russett, "Elite Perspectives and Theories of World Politics," in Geoffrey Goodwin and Andrew Linklater, eds., *New Dimensions in World Politics* (London: Croom Helm Ltd., 1975); and a version of Chapter 5 appeared as Betty C. Hanson and Bruce M. Russett, "Testing Some Economic Interpretations of American Intervention: Korea, Indochina, and the Stock Market," in Steven Rosen, ed., *Testing the Theory of the Military-Industrial Complex* (Lexington, Mass.: D. C. Heath, 1973). Both articles, however, have been extensively revised and expanded here.

B. M. R.
E. C. H.

New Haven, Connecticut
April 1975

INTEREST AND IDEOLOGY

CHAPTER ONE

Business Elites
and
World Politics

*What brought about this extraordinary
occurrence? What were its causes? . . .
The deeper we delve in search of these
causes the more of them do we discover;
and each separate cause or whole series of
causes appears to us equally valid in itself
and equally unsound by its insignificance
in comparison with the size of the event,
and by its powerlessness (without the cooperation of all the other coincident
causes) to occasion the event.*

Leo Tolstoy, War and Peace

Why Perceptions Matter

"International politics" have changed greatly in recent years. But
precisely how? Faced with the evidence of change in many spheres,
we can easily ignore continuing aspects of stability, or fail to take
appropriate measure of the depth and consequences of change.
Consider, for example, three distinct elements of interest: the basic
structure of international power relationships; the *behavior* of national governments toward one another and toward various non-
national groups within or transcending nation-states; and the
perceptions of politically influential figures about the structure and
behavior of world politics. Changes in each of these elements need
not be of the same degree nor have the same timing.

The policy orientation and behavior of the major national governments have changed fairly dramatically over the past two decades. Limited détente between the United States and the Soviet Union, and between the United States and China; a general relaxation of the cold war and avoidance of overt military threats between East and West; modest achievements in arms control; the intensified, protracted hostility between the Soviet Union and China, formerly closely allied; the increasingly independent behavior of the major European states: all these changes are well recognized. Indeed, most people's perceptions of world politics have changed even more drastically. Consider the widespread expectations of continuing and deepened détente and peaceful coexistence; the nearly complete erosion of fears of a communist invasion of Western Europe; the genesis and broad acceptance of more or less revisionist histories about the origins of the cold war; the recognition of new power centers in China, Japan, and Western Europe; the acknowledgment of the decay of American military supremacy; the American turning away from the so-called responsibilities of world power to a posture typified by a limited degree of political "isolationism," coupled with a general belief in the economic and physical interdependence of the globe, which demands concerted action to preserve the earth from the consequences of pollution, resource depletion, and overpopulation—these problems were hardly considered in the early 1960s. In short, the perceptions of most persons concerned with world politics have changed at a faster rate, and at more-nearly discontinuous jumps, than has the behavior of governments. With those changes in perceptions have come equally significant changes in preferences.

Equally important as these changes, however, is their contrast to the much more modest changes that occurred—especially through 1970—in international power relationships, the underlying structure of much of international politics. For example, the figures in Table 1.1 show relationships among the major states at two different times: 1955, at the height of the cold war, and 1970, when détente and the American retreat from certain overseas political involvements were well under way. The figures in the two left-hand columns represent energy consumption, in 10,000 metric tons of coal or coal equivalent and in percentages of the seven-country total. Such figures give us a rough but not seriously inaccurate picture of relative national productive capacity—of the range of resources that can be turned to peaceful uses or, in the middle term, in large part diverted to military purposes. (In current times, of

Table 1.1 *National Power Bases, 1955-1970*

	Energy Consumption			Military Expenditures	
Country	10,000 metric tons of coal or equivalent	% of 7-country total	Country	Millions of U.S. dollars	% of 7-country total
			1955		
United States	1,314	53.0	United States	35,791	48.7
Soviet Union	439	17.7	Soviet Union	26,399	36.0
United Kingdom	254	10.2	United Kingdom	4,393	5.9
West Germany	175	7.1	France	3,310	4.5
France	114	4.6	China	3,119	4.2
China	97	3.9	Japan	414	.6
Japan	88	3.5	West Germany	0	0
			1970		
United States	2,859	49.9	United States	77,827	52.1
Soviet Union	1,183	20.6	Soviet Union	42,619	28.5
China	409	7.1	China	8,500	5.7
Japan	400	7.0	West Germany	6,188	4.1
West Germany	336	5.9	France	6,014	4.0
United Kingdom	318	5.5	United Kingdom	5,850	3.9
France	229	4.0	Japan	2,506	1.7

SOURCES: J. David Singer, et al., *The Strength of Nations* (forthcoming); except for 1970 data on military expenditures, which are from Stockholm International Peace Research Institute, *Yearbook of World Armaments and Disarmament, 1973* (New York: Humanities Press, 1973), pp. 235, 243.

course, energy consumption paradoxically implies vulnerability as well as strength.) The figures in the two right-hand columns are military expenditures, expressed in millions of dollars and percentages of the seven-country total. There are problems in obtaining accurate estimates and in converting currency, but these figures are accepted among strategic and economic analysts as reasonably accurate. They indicate a short-term or immediate power potential, at least in those circumstances where military capabilities are an appropriate instrument for exerting national influence.

What is striking, we think, is how little the relationships among nations' power bases changed during the fifteen-year period. In energy, our measure of basic productive capacity, the United

States slipped, but only slightly, in relation to the Soviet Union, and China and Japan moved up in the rankings at the expense of the United Kingdom and West Germany. But the relative predominance of the United States and the Soviet Union over the smaller economies remained as strong as ever; in fact, the gap between the second and third places actually widened. The data on military expenditures, used for immediate military power, show roughly the same picture. China and West Germany came up, and the United Kingdom especially dropped, but the predominance of the big two over the lesser powers was not affected. Even modifying the American figures by deleting expenses for the Vietnam war in 1970 would reduce the United States percentage by only about 4 percent and increase the Soviet percentage by roughly the same amount. Both countries would remain roughly where they were in 1955, more than six and eight times the third-ranked power, respectively. Despite China's accession to the ranks of thermonuclear powers, a big gap remains.

There are real limits to the purposes for which military or economic power bases are relevant. They do not take into account all the new restraints on the exercise of military power by nation-states, or the growth of such transnational organizations as multinational corporations, or the rise of guerilla groups, for which the traditional power capabilities of nations have little meaning. Even the power relations should be modified for the waxing and waning of alliance links, such as European integration or the Sino-Soviet split. The meaning of the figures is nonetheless indisputable: the structure of international power relationships did *not* change greatly during the cold war period. Our perceptions have changed greatly, and often appropriately so. But they deceive us if they lead us to imagine a change in power relationships that did not really occur.[1]

Most emphatically, this is not to say that because power relationships did not change substantially we should return to the perceptions and attitudes of the cold war era. If our perceptions are currently out of step with reality in any noteworthy degree, they probably were equally so early in the cold war. Then the bipolar structure of world politics, and especially the magnitude of the "Soviet threat," were almost surely exaggerated, and it would

---

[1]See Chapter 2, "A Macroscopic View of International Politics," in Bruce M. Russett, *Power and Community in World Politics* (San Francisco: W. H. Freeman, 1974), for a more general argument about the long-term stabilities in the structure of world politics.

not help to reincarnate previous error. Furthermore, the major powers have exhibited important behavior changes, affecting a variety of policies, that have profoundly modified the *effect* of the power relationships. Behavior has changed notably, probably less than have perceptions but more than power relationships. How is it, then, that what we formerly perceived as an appropriate set of policies neither is nor is perceived to be appropriate any longer? Why did policy and especially perceptions change so much? Can we identify different individuals' current perceptions, and produce better evidence concerning the details, timing, and causation of changes? Certainly the feedback effect of changed perceptions on policy will be great. After all, "objective" conditions in the "real world" must always be filtered through our perceptual lenses; it is what we "see," as well as what "is," that affects our response.

We think it is important to look carefully at whatever evidence is available about elites' preferences and perceptions about international politics. Use of the word "elite" in this context does not imply acceptance of any "power elite" theories or of any ideas about interlocking interests or even conspiracies that direct the government. We simply use the word to mean "leaders" or prominent individuals. We mean first those people who participate at high levels in the political process, such as party politicians and officials, senior civil servants, leaders in the mass media, and leaders of interest groups involved in political activities. Along with them we include high-level executives of major corporations and labor unions, and more generally the kind of professional and upper-status people who we know are especially likely to vote, to take an interest in international affairs, to make campaign contributions, and to lobby. We thus are identifying the sorts of people especially relevant to political decision making, but we are making no prior assumptions that particular individuals or types of people directly affect particular decisions or that they can in any way be identified as sharing particular interests or preferences. We will be looking at the beliefs of some of these people in the United States, because of that country's crucial role in world politics and because the beliefs of such people in America are much more accessible than are those of their counterparts in other nations that are classified as superpowers. Our substantive interests focus on the United States, but perhaps we can use the opportunity to develop some ideas and findings that may be applicable elsewhere.

We want to know these people's policy preferences and perceptions regarding the foreign political and military activities of the

United States—in other words, what they conceive to be the proper role of the United States in the contemporary world. We will be looking at their attitudes on national security questions, and especially their attitudes toward the Vietnam experience and future military and political involvements of the United States in the world and particularly in the less developed countries. We want to understand the attitudinal basis for what is variously termed the "internationalist," "globalist," "activist," or "interventionist" policy of the United States in the post-World War II era, and how and to what degree that basis has changed.

Even more than with most countries, we think it important to look at intranational and specifically societal influences on the foreign policy of the United States. Almost by definition, the foreign policy of a small, poor country on the periphery of world politics, a state deeply penetrated or dominated by one or more great powers, will be very heavily influenced by inputs from the international system, and its leaders' autonomy in decision making thus will be restricted. On the other hand, the governmental leaders of a country with a relatively closed political system may be able, to a substantial degree, to ignore pressures from within their own societies to pursue certain kinds of foreign policies. But neither of these sets of attributes describes the United States. It is a big superpower at the center of world politics, more dominant than dominated in its relations with other states, and by common agreement possessing a relatively open political system where societal influences matter more than they do in most countries. Of course, no nation is a purely autonomous actor in the highly interdependent world in which we now live. But on purely theoretical grounds it is hard to find another country where we would expect the perceptions and policy preferences of its public—at least that portion attentive to and informed about foreign policy—to matter more.[2] Moreover, insofar as power relationships and nations' behavior

---

[2]For characterizations suggesting the kinds of states where societal influences will be most influential in foreign policy making, see Helge Hveem, *International Relations and World Images: A Study of Norwegian Foreign Policy Elites* (Oslo: Universitetsforlaget, 1972), p. 43, and the pre-theory of James N. Rosenau, described in *The Scientific Study of Foreign Policy* (New York: Free Press, 1971), ch. 5. For a quantitative analysis of recent events in the United States, see the conclusion of Jong Ryool Lee and Jeffrey S. Milstein, "A Political Economy of the Vietnam War, 1965–1972," *Peace Science Society (International) Papers* 21 (1973), 51: "The war in Vietnam . . . demonstrates that the President is as much limited in his choice of foreign policy by the internal political environment as by the external events."

have changed importantly in recent years, it seems reasonable to expect intranational influences to matter more in such periods than during times of long-term continuity in nations' foreign policies.[3] We think that an understanding of what has happened and is now happening in the United States is important for reaching any conclusions about the future world order, and for planning any action to influence the shape of that order. We start, then, with a policy problem and a need for information, which in turn demand theoretical explanation.

Theoretical Overkill

Theories about what drives or has driven American foreign policy are much in evidence. American foreign policy has, in terms of its expressed aims, achieved a mixture of success and failure during the past thirty years. Perhaps the successes have, on balance of quantity and importance, exceeded the failures. Nevertheless, one vibrant failure stands out to color the view of almost everyone: Vietnam. Just as there are many theories about the sources of American foreign policy generally, there have been many attempts to apply those theories specifically to the Vietnam case, because that case has had such important consequences for America and the world, and primarily because the experience was so searing for Americans. It represents a puzzle that demands understanding.

The puzzle stems from the obvious failure of American policy in Vietnam, even in terms of the goals officially declared for that policy.[4] Variously described as aimed at defending the Vietnamese, halting the spread of communism, or establishing the credibility of the American security guarantee for small countries, it effectively did none of those. The war virtually destroyed the society and culture of those it was supposed to defend. The American-supported regimes in Saigon and Phnom Penh have fallen. The credibility of the United States guarantee to defend small allies has been drastically weakened, not reaffirmed, by the effect of the Vietnam war on that country and on the United States itself. Given the death and

---

[3]For evidence that intranational changes did not produce many important changes in most countries' foreign policy during the stable cold war years, see Bruce M. Russett, *International Regions and the International System* (Chicago: Rand McNally, 1967), ch. 5.

[4]For a well-documented review of the rationales, see F. M. Kail, *What Washington Said: Administration Rhetoric and the Vietnam War* (New York: Harper & Row, 1973).

devastation in that unhappy Asian country, few peoples or governments would now choose to be defended in similar manner. Although the costs to America were in every way less severe than to Vietnam, they were bad enough: lives, money, and social and political disruption of a degree virtually unprecedented in the past century. Thus quite on its own terms, even without challenging the essential wisdom or morality of those terms, the war was an utter failure.

It was a failure, moreover, not just in our opinion, but in the opinion of most Americans. As early as 1967 and 1968 this was clear to a majority. In a Gallup poll taken in October 1967, only 42 percent denied that "the United States made a mistake sending troops to fight in Vietnam."[5] The failure became apparent to the majority of careful observers, not to mention the populace in general, long before the effort was abandoned in 1973. Yet the American government, with its vast apparatus for intelligence gathering and evaluation, "must" surely have been aware of the failure at least as soon as was the populace at large. Why then did so much time pass before a decision to get out was finally made and implemented? Four, or perhaps four and a half, different theories attempting to explain this can be singled out. We term them respectively "strategic," "bureaucratic," "economic," and "ideological" (the last with a subset of "democratic") theories. There are still others, but these are the most prominent and will suffice to make our point.[6]

The first is the set of *strategic* theories, attributing the actions of American policy makers to their perceptions of security requirements and realpolitik. By this explanation, policy makers think in terms of military security, balance of power, containing Soviet and/ or Chinese expansion, containing power centers in general, and the importance of honoring commitments to defend one's military allies. This perceived need to match, contain, or repress rival world power centers stemmed in part from, or at least was reinforced by, the experiences of Great Britain, France, and the United States in

---

[5]*Gallup Opinion Index*, Report No. 39, September 1968, p. 3.

[6]Although we arrived at our basic fourfold scheme independently, it is remarkably similar to that of James Kurth, as laid out in his "Aerospace Production Lines and American Defense Spending," in Steven Rosen, ed., *Testing the Theory of the Military-Industrial Complex* (Lexington, Mass.: D. C. Heath, 1973). Also see Kurth's "Testing Theories of Economic Imperialism," in Steven J. Rosen and James R. Kurth, eds., *Testing Theories of Economic Imperialism* (Lexington, Mass.: D. C. Heath, 1974). In the following discussion we will draw rather heavily on some of Kurth's incisive comments. Other theories, such as personality-oriented ones, are possible but less applicable to long-term policies sustained through several administrations and similarly implemented by different personalities in high office.

World War II. The Munich analogy was frequently drawn,[7] as were explicit allusions to the failure to resist Japanese aggression in the 1930s. In some versions the balance of power is always seen to be precarious, and a secure "balance" really is considered to rest only on American predominance. In any event, by this line of thought communism is incidental except as it is thought to add to the expansionist impulse, capability, or attractiveness of the post-World War II opponent. Policy makers holding strategically oriented views basically are concerned with containing *any* rival power center, regardless of its ideology or form of domestic organization. An almost perfect example of this line of reasoning is Joseph Alsop's comment on World War II:

The choice the British and French made in 1939 was to fight like cornered rats rather than to submit to Adolf Hitler. But with the vast tilt in the power balance that had then occurred, the same choice would have had to be made even if Adolf Hitler had been miraculously replaced by another German leader of undoubted rectitude. The mere presence of overweening power almost always begets this choice.[8]

People who espouse strategic theories argue that in the 1960s and earlier, American policy makers exaggerated the strategic importance of Vietnam, and exaggerated the ability of any major power—whether Russia, China, or the United States—to control that country for the major power's purposes.

Bureaucratic theories are quite different. Strategic theories postulate the widespread existence of images of the *national* interest as expressed in power or security terms, in which policy makers make decisions that are rational at least as defined by their conceptions of the nation's security needs and threats thereto. Bureaucratic theories emphasize the competing interests of many rival individuals and agencies within the vast policy-making organizations, each caught up in pursuing its own interests or, at best, its own parochial view of the national interest when that national

---

[7]For some representative quotations by American leaders, referring to the Munich analogy after World War II, see Bruce M. Russett, *No Clear and Present Danger: A Skeptical View of the United States Entry into World War II* (New York: Harper & Row, 1972), pp. 83–85.

[8]"History and the Balance of Power," *Washington Post*, December 6, 1974, A31:3. More generally, theories of national interest and concern for power are extremely common. The most influential among academics, and probably among policy makers as well, is doubtless Hans J. Morgenthau, *Politics Among Nations: The Struggle for Power and Peace* (New York: Knopf, first edition 1948). Certainly one sees it in Lyndon B. Johnson, *The Vantage Point: Perspectives on the Presidency* (New York: Holt, 1971).

interest conveniently happens largely to coincide with the narrow bureaucratic interest. Organizations and governmental institutions thus get embroiled in bureaucratic politics, with each agency or branch chief seeking to aggrandize or at a minimum protect the status of his agency and ensure the continuation of agency policy.

To this end bureaucrats control information and intelligence passing up through the agency hierarchy, trying to make the agency look good and to persuade their superiors that current policy, as they are executing it, is succeeding and should be maintained. As a result, policy makers at the very pinnacle may really be among the latecomers in getting accurate information on what is going on. Dependent on subordinates for intelligence, officials at the top may become aware of a failure only after it has become widely manifest, even to the general public, which does not derive its information so totally from the governmental bureaucracy as some political leaders may allow themselves to do. Under these circumstances the easy assumption that decision makers must have known early about the Vietnam failure needs to be questioned. Public skepticism and disapproval might well lead rather than follow the man at the top. This would be especially true if the political leadership tended to give special weight to information from particular sources on the ground that it generally seemed "harder" or more data-based than information from other sources. Allegedly this happened when some "softer," more pessimistic political estimates of the status of the military in Vietnam were ignored in favor of the deceptively solid and fully as self-serving estimates coming from the military itself.

Bureaucratic theories are concerned with difficulties in co-ordinating policy execution as well as with information processing. Just as agency chiefs and their subordinates may distort information, they may ignore or bend their superior's orders so as not to conflict with their own purposes. They may continue to pursue their own policies, or even take independent and unauthorized initiatives. The famous incident over American missiles in Turkey during the Cuban missile crisis is a good example of the former. Premier Khrushchev intimated he might dismantle the Soviet missile bases in Cuba if the Americans did likewise with theirs in Turkey. President Kennedy's response was one of surprise and anger with his own military and political subordinates. He had in fact ordered the American missiles taken out of Turkey months before; by the time of the Cuban crisis he was not pleased to have them available as a quid pro quo for Khrushchev to demand. The general problem is simply that, faced with determined bureaucratic interests having their own priorities and preferences, a Chief Executive can effectively change policy only by repeated and forceful intervention. There are severe limits to the number of times and places he can effect such intervention, especially if he is also to maintain the morale and general loyalty of the members of the bureaucracy. The larger the bureaucracy—and the United States defense and foreign policy bureaucracy is certainly large—the more severe these problems are likely to be.[9]

In trying to explain the Vietnam embroglio various observers have noted cases of biased intelligence and deliberate "ignorance" or disregard of unwelcome orders within military and civilian agencies, bureaucratic infighting between agencies, and excessive zeal in continuing discredited policies on the part of advocates of the Green Berets or "pacification." Military activities during the long tacit bargaining period before the Paris Peace talks have come in for special attention, including the choice and timing of bombing raids. Different agencies, each "doing its own thing," provided sharply conflicting signals—sometimes intentionally, sometimes accidentally—about American conciliatory intentions or their absence. By all these explanations, the United States remained in Vietnam not because to do so in any way suited the national interest, but because particular policies suited the interests of particular agencies, which thus frustrated rather than coordinated understanding and execution.

Economic theories come in various shapes and sizes, but all in one way or another attribute political and military acts to the needs of the American capitalist economy. Since economic theories will be the subject of intensive investigation in this volume, we shall outline them only very briefly here, and devote the following chapter entirely to a more extensive and critical review. In bare outline, some theories trace war to activities of the arms industries, "merchants of death" in a military-industrial complex who promote

---

[9]The argument about size is well expressed by Anthony J. Downs, *Inside Bureaucracy* (Boston: Little, Brown, 1967). The recent surge of academic interest in the effects of bureaucratic politics began with Richard Neustadt, *Alliance Politics* (New York: Columbia University Press, 1970) and was given further impetus by Graham Allison, *Essence of Decision: Explaining the Cuban Missile Crisis* (Boston: Little, Brown, 1971). On the Kennedy-Johnson administrations in general, and on Vietnam in particular, see the books by various participants: Schlesinger, Sorensen, Hilsman, Cooper, Hoopes, McNamara, et al. A useful interpretation is David Halberstam, *The Best and the Brightest* (New York: Random House, 1972).

militarization, international hostility to justify military spending, and wars to require still more arms purchases. It may be hard to see how the defense industries alone (large in terms of absolute sums of money spent, perhaps, but less than 10 percent of the total economy) could determine vital decisions of war and peace. A more comprehensive version of this theory insists that the aggregate level of demand in the entire capitalist economy can be maintained only by "excessive" military spending, and that, in turn, requires a level of international tension and even active hostilities. Without military spending, it is alleged, the economy would collapse into depression.

More generally still, American capitalism is said to demand the defense of American markets or investments in Vietnam, Indochina, and the rest of Southeast Asia. Of course, such markets and investments are in fact minimal; less than 1 percent of all United States foreign economic activity is directed to Southeast Asia as a whole. The defense of economic interests in Southeast Asia alone, then, is just too small a tail to wag such a very big dog. But according to an economic variant of the domino theory, the purpose of American intervention was to prevent a nationalist or socializing regime from coming to power in Saigon not because South Vietnam was economically significant, but as a clear warning to groups with similar aspirations in nations that were more economically significant. These theorists postulated that nationalist takeovers in the less developed countries and attempts to remove those countries from the capitalist world economy should everywhere be resisted on the ground that it was better to make the case precisely where the immediate importance was minimal, so that American economic access could more easily, and more peacefully, be kept where it mattered. A further refinement of these theories emphasized the key nature of certain raw-material supplies (for example, offshore oil deposits in the China Sea) or the peculiar political leverage of certain key pressure groups.

Finally, there is a class of *ideological* theories that carry a certain persuasiveness. Certainly cold war ideology, militant anticommunism, and determined (sometimes hysterical) demands for resistance to communist expansion have played a part in American foreign policy. Even in the 1960s there remained in many quarters the vision of a fairly close, still quasi-monolithic world communism, headed by a Moscow-Peking axis that controlled dedicated instruments of war and subversion throughout the world. People with this vision typically were ideological conservatives on domestic

THEORETICAL OVERKILL   13

American political issues. They feared "communist-inspired" economic "levelers," dreaded communist subversion of democratic and capitalist institutions, and favored severe restrictions on civil liberties in order to control radicals and subversives. According to one theory, anticommunist "interventionist" policies stemmed from a broad spectrum of interwoven beliefs, and were not limited to strategic or economic motivations or realistically evaluated by strategic or economic criteria. Intervention in Vietnam thus was seen as an almost reflexive anticommunist act. To some radicals, anticommunist ideology is but a superstructure lending legitimacy and energy to policies directed to the protection of economic interests; without these interests the ideology could not be sustained. We shall have more to say about this idea later. For the moment we may cast the argument in a form not dependent on economic origins, and speak of ideology as "composed largely of symbols, visible in the public domain, with an independent capacity to influence behavior."[10]

An important variant of ideological theories, deserving separate attention, is that of *democratic* theories, which stress the importance of ideology at the mass level rather than the elite level of the political process. According to such theories, high-level policy makers feared a backlash of militant anticommunism from the general populace in reaction to major foreign policy reverses. They remembered, for example, the domestic political costs resulting from the trauma of "losing" China that were incurred by the administration in the late 1940s, and the witch-hunting of the Joseph McCarthy era, which was so hard on liberals as well as radicals in the United States. In the words of former Senator Sam Ervin, "You can't believe the terror that man [McCarthy] spread among politicians."[11]

Thus politicians feared to loose a popular anticommunism that would punish them for foreign policy defeats, and were therefore constrained by anticommunism even though they themselves were too sophisticated really to believe its premises. Believing that the people would not tolerate the "loss" of Vietnam, senior elected and appointed officials in Washington resolved that Vietnam would not be lost—at least not during their terms in office. They would hang on, and escalate where necessary to avoid defeat, even though they

---

[10]Douglas Rosenberg, "Arms and the American Way," in Bruce M. Russett and Alfred Stepan, eds., *Military Force and American Society* (New York: Harper & Row, 1972), p. 160.
[11]Seminar at Yale University, February 13, 1974.

knew the long-term prospects for holding the country were poor. They could hope to postpone the day of reckoning to a time when they themselves would not be held responsible, and perhaps hope, against the evidence available to them, that events would break favorably so that the ultimate outcome would not be disastrous. According to some analysts, this kind of thinking can be found in every administration from Truman to Nixon.[12]

Our example here is the Vietnam horror, but the different theoretical perspectives listed are of general interest, and are not limited to that set of events, nor to American foreign policy alone. They are general perspectives that could be applied to the policy orientation of almost any major power, with only some adaptations for the specific context. Similar reasoning could be applied to French policy in Indochina or in Algeria, or for that matter to the reasons for Soviet intervention in Czechoslovakia in 1968. Consider, for example, rationales about the power interests of the Soviet state, Brezhnev's problems of bureaucratic politics in the Kremlin, and the distorting and possibly fear-inducing effects of communist ideology; and perhaps substitute, for economic interests, worries that the potential example of a mixed economy in Czechoslovakia would be its own kind of domino to endanger state socialism through-out Eastern Europe. With appropriate adaptations these are virtu-ally universal considerations that are applicable to virtually all international actors.

Because they are indeed virtually universal, each of the kinds of theories carries substantial plausibility.[13] As applied to Vietnam, each includes much that is persuasive, although a sophisticated observer would want to attach significant caveats or reservations to each. And evidence can be found to support each type of theory, at least in part. Doubtless each does in fact explain a part of the policy outcome. But that does not give us a satisfactory scientific explana-

[12]This seems basically to be the interpretation of Daniel Ellsberg, "The Quagmire Myth and the Stalemate Machine," *Public Policy* 19, 2 (Spring 1971): 217–274. See also Leslie Gelb, "Vietnam: The System Worked," *Foreign Policy*, No. 3 (Summer 1971), and Halberstam, op. cit. To an impor-tant degree this popular anticommunism was built up by policy makers themselves, as in Senator Vandenberg's advice to Truman that he must "go and scare hell out of the country." Once this force was unleashed, policy makers felt more constrained by it than they wished to be.

[13]For a useful statement on the relevance of strategic, ideological, and economic influences on Vietnam policy—though downgrading the last—see Marek Thee, "War and Peace in Indochina: U.S. Asian and Pacific Policies," *Journal of Peace Research* 10, No. 1 (1973): 51–70.

tion, nor help us arrive at an understanding that would permit us to predict the outcome of a similar set of pressures in another situation. Just because each has important elements of plausibility, we must ask with special vigor, what kinds of evidence would be required effectively to *refute* each theory? That is, what kind of evidence would establish that a particular kind of influence did not operate to affect the result? Or perhaps rather, only after conducting what kind of diligent search, where and how, *without* discovering evidence to support the theory, could we then reliably regard the theory as refuted? If a theft has been committed, and the detective suspects the building was not entered from outside, it is not enough simply to establish that the doors remained locked. Until the windows too have been carefully checked, burglary remains a viable hypothesis.

Still more important is the difficult question of evaluating the *relative* importance of each theory. Assuming that there is some evidence to support each, as is likely, we cannot merely throw up our hands and express some vague notion of multiple causation. Some influences surely must matter more than others. Speaking quantitatively, what percentage of the variation in the total outcome can be accounted for by each explanation? An explanation accounting for half the variation is usually a good deal more interesting than one accounting for just 2 percent. Estimation becomes especially difficult when there are interacting causes—that is, when two influences in combination produce an event that neither could cause by itself. Thus what began as a policy problem and turned into a theoretical one now has become a problem of evidence—we cannot carry the discussion of theory much further without devoting some attention to the question of what are the relevant pieces of evidence for testing various theories.

The Unintended Bias of Traditional Methods

Classical, "traditional" methods of political and historical analysis concentrate on examining documents, personal and state papers, and memoirs, supplemented by interviews with top policy makers whenever possible. They often seek to determine the reasons that chief decision makers gave for their policy and the motivations that they attributed to other major actors. Overwhelmingly, the resulting statements stress strategic explanations and emphasize concern for power, security, and national interest. It is, after all, a basic element of political myth that a Chief Executive, especially in democratic systems, is concerned for the national interest, must surmount narrow personal, group, or partisan interests that may motivate his constituents, and must act, to use the American phrase, as "President of all the people." Top decision makers will invoke this kind of argument. When they do, they may well be describing their conscious motivations quite accurately; surely they do frequently think in such terms, for in their positions at the apex of so many conflicting pressures they have many reasons to take a broad overview.

Furthermore, they are encouraged by the myth to give such reasons, and discouraged from emphasizing other kinds of explanations. Presidents are unlikely, for instance, to stress the frustrations of bureaucratic politics. Of course, a President will mention some of his difficulties, and his need to present his wishes forcefully to his subordinates and to monitor their execution of his directives. Some appreciation of bureaucratic obstruction and self-interest is essential to any sympathetic evaluation of a President's lot in trying to carry out a coherent sustained policy in the general interest. Yet even though Presidents want their difficulties to be appreciated, they rarely want to give the impression of having been overwhelmed by those difficulties. They will not want observers to think that they have been systematically unable to control their subordinates, or that they have been regularly duped by them. They hardly will want to risk looking like incompetent executives.

Nor certainly should anyone expect them to tell us much about economic interests and the kinds of parochial pressures to which they may have been subjected—especially when such pressures were successful. We recently have vividly seen how very reluctant policy makers are to disclose the activities of those who have lobbied them, or made political campaign contributions. Nor, finally, is any President or other top official likely to admit, however obliquely, that he placed the priority of holding his office above the longer- and broader-term perspectives of the national interest. Louis XV may have said, "Après moi le déluge," but no democratic leader is about to admit he pursued that as a deliberate policy.

Mentioning these other possible motivations—bureaucratic conflict, economic interest, and considerations of democratic electoral politics—is not to imply that in any particular case, or even in most cases, these are driving motivations behind the actions of major political figures. They may or may not be—but we are very unlikely ever to know merely by studying the kind of documentation and interview material that is publicly available, especially the publicly available material about events within the past few decades. Substantial evidence supporting other interpretations is likely to emerge, if at all, only to future historians not operating within the constraints of contemporary security classification. Thus the absence of evidence supporting those interpretations cannot disprove the interpretations, since we should not expect to find much evidence there. The case necessarily remains open.

To probe further we can look at other kinds of documentary material, and interview and read the memoirs of officials who operated below the very highest levels of the policy-making process. The materials compiled by bureau chiefs, undersecretaries, ambassadors, and speech writers, and by journalists who have talked extensively with such people, are rich with explanations. But here again, the people involved are human, and must be expected to try to put a good face on their actions, to make themselves look reasonably good at the expense of their bureaucratic rivals. So here, in addition to perceptions of national interest, we would expect the mechanisms of deliberate or unconscious recall to lead these officials to emphasize the jungle of bureaucratic politics, and how their aims were thwarted by the narrow interests of others. The memoirs of all the bureaucratic survivors (wounded and otherwise) from the Kennedy and Johnson years are full of this sort of material. Some of these individuals have even returned to academia, and they and their students, among others, have written fascinating and often deeply insightful accounts of bureaucratic politics and the hazards they pose to rational policy making. At the same time, economic and ideological influences do not figure prominently in these explanations. Sometimes they are mentioned, surely more often than by top-level decision makers, but as exceptional cases and exceptional influences (always affecting *other* people's acts), and not as pervasive factors. Again, we cannot make the mistake of assuming they *must* have operated, however sparse the evidence. But the sparseness of evidence does not prove they did not operate; there is little reason to expect much of such evidence to emerge, and much reason to expect ex-bureaucrats, especially frustrated ones or men who wish to disassociate themselves from unpopular policies, to tell us how red in tooth and claw are the struggles of bureaucratic politics.

Radical critics who wish to highlight the role of economic interests will, in their own way, also stress those kinds of evidence that will highlight the kinds of influences they think important. One variety of analysis examines aggregate data on foreign markets and investment patterns, showing the importance to key firms or industries of economic activities in countries that were the target of special political attention. It is practically always possible to find some such investment, sales, or import interest—but very difficult indeed to judge its importance in the political process relative to a host of actual or potential countervailing interests.

Another type of analysis looks at particular cases of foreign policy decision making, and at the interests and connections of key participants. There surely are many instances in which the policy and economic interests of the participants are more than suspiciously close, or even where direct action by economically motivated actors can be identified beyond doubt. A notable example is the American military intervention in the Dominican Republic in 1965, when many senior United States policy makers or advisers—Ellsworth Bunker, Adolf Berle, Abe Fortas—were officers or directors of big sugar companies. But especially in the American political system, the great majority of senior policy makers have close past or current corporate ties—as directors, officers, lawyers, shareholders, or at least relatives of same. It often becomes difficult not to find someone with a corporate interest somehow affecting the outcome. Moreover, many other individuals without such apparent interests usually can be found advocating similar policies. And as with Bunker in the Dominican case, it is not always those with the apparent economic interest who vigorously press the expected arguments, in this instance for intervention.

The matter is all very complicated, and it is rarely easy to trace an unambiguous causal sequence from interest to influence to decision. Indeed there are many cases where economically interested actors are known to have advocated self-serving policies, and then failed utterly to implement them.[14] Despite the nontrivial number of American political and military interventions in the third world during recent decades, there are far more cases where the actual or imputed desires of economic interest groups would have pointed to interventions that in fact did not occur. Simply identifying examples and illustrations of interests, or even attempts to influence policy, will not suffice. Both a carefully developed theory of circum-

---

[14]For various examples of both successful and unsuccessful efforts Anthony Sampson's *The Sovereign State: The Secret History of ITT* (London: Coronet, 1974) is illuminating. See also the brief but useful discussion in Kurth, "Testing Theories," op. cit.

stances favoring or hindering the success of such efforts, and much additional information on perceptions, motivations, and pressures, are required to bring predictive order to a persuasive economic interpretation.

As a result, these traditional, classical tools of analysis cannot alone provide satisfactory answers to questions about the relative power of various kinds of influences on foreign policy making. Actually, the pieces of evidence supporting different kinds of theories frequently slip past each other without ever meeting. One adviser may have an economic interest behind his advice, another may be moved in the same direction by ideological anticommunism, and yet another may be influenced by "hard-nosed" strategic considerations. If they all give the same recommendation and the President accepts, who has the "real" power? These and other difficulties, all too familiar to close students of power and influence theory, bedevil the most careful and perceptive analyst. The analytical problems are extraordinarily difficult; bitter disputes over the relative importance of economic influences on foreign policy go back many years, at least to Hobson and the Marxists, and hardly seem closer to resolution now than they were in their early days. The fault does not stem from lack of insight or effort on the part of analysts. The subject of politics is very complex—"harder than physics"—and this problem is especially difficult. But the problem is also an extremely important one; although we may never "settle" these matters once and for all, they deserve better answers than have so far been devised. To get those answers we must ask somewhat different questions, and most importantly ask them in different ways, demanding different kinds of evidence.

The traditional research procedures are, by themselves, inadequate—not "wrong," necessary in fact, but insufficient. They must be supplemented, especially because each of the basic traditional methods tends to be biased in terms of the kind of theories it tends to support. Some lead us to answers stressing strategic conceptions, others to answers emphasizing bureaucratic politics, or economic interests. These biases are rarely intended by the methods' practitioners; the methods seem the best and fairest that can be brought to bear on a particular decision or set of decision makers. But the biases, in terms of the kinds of evidence the methods find and cannot be expected to find, are there and, for each of the individual methods by itself, virtually unavoidable. The evidence problem therefore has become a methodological one: how can we get the needed evidence, especially to test economic and ideological theories since they are probably the least satisfactorily investigated with the traditional procedures?[15]

Methods for Studying the Views of Corporate Executives

We have no world-shaking solution to this problem, but we have developed some methods of inquiry in this book that should help to right the imbalance. In a variety of ways we shall be looking at the perceptions, attitudes, and preferences of major "elite" groups, and especially at those of high-level executives of major corporate enterprises. We will be asking whether their perceptions and preferences are significantly different from those of other elite groups, and if so, how and on what kinds of foreign policy issues? We shall be comparing them systematically with those of other civilian and military elite groups, and where possible examining changes over time. How do members of the large group of business executives differ among themselves? Does the foreign policy orientation of men employed by heavily defense-dependent firms differ markedly from that of executives in other industries? Similarly, is the orientation different for men from firms heavily dependent on sales or investments abroad, or, more specifically, on sales or investments in underdeveloped countries? Do these men express economic motivations, and are these motivations then related to the choice of particular policies, such as intervention or the support of certain kinds of regimes in less developed countries? Or is policy choice related less to economic interest or motivation than to "ideological," liberal-conservative differences on domestic policy, or to conceptions about strategy and international power relationships?

These questions are explored first by describing a sample survey we conducted of top-level executives, and comparing the

---

[15]For two studies that have examined a variety of interventions and other policies to try to establish some general patterns, see John Eley and John Petersen, "Economic Interests and American Foreign Policy Allocations, 1960–69," in Patrick J. McGowan, ed., *Sage International Yearbook of Foreign Policy Studies*, I (Beverly Hills: Sage, 1973), and Frederic S. Pearson, "American Military Intervention Abroad: A Test of Economic and Non-Economic Explanations," in Craig Liske, ed., *The Politics of Trade and Aid* (Beverly Hills: Sage, 1975). These efforts, using aggregate data on many cases rather than looking at decision making, suggest a nonzero but still relatively unimportant role for economic influences relative to ideological and strategic ones; however, the difficulties with this mode of research are also formidable.

results with those obtained from similar surveys that were carried out on other elite groups. We asked these executives a wide range of questions, hoping to tap their attitudes in suitably subtle and mixed ways. The individuals concerned are highly intelligent; the task of inquiring into their beliefs with reasonably accurate results was far from easy. There are serious limits on the ability of survey research to probe complicated matters with sophisticated respondents, and we were obliged to supplement the large-scale survey results with substantial numbers of intensive face-to-face interviews, to test the validity of our survey responses and develop some of the subtle undertones. But the survey approach has great advantages as well as hazards attached to it; with a sufficiently large and well-designed sample it becomes possible to generalize statistically about the relative effect of various influences with a confidence that can never be achieved from a score or two of interviews, however intensive and probing. The two methods again are not mutually exclusive, but mutually supportive when used in tandem.

Another methodological approach of this book is to look intensively at what businessmen say to each other, or more precisely, what journalists say to businessmen through the medium of their specialized business and financial press. What policy recommendations do writers make, based on what kind of justifications (economic, ideological, strategic)? How have these recommendations and justifications changed over recent decades in response to different kinds of international events, and how do they compare with the kind of political recommendations and justifications to be found, for example, in journals edited for and by military men?

Finally, we look in some detail at share prices on the New York Stock Exchange—how they have moved up and down in apparent response to international events, particularly to war-related events during the Korean and Indochina conflicts. Stock prices can serve as one indicator of expectations, in the business and financial community, of how major segments of the economy may fare as a result of international developments. Has the market been bullish or bearish in response to escalatory events during the wars, or in response to conciliatory acts by either side? Has the pattern varied over time, showing differences between the two wars or during the course of either? Perhaps more importantly, have particular kinds of stocks, such as those of defense-oriented firms, or of firms with heavy stakes in the less developed countries, behaved differently from those of most other firms? Used cautiously and with discrimination, stock prices become one more partial indicator of attitudes and beliefs in the corporate world. For the researcher, they have the singular virtue, even more than the content analysis material, of being "nonreactive" measures. That is, unlike responses to a survey, the data are compiled by businessmen in the course of their normal acts and without thought to how a researcher might interpret those acts.

Taken together, all these pieces of evidence should give us some information of a sort previously unavailable. None of these pieces is by itself unassailable; serious questions can and should be raised about the validity of each. Skepticism is appropriate about the interpretations we give to changes in stock prices, or about how much candor we really can expect to find in the business and financial press. But as noted, similar questions, no less profound, can be raised about the validity of interviewing or documentary analysis of the kind of material usually available to journalists or historians. Our purpose is not to replace traditional analysis with our newer sorts of material, but merely to supplement, to complement, the conclusions obtainable through the more traditional methods. The techniques we are employing are not all that new; basically they have already been developed by other scholars and applied, usually individually, to other matters. But they have not previously all been collectively brought to bear on a major issue of foreign policy. We believe that by drawing on multiple streams of evidence here, each with its own limitations but also with its own strengths in terms of the kinds of material it is likely to uncover, we can deepen our understanding of these very complex yet important political phenomena.

In some ways, our attempt to bring new kinds of evidence to bear resembles the different things one "sees" by "looking" in various ways at the human body. By looking with your eyes in ordinary light, you see the color and texture of the surface: skin, hair, clothing. But by looking with heat-sensitive infrared instruments, you see varied patterns of warmth, spots and periods of intense activity, or absence of it. Or by looking at an X-ray picture, you see the basic underlying structure of support, strength, and vulnerability. None of these is "the" picture of the human body, but each tells us very different things about how it functions, what its capabilities are, and what to expect of it. In our study we engaged in methodological eclecticism not for its own sake, but to broaden understanding in directions that the traditional methods cannot so easily reach.

We do not for a moment imagine that beliefs, preferences, and attitudes about politics are to be equated with political acts, attempts to influence, or the successful exercise of political power. All those give rise to other questions requiring very different inquiries and evidence.[16] This is not a search to find who has power, who makes decisions, and certainly not who constitutes a "power elite" deciding what foreign policy issues. Questions about power and its exercise surely are not trivial; they remain some of the most central questions of political science. But these questions, although very interesting, are extremely difficult matters for investigation. Probably no aspect of political science has been analyzed so thoroughly as has the problem of power, with such indeterminate empirical results. Efforts to establish convincingly the existence and scope of a power elite, for example, have generally failed to be convincing by the standard criteria of empirical social science. This failure is partly the result of conceptual, theoretical difficulties in the approach, but it is due at least equally to the extremely complex and abstruse nature of the world at issue. Especially when power is defined as the ability to get someone to do something he would not otherwise do, the barriers to establishing such hypothetical circumstances are virtually insuperable. These same barriers bedevil the pluralist critics of power elite theories. However cogent their critiques or ingenious their counterpropositions, it remains almost impossible ever to prove that there is *not* a power elite, or even at the more modest level that economically motivated individuals do not exert great power over decision making. We are avoiding these questions out of respect for their difficulty, not out of disrespect for their importance. Similarly, we will have nothing more to say here about bureaucratic politics.

Instead, we have moved to a logically *prior* step of inquiry. By asking about the beliefs, preferences, and attitudes of corporate executives we are trying to discover whether those attitudes are

---

[16]The relation of beliefs, attitudes, and so on to political behavior is a more complicated matter, empirically and theoretically, than we can deal with in this book. Some of the relevant literature is reviewed by Patrick J. McGowan and Howard B. Shapiro, *The Comparative Study of Foreign Policy: A Survey of Scientific Findings* (Beverly Hills: Sage, 1973). Obviously behavior is a function of both attitudes and environmental stimuli; when attitudes predispose an actor in a certain direction, presumably the stimulus necessary to produce behavior can be less than if his attitudes were otherwise. In some areas (e.g., party identification and voting behavior) the correlation between attitudes and behavior seems rather high, and in others (e.g., race relations) it seems more problematic.

consistent with what various theorists about economic or other motivations would have us expect. A question that we ask prior to that about their behavior is simply, are their attitudes what would be predicted? In what ways do businessmen think differently about foreign policy than do other leaders, and what kinds of differences, associated with what ideological or economic characteristics, exist within the business community?

Without making assumptions that businessmen or other elite groups play a particular role in policy making, we nevertheless consider the beliefs of such people as contributing "to the formation of images and attitudes through advice or information."[17] Although they do not hold official positions in the policy-making arena, such people have an importance, actual or potential, in forming the climate of opinion within which policy makers must operate. It is well known that political interest and activity are closely correlated—though certainly in no one-to-one correspondence—with high socioeconomic status. Such people are, on the average, more likely to be informed about politics (especially international politics), and to take part in political activities. In so doing they help to define the limits of action available to policy makers. A policy maker, particularly in the area of foreign policy, can to some degree and for some time pursue actions that do not have broad approval among the politically relevant segments of the population. But serious deviations from approved norms, certainly if continued over a long term, will bring political penalties. The positions of opposition leaders will be strengthened, and some of the basic instruments needed to pursue the policy (appropriations, for example) are less likely to be forthcoming. Policy makers must depend on thousands of individuals, from top civil servants to footsoldiers in the field, to execute policy; and widespread disaffection for a policy will be reflected in its indifferent execution. Moreover, policy makers are dependent on information coming up to them; and their own images and perceptions are unavoidably shaped by those around them. No man is an intellectual island. Moreover, businessmen of high status who are interested in politics inevitably form the reservoir from which new policy makers will be recruited. We do not need a C. Wright Mills to remind us that many senior government officials are customarily recruited from the ranks of senior business executives. For all these reasons the study of elite perspectives becomes important, and in looking

---

[17] Hveem, op. cit., p. 17.

closely at those of businessmen we need not assume that top business executives are especially important—only that they form a part of the wider elite that cannot help but matter in politics.

This is not a broad study of the political views of businessmen, nor of the sociology of business. We have sought no information on the effect of religion, upbringing, education, or social origin, for instance. But it is, we think, addressed to a few central matters about economic and other motivations; it is an inquiry that could in principle serve almost as a "critical experiment" to determine the direction of future investigation into questions about economic influence. If the attitudes are such as would be predicted by economic influence theories, then there will be good reason to redouble efforts to trace the exercise of power and influence. If, on the contrary, the attitudes do not bear much resemblance to those predicted, then it may be time to move on to other, more promising kinds of inquiries.

And the questions *are* important, from a policy-oriented point of view, with which we began, as well as from one concerned with theory. If economic interests have truly been powerful influences impelling American intervention in Vietnam and elsewhere in the underdeveloped world, then presumably they could produce the same effect again, on an occasion when the prospective cost/benefit ratio looked more favorable. If economic pressures have been powerful, then the possibility of "imperial" rivalry with other economically motivated major powers exists for the future. If strategic considerations were paramount, then diminished world bipolarity and the rise of new power centers will somehow, in ways not always easy to discern, affect future willingness to intervene on behalf of strategic power. If ideology, or the fear of an ideologically motivated mass public, were paramount, then maybe there are special grounds for optimism that future interventions can be more readily avoided. There is substantial evidence, which we will scrutinize in detail in this book, of a major shift in ideology, a shift that has left vast numbers of people, especially of the younger generation, barren of many of the fears and ideologically motivated ambitions of the cold war years. Whatever the facts, prescriptions for avoiding a repetition of past tragedies will depend centrally on the diagnosis of why past ones occurred. We cannot comprehend the future until we understand how people view their past and present.

CHAPTER TWO

Economic Theories
of
Foreign Policy

Absence makes the heart grow fonder.

Sextus Aurelius Propertius, Elegies

Out of syght, out of mynd.

Barnabe Googe, Eglogs

$\left[\begin{array}{c}\textit{One can find opposite plausible hypotheses} \\ \textit{about almost every human relationship.}\end{array}\right]$

Types of Theories

Men have always pursued material interest as one of their most
important goals, and since the dawn of government have tried to
use the state as an instrument of that pursuit. No one doubts this.
What is at issue are questions like these: Do states with different
kinds of economic systems pursue different kinds of foreign policies?
If so, just how do their foreign policies differ? Merely in terms of
foreign political activities, or in degree of military preparation, or
actually in warproneness? To the material benefit of what groups
or classes within the state are these policies pursued? Do all groups
benefit, or at least not lose, from them? In the terms of the last
chapter, how much of the variation among states' foreign policies
(none, a little, or a lot) can be attributed to their economic systems?

These questions are old, but they have been asked with particular force during the last century or so, and they have been applied especially to capitalist economic systems.

Both liberal and Marxist traditions assert that there is something very special about the advanced capitalist economies dating from the industrial revolution. Some elements of liberal theory emphasize features in capitalism that are alleged to promote world peace, but other elements of liberal theory, and certainly most of Marxist thought, claim that capitalist countries are likely to have particularly aggressive foreign policies. Many, indeed, attribute virtually all acts of Mars to the not-always-invisible hand of the modern capitalist. This concern is not limited to acts of war. Capitalism is sometimes blamed for a variety of imperialist acts, defined loosely as efforts to exert political or economic control over smaller or weaker states. Political and military interventions in less developed countries are of special interest. Other foci include military spending, "militarism," and arms races.

The theories differ substantially according to the particular aspects of capitalism that are considered of primary causal significance. Some are addressed to the alleged imperatives of the aggregate capitalist economy—that the capitalist system *as a whole* (or at least the capitalist economy of any major nation-state) is structurally dependent on military spending, or on continued access to foreign markets for goods or investment opportunities. Another strain is largely concerned with the interests and power of *particular groups or classes*. Foreign investors, or the military-industrial complex, or other economically defined groups may have an interest in an aggressive or expansionist foreign policy, which has potential great gains for them, even though many other members of the system, capitalists as well as workers, will suffer net losses from such a policy. A minority of economic interests, therefore, may successfully maintain a policy that benefits them but is not required by, and may even be detrimental to, the capitalist economy as a whole. Finally, there are some theories that are addressed less to readily definable material interest than to the *value structure*, that is, the ideology, that characterizes capitalist systems. According to these theories, this value structure, concerned as much with the desire to preserve the capitalist system as to extend it, produces behavior excessively responsive to economic growth and the incentive of material rewards. The resultant foreign policy is thus both expansionist and hostile to socialist states with different value structures whose adoption by major segments within the capitalist system would undermine its viability and the privileged place of the capitalist classes within it.

Contradicting each of these types of theories are others that stress the relative unimportance of economic motivations in influencing foreign policy, and as an explicit refutation emphasize political and cultural ends and other kinds of ideological motivations. The area, so defined, is extraordinarily broad, and we could not possibly provide a comprehensive overview here. We shall, however, consider a number of variants within each of the three categories just identified, including some counterarguments as well as economically oriented theories. Our attention will be mainly devoted to the economic theories, and we will at least mention most of the major ones.[1] The purpose will be to derive some hypotheses so that we may test them in subsequent chapters.

The Imperatives of Capitalist Economies

Most of the classical economic interpretations of imperialism fall largely into a group of theories that, in one way or another, attributed it to demands arising from the organization of production in capitalist economies. Many eighteenth- and nineteenth-century economists believed that the normal tendency of profit rates in industrialized countries was to fall over long periods. They had differing explanations for this phenomenon, but according to one review, Adam Smith, Sismondi, and even Malthus "all suggested that if part of the savings of the industrialized countries of Europe were invested overseas instead of at home, the moment when the rate of profit dropped below the minimum required to encourage capitalists to invest could be postponed."[2] These economists did

---

[1]We will not attempt to provide a comprehensive bibliography. Good bibliographies can, however, be found in Roger Owen and Bob Sutcliffe, eds., *Studies in the Theory of Imperialism* (London: Longmans, 1972); Douglas H. Rosenberg and Major Raoul Alcala, "The New Politics of National Security: A Selected and Annotated Research Bibliography," in Bruce M. Russett and Alfred Stepan, eds., *Military Force and American Society* (New York: Harper & Row, 1972), esp. pp. 322 ff.; and several of the more recent and wide-ranging materials cited later in this book.

[2]D. K. Fieldhouse, ed., *The Theory of Capitalist Imperialism* (New York: Barnes and Noble, 1967), p. xvii. Also see Edmund Silberner, *The Problem of War in Nineteenth Century Economic Thought*, translated by Alexander H. Krappe (Princeton, N.J.: Princeton University Press, 1946). A number of conservative political figures also asserted a causal connection between capitalism and imperialism. See Karl W. Deutsch, "Theories of Imperialism and Neocolonialism," in Steven J. Rosen and James R. Kurth, eds., *Testing Theories of Economic Imperialism* (Lexington, Mass.: D. C. Heath, 1974), p. 17.

not always then link this interpretation to the acquisition of colonies, but J. A. Hobson, the liberal English economist writing at the end of the nineteenth century, developed it more completely. He saw the maldistribution of income and wealth in capitalist countries—especially England—as leading to underconsumption, which in turn forced the export of capital and competition for control of foreign markets.[3] The capitalist system of the time was to blame, but imperialism was not, by his theory, inherent in capitalism. If there were a more equal distribution of income, underconsumption—and thus the export of capital—could be avoided.

Thorstein Veblen also sometimes wrote in a similar if far less theoretically developed vein:

The great business interests are the more inclined to look kindly on an extension of warlike enterprise and armaments, since the pecuniary advantages inure to them, while the pecuniary burden falls chiefly on the rest of the community. It is, to say the least, highly improbable that the business gains which accrue from a well-conducted foreign policy over, in modern times, equal the cost at which they are secured; but that consideration scarcely enters, since the costs are not paid out of business gains, but out of the industry of the rest of the people.[4]

And Charles A. Beard, identifying what he called the "Hamiltonian conception of national interest," described it as supporting the "acquisition of distant territories offering naval bases and opportunities for the extension of American commerce," as well as the idea that "the whole weight of the Federal Government, including an efficient naval establishment, is to be thrown into the operation of promoting the export of American goods and importation of materials that will not 'harm' American industries."[5]

Karl Marx himself had comparatively little to say about the international consequences of capitalism, but many writers of the early twentieth century developed extremely influential theories on imperialism that were in the Marxist tradition. Most famous is the work of Lenin. According to him, surplus capital arises inevitably from the processes of monopoly capitalist production; no feasible redistribution of income could avoid it. Industrial and banking capital ("finance capital" in the phrase of Rudolf Hilferding) merge to gain effective control of the state. Thus the drive to export surplus capital becomes a competition among nations, rather than simply a competition among corporations. The capitalist nations, in turn, divide the world among themselves, and their

---

[3]J. A. Hobson, *Imperialism: A Study* (London: Allen and Unwin, 1902).
[4]*The Theory of Business Enterprise* (New York: Scribner's, 1904), p. 297.
[5]*The Idea of National Interest* (New York: Macmillan, 1934), p. 550.

competition for territory ultimately leads to war among the capitalist powers.[6]

In regarding imperialism as an inherent stage of capitalism, required by finance capital, Lenin expressed the predominant Marxist view, in contrast to the views of the liberal Hobson and the Marxist Karl Kautsky, which he explicitly tried to refute. For Kautsky the international cartels might become a force for peace, a "super-imperialism" that would dominate the world and impose peace and order. Lenin rejected this view: if such events happened they would only be temporary. When capitalists' interests changed there would be a renewed struggle along national lines.

Kautsky was concerned not just with the export of capital, but with capitalist countries' need for market outlets. So too were Nikolai Bukharin and Rosa Luxemburg, who like Lenin believed militarism and colonial expansion to be inherent in capitalism. "Imperialism is the political expression of the accumulation of capital in its competitive struggle for what remains still open of the non-capitalist environment." Manifested in political expansion, violence, and war, "imperialism grows in lawlessness and violence, both in aggression against the non-capitalist world and in ever more serious conflicts among the competing capitalist countries."[7] Kautsky, Luxemburg, and Bukharin also gave some attention to capitalist countries' continual need for new sources of raw materials.

All these theories were designed essentially to explain the phenomenon of European colonialism, which was at its height in the decades preceding World War I, and they have been the subject of intensive criticism; on a variety of grounds they are said to provide poor explanations of the phenomenon. A number of studies have pointed out empirical evidence that contradicts them. For example, income from overseas investment *exceeded* capital outflow for Great Britain (the chief capitalist and imperialist power) during most of the nineteenth century and up to 1914—hardly consistent with the idea of ever-expanding surplus capital at home. Moreover, most of British foreign investment did not go to the African and Asian colonies or to other less developed countries (LDCs); instead, more than three-fourths went to the United States, the white

---

[6]V. I. Lenin, *Imperialism* (New York: Vanguard, 1929 edition).

[7]Quotations from Rosa Luxemburg, *The Accumulation of Capital* (New Haven, Conn.: Yale University Press, 1951 edition), p. 446; cited in Tom Kemp, *Theories of Imperialism* (London: Dobson, 1967), p. 59. Also see Nikolai Bukharin, *Imperialism and World Economy* (London: Merlin Press, 1972).

Commonwealth, and other advanced capitalist countries, which should have been plagued by surplus capital conditions similar to those that were supposed to have been occurring in Great Britain. Then too, the formation of monopolies in Great Britain took place mainly toward the end of this period, not during the time of greatest colonial expansion.[8]

In response to this evidence, other theorists have offered primarily political or strategic explanations for colonialism, taking account of economic factors but putting them in a relatively subordinate place. Diplomatic and strategic rivalries among European powers assume prominence, as does emphasis on mass support, that is, nationalism. For instance, D. K. Fieldhouse writes, "Imperialism owed its popular appeal not to the sinister influence of the capitalists, but to its inherent attractions for the masses"[9]: practically an ideological or "democratic" theory as we characterized them in Chapter 1. Primary among the theorists of *political* rivalry was Eugene Staley. He did note the force of economic interests in some instances:

The permanent investor of bona fide capital wants a long-run promotion of stability, a strong government which can guarantee tranquility and the security of property. . . . It may help to produce a policy of active diplomatic interference in the affairs of nominally independent states with the purpose of preventing chronic revolution and fostering security of property.

Generally, however, he considers this unimportant.

The caricature of the banker burdened with bags of "surplus capital" forced to seek outlets for his excess funds in hazardous territory, then calling upon his government for protection, belongs mainly in mythology. The truth is that enterprises involving considerable amounts of capital . . . are ordinarily undertaken with reluctance in regions where there are obvious financial hazards, and very often only after considerable persuasion from a government with a political axe to grind.

---

[8]For this counterevidence see, for example, A. K. Cairncross, *Home and Foreign Investment, 1870–1913* (Cambridge: Cambridge University Press, 1953); Herbert Feis, *Europe: the World's Banker, 1870–1914* (New Haven, Conn.: Yale University Press, 1930); D. K. Fieldhouse, *The Theory of Capitalist Imperialism* (London: Longmans, 1967); and, for an acknowledgment of the force of this argument by one now writing in the Marxist tradition, see Michael Barratt Brown, *After Imperialism* (London: Heinemann, 1963); and Brown, "A Critique of Marxist Theories of Imperialism," in Owen and Sutcliffe, eds., op. cit.

[9]"'Imperialism': An Historiographical Revision," *Economic History Review* 14, No. 2 (December 1961): 195.

The typical situation, according to Staley, is one of investments in the service of diplomacy, not vice versa:

Private investments have usually, in actual practice, been subordinated by governments to factors of general political or military strategy which have a more direct bearing on power. Thus it is that private investors have received strong, even outrageously exaggerated governmental backing where they have been tools and agents of power and prestige politics, while other investors whose projects seemed to run counter to the government's line of political endeavor have experienced official indifference or even active opposition.[10]

Other largely politically based theories are widespread; one of the most notable examples is that expressed by Raymond Aron, who wrote of the power of patriotism and the myth of national and racial superiority.[11] Another theory, carefully examining British actions in Africa, declares that their object was political and strategic, not economic.[12]

Some prominent writers incorporated economic motivations into their understanding of the period, but not in the way of Hobson or the Marxists. For William L. Langer, British imperialism of the late nineteenth century was basically reactive, protective, as witnessed by the fact that other countries imitated earlier British imperial expansion and erected trade barriers in their new colonies to keep British goods out:

At bottom the movement was probably as much economic as anything else. It resulted from the tremendously enhanced productive powers of European industry and the breakdown of the monopolistic position of England through the appearance of competitions. The feeling that new markets must be secured was very widespread and the need for new fields of investment, though not much discussed at the time, was probably even more important. These needs, however, had been met in the past without any corresponding expansion of territory. It was the embarkation of France, Germany, and other countries on the course of political control that brought the British to the conviction that only political control could adequately safeguard markets.[13]

---

[10]All quotations from Eugene Staley, *War and the Private Investor* (Garden City, N.Y.: Doubleday, 1935), pp. 161, 273, 361–362.

[11]See his *The Century of Total War* (Garden City, N.Y.: Doubleday, 1954), esp. the chapter entitled, "The Leninist Myth of Imperialism."

[12]R. E. Robinson and John Gallagher, *Africa and the Victorians* (New York: St. Martin's, 1961). But note the important caveat of Kemp, op. cit.: the strategic interests arose for Britain because of her *existing* imperial holdings in India, which leaves open the possibility that the basic motivation was to protect the economic interests there.

[13]William L. Langer, *The Diplomacy of Imperialism, 1890–1902* (New York: Knopf, 1935), p. 95.

And Karl Polanyi, acknowledging the responsibility of commercial interests for many fairly small wars, noted their concern for avoiding large-scale violence among the colonial powers:

Actually, business and finance were responsible for many colonial wars, but also for the fact that a general conflagration was avoided. Their affiliations with heavy industry, though really close only in Germany, accounted for both. For every one interest that was furthered by war, there were a dozen that could be adversely affected. International capital, of course, was bound to be the loser in case of war; but even national finance could gain only exceptionally, though frequently enough to account for dozens of colonial wars, as long as they remained isolated. Every war almost, was organized by the financiers; but peace also was organized by them.[14]

Best known of the noneconomic theories surely is that of Joseph Schumpeter. Although he acknowledged that some monopolists have an interest in the conquest of lands producing raw materials and foodstuffs, he regarded it as "a basic fallacy to describe imperialism as a necessary phase of capitalism, or even to speak of the development of capitalism into imperialism."[15] Some capitalists may gain, but only a small minority. The gains of capitalists as a class from war are more than offset by its losses and burdens. Though economic interests play a part, imperialism is *primarily* an affair of politicians and military men, not capitalists. Basically it is the result of attitudes and behavior patterns among the militarists who evolved historically, in the precapitalist era, to defend the state and establish its security. Atavistic psychological dispositions and social structures, having outlived what Schumpeter called their "meaning and their life-preserving function," retain an interest in war itself rather than in the material advantages to be gained by conquest.

Despite the relative age of these theories, the fact that they were developed mainly to explain the acquisition of overt political control of colonies, and the empirical difficulties with many of them, they most certainly are not dead. Those in the Marxist tradition have the strength of a relatively deductive system of reasoning, but all of them suffer from the methodological problems of evidence and selective perception that we discussed in Chapter 1. We shall

[14]Karl Polanyi, *The Great Transformation* (Boston: Beacon Press, 1957), p. 16. For other interpretations generally along this line, see Lionel Robbins, *The Economic Causes of War* (London: Jonathan Cape, 1939); and Jacob Viner, "International Finance and Balance of Power Diplomacy, 1880–1914," *Southwestern Political and Social Science Quarterly* 9, No. 4 (March 1929).

[15]*Imperialism and Social Classes* (New York: Meridian Books, 1955), p. 84.

deal with some modern developments of all these theories later in this chapter, but it is convenient at this point to derive from them a few hypotheses we can test from our data:

1.1 *Businessmen will be more favorable toward military preparedness than will other elites.*

1.2 *Businessmen will be more favorable than other elites toward United States government activities to protect American business interests abroad, and toward the promotion of governments in less developed countries that are well disposed to the activities of foreign investors and maintenance of the free enterprise system; similarly, they will be more hostile toward socialist and communist governments in less developed countries.*

The two hypotheses seem to follow from both the liberal and Marxist economic interest traditions as reviewed so far. Both indicate, for somewhat different reasons, an interest on the part of capitalists as a class—a greater interest than that evidenced by other classes—in economic and political expansion overseas, and in equipping and maintaining the military forces necessary to support expansion. A hypothesis that probably would be endorsed by critics of economic theories like Staley and Aron would be that businessmen would not significantly differ from other elite groups. A largely contrary pair of hypotheses, derivable from a Schumpeterian perspective, would be:

1.3 *Military men will be more favorable toward military preparedness than will civilian elites, including businessmen.*

1.4 *Military men will be more "hawkish" on a variety of foreign policy issues than will civilian elites, including businessmen.*

Of course, these hypotheses, especially the first, can also be derived from a variety of perspectives on bureaucratic politics or military sociology that owe little specifically to Schumpeter.

Modern Theories about the Imperatives of Capitalism

Few modern theories accept the full "surplus capital" version of the classical Marxist tradition, though several employ major aspects of it. Baran and Sweezy express the neo-Marxist position well. Their basic argument is that heavy military expenditures serve the capitalist purpose of maintaining prosperity at home while fighting socialism abroad. According to them, monopoly capitalism does generate a surplus, which must be absorbed. This can only be done by government spending and taxing. "It is to the interest of all classes—though not of all elements within them—that government should steadily increase its spending and taxing." Some "welfare state" spending is broadly acceptable, but not to the point of damaging work incentives in the labor market or providing major competition to private enterprise. Capitalist desires not to lose potential areas of productivity to public enterprise, and the need to maintain capitalist ideological premises that social welfare is best provided by the private production of goods and services, limit the scope of government activity. Thus neither private demand nor public spending for civil purposes can sustain the economy. Under these circumstances, military spending is entirely acceptable because it does not compete with any vested private interests, and it has the extra advantages of quick obsolescence and effective central control over levels and locations.[16]

The military capabilities so acquired are, it is alleged, also of great utility for defending the international capitalist system. Socialist revolutions in less developed countries must be opposed, by force if necessary. To American capitalists particularly, governments aiming to abolish private ownership and private enterprise

... are profoundly objectionable not only because their actions adversely affect foreign-owned interests and enterprises or because they render future capitalist implantation impossible; in some cases this may be of no great economic consequence. But the objection still remains because the withdrawal of any country from the world system of capitalist enterprise is seen as constituting a weakening of that system and as providing encouragement to further dissidence and withdrawal.[17]

It is difficult to make an unambiguous test of these ideas. One side can point to the unprecedented high level of peacetime military spending in the United States over the past three decades (coinciding until 1974 with satisfactory maintenance of adequate aggregate demand for the first time ever over such a long period), sometimes at a level double that of all government spending on health and

---

[16]Paul A. Baran and Paul M. Sweezy, *Monopoly Capital: An Essay on the American Economic and Social Order* (Harmondsworth: Pelican, 1968), esp. chs. 6 and 7. See also, for example, Michael Kidron, *Western Capitalism Since the War* (Harmondsworth: Penguin, 1970), ch. 3; Michael Reich, "Military Spending and the U.S. Economy," in Steven Rosen, ed., *Testing the Theory of the Military-Industrial Complex* (Lexington, Mass.: D. C. Heath, 1973); and Michael Barratt Brown, in Owen and Sutcliffe, eds., op. cit. Some of this can also be found in recent writings of liberal critics, such as J. K. Galbraith, *The New Industrial State* (Boston: Houghton Mifflin, 1971).

[17]Ralph Miliband, *The State in Capitalist Society* (New York: Basic Books, 1969), p. 86. See also Helmut Kramer and Helfried Bauer, "Imperialism, Intervention Capacity, and Foreign Policy Making: The U.S. Intervention in Indochina," *Journal of Peace Research*, No. 2 (1972): 285–303.

education combined. The other side, however, can answer that military spending as a proportion of GNP has been falling ever since 1968, was in 1973 lower (at 6.4 percent) than at any time since 1950, and was surpassed by government health and education spending in 1972.[18]

Which is the proper perspective? Or can it be that the evaluation of Baran and Sweezy and others was largely correct, but that recently capitalists have changed their spots? Even Soviet theorists now explicitly *reject* the idea that in the long term military spending is beneficial or necessary to capitalism. Acknowledging that a boost in military expenditures may temporarily stimulate the economy, a recent study by the Institute of Philosophy of the Soviet Academy of Sciences approvingly quoted a United Nations report: "There should thus be no doubt that the diversion to peaceful uses of the resources now in military use could be accomplished to the benefit of all countries and lead to the improvement of world economic and social conditions."[19]

Nevertheless, we can make a partial test of the theory by adding to our previously derived hypotheses 1.1 and 1.2 the following:

1.5 *Businessmen will be more hawkish on a variety of foreign policy issues than will other elites.*

1.6 *Businessmen will be more opposed to income redistribution (in an egalitarian direction) than will other elites.*

Arguments about the critical role of foreign trade and/or investments (e.g., Lenin) face some problems when applied to the

---

[18]U.S. Bureau of the Census, *Statistical Abstract of the United States, 1974* (Washington, D.C.: Government Printing Office, 1974).

[19]*Economic and Social Consequences of Disarmament*, Report of the U.N. Secretary General transmitting the study of his consultative group, Vienna, 1962, p. 57, as cited in *Problems of War and Peace: A Critical Analysis of Bourgeois Theories* (no author given; Moscow: Progress Publishers, 1972), p. 107. Also see Georgi Arbatov, *The War of Ideas in Contemporary International Relations* (Moscow: Progress, 1973), p. 74, discussing ". . . aggravation of the social contradictions of American society and the emergence of a wide range of internal problems linked with poverty, the urban crisis, the condition of the Negro population and the growth of crime. . . . Most of these difficulties have been caused by the huge spending on armaments and the war in Vietnam. They have aggravated the political situation in the United States itself." A neat counterargument to neo-Marxist theories is the recent one that the Soviet Union is now dependent, if not for adequate overall demand, at least for vital foreign exchange, on its arms sales to Arab nations.

contemporary United States; American industry and commerce is overwhelmingly oriented toward the domestic, not the foreign, market. Long-term foreign investment by American firms amounts to only 10 percent of the total United States GNP. Even this gives an exaggerated impression of its importance, since the proper comparison of the value of foreign investment ought to be with the value of domestic productive capacity, not GNP. That would work out to something like 3 or 4 percent. Similarly, merchandise exports plus imports amount to only about 9 percent of GNP. Adding trade in services but subtracting for a bit of double counting (even in 1968, 8 percent of the production of United States-owned foreign manufacturing subsidiaries was imported back into the United States),[20] private foreign-oriented economic activity in the United States accounts for under one-sixth of total economic activity, or less than one-fifth of private economic activity (excluding government).[21] Furthermore, although this proportion has grown modestly during the post-World War II years, it remains well below the levels reached before that war (see Figure 2.1.). The classical Marxist arguments about an advanced capitalist economy's dependence on foreign investment (or trade) to absorb surplus capital thus encounter some difficulty, although it is still possible to argue that this foreign-oriented activity, though relatively small, is nevertheless critical to the economy's health. All of the foregoing is roughly compatible with the results of our survey of executives from the major industrial and financial corporations of America; 62 percent of them indicated that business with foreign countries (excluding Canada) accounted for less than 10 percent of their firms' total sales or assets.

Perhaps more plausible to most readers will be some theories about the benefits certain kinds of capitalists obtain. In some de-

---

[20]Theodore Moran, "Foreign Expansion as an 'Institutional Necessity' for U.S. Corporate Capitalism: The Search for a Radical Model," *World Politics* 25, No. 3 (April 1973): 384.

[21]Some writers like Harry Magdoff, *The Age of Imperialism* (New York: Monthly Review Press, 1969), p. 183, have produced related calculations that are substantially higher, but they do not seem valid. See, for example, Benjamin J. Cohen, *The Question of Imperialism* (New York: Basic Books, 1973), ch. 4, Table 4.9. Other writers emphasize that, though relatively not large, foreign economic operations are important at the *margin* to American firms. See, for example, William Appleman Williams, "The Large Corporations and American Foreign Policy," in David Horowitz, ed., *Corporations and the Cold War* (New York: Monthly Review Press, 1969), p. 75.

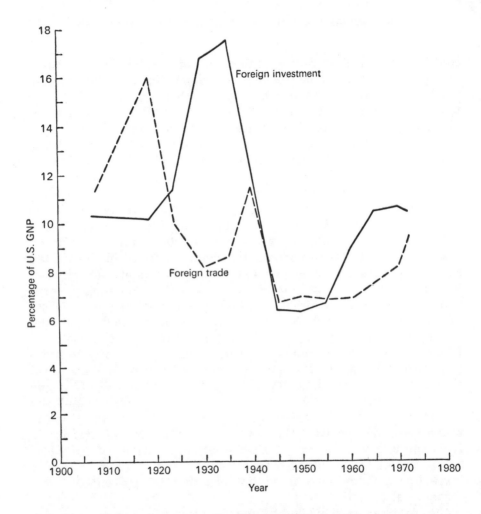

Figure 2.1. Foreign trade in merchandise and long-term foreign investment as a percentage of United States GNP. [Sources: United States Bureau of the Census, *Historical Statistics of the United States, Colonial Times to 1957.* Washington, D.C.: Government Printing Office, 1962, pp. 139, 539, 565. United States Bureau of the Census, *Statistical Abstract of the United States, 1973.* Washington, D.C.: Government Printing Office, 1973, pp. 320, 766, 767.]

gree the theories share the same perspectives as the previously described theories. They consider the imperatives facing virtually all capitalists in advanced industrial economies, but attribute enough special importance to particular groups to allow us to develop a different set of hypotheses.

Several modern theories allege that foreign-oriented firms play a particular role in overseas political as well as economic expansion. A perceptive article by Theodore Moran suggests that foreign investment results from barriers to overseas trade in addition, perhaps, to certain pressures of surplus capital. When opportunities for expanding the home market no longer suffice, manufacturing enterprises in advanced economies will seek overseas markets for their products—but markets with similar demand structures, able to absorb goods similar to those the enterprises are already producing. This will be satisfactory for a while during the life of a product, but soon the exporting firm's successes will be imitated in the importing country. The new competition is likely to be protected by means of quotas, tariffs, and other restrictions imposed by the home government. To leap these import barriers the previously exporting firm will have to develop or acquire productive capacity abroad; that is, it will have to invest overseas. Otherwise it will lose its foreign markets, and indeed possibly face the threat that its new foreign competitors may even send their goods back to take away its domestic market. Innovative enterprises relying on advanced technology, like many of those in the United States, are particularly subject to this cycle, and so are driven to foreign investment. Thus, according to Moran, the absolute size of foreign investments relative to GNP at any particular time is less important than the opportunity or expectation of expanding them: "Any interpretation of an *accumulated* stake far understates the interest that the most dynamic domestic corporations have in keeping the possibility of foreign expansion open to them in *the future*." Moreover, this interest is likely to lead to pressures for general forms of political support from the American government:

There *is* something fundamental to American corporate capitalism— the capitalism of tightly held technology, uncertain information, large economies of scale, and unstable imperfect competition ... —that creates strong pressures for foreign investment. As long as American corporations exercise their virtues of inventiveness and aggressiveness, their government will feel intense, even frantic pressures to create and preserve an international system that facilitates foreign economic expansion.[22]

In supporting his description of the product cycle and the incentives for overseas investment Moran draws on a substantial volume of research conducted at Harvard University. Neverthe-

---

[22]Moran, op. cit., pp. 371, 386; italics in original.

less, there are severe difficulties with this theory, among them the still fairly modest rate of increase in overseas investment. More important, however, the theory is of only moderate utility as a *political* theory. It would explain some pressures for maintaining NATO and other military or political ties with developed states (European countries, Canada, Japan), and some efforts by the American government to obtain favorable treatment for its investors in those countries. But as a radical theory to explain American "interventionist" policy in underdeveloped countries, it is entirely inappropriate. Because it focuses on American investments in the developed states (where in fact approximately 70 percent of such investments are to be found), it is not a theory about the sources of policy toward the LDCs.

The virtue of Moran's theory is its attempt to incorporate the fact that American foreign investments are predominantly in the other advanced capitalist countries—a fact that weakens any "surplus capital" theory. Other attempts to cope with this difficulty have stressed the differential rates of return to investment in different areas. Some studies seem to show that the average rate of return on foreign investments in general is not higher than the return on domestic investments in advanced economies; others suggest that the rate is higher, especially for investments in underdeveloped countries. But the results are inconclusive, largely because big multinational corporations have some freedom to juggle prices among their subsidiaries and to show their profits where they wish, largely for tax considerations.[23]

Yet another line of attack is to recognize the quantitative unimportance of American investments in LDCs, or trade with LDCs (barely more than 2 percent of GNP), but to emphasize their crucial nature. Polanyi believed that objectively, and taking the long view, the economic benefits of nineteenth-century imperialism to the European states were very slight, but he saw those states as competitively acquiring colonies so as to avoid short-term dislocation from loss of markets and raw-material sources (a view not dissimilar from Langer's):

To expect that a community would remain indifferent to the scourge of unemployment, the shifting of industries and occupations and to the moral and psychological torture accompanying them, merely because

---

[23]See, for various views, Magdoff, op. cit.; Cohen, op. cit.; Frank Ackerman, "Magdoff on Imperialism," in *Public Policy* 19, No. 3 (Summer 1971): 325–331; and Michael Barratt Brown, in Owen and Sutcliffe, eds., op. cit.

economic effects, in the long run, might be negligible, was to assume an absurdity.[24]

Staley noted that British purchase of control over the Anglo-Persian Oil Company was impelled by the Royal Navy's need for oil, and quoted Churchill: "The supreme ships of the navy on which our life depended, were fed by oil and could only be fed by oil. . . . A decision like this involved our national safety as much as a battle at sea."[25] This is consistent with Staley's general view that the government intervened more often to promote investment or exploration for political or strategic purposes rather than to act as the subordinate agent of private enterprise. Something like this might surely be going on now, given the substantial and very rapidly growing dependence of the United States on foreign sources of raw materials: among others, chromium, copper, nickel, cobalt, bauxite, iron, and most notably oil. Figure 2.2 shows the situation for four of these materials even in 1970; American overseas dependence is increasing rapidly, and is expected to increase, for each of them. *Any* industrial economy in the United States, whether capitalist or socialist, would be dependent on these sources, but it is alleged that the existing capitalist economy is particularly vulnerable for two reasons: the especially high valuation that is placed on growth (and hence ever-greater resource needs), and the global rivalry with the socialist states. Any danger that developing countries will adopt socialist governments, and hence either cut off the resource flow for cold war reasons or divert the resources to their own development, is peculiarly threatening. Low prices, as well as simply adequate supplies, are at issue.[26]

Surely the idea of intervening to assure access to strategic raw materials is not dead, though whether capitalist systems are especially prone to such acts is not clear. That view will not explain every case of intervention in a less developed country (e.g., the Dominican Republic), but then no single theory should realistically

[24]Polanyi, op. cit., p. 215.

[25]Staley, op. cit., p. 76.

[26]See especially Magdoff, op. cit.; Magdoff, "Imperialism without Colonies," in Owen and Sutcliffe, eds., op. cit.; Michael Barratt Brown, in Owen and Sutcliffe, eds.; Heather Dean, *Scarce Resources: The Dynamic of American Imperialism* (Boston: New England Free Press, 1969); and Gabriel Kolko, *The Roots of American Foreign Policy: An Analysis of Power and Purpose* (Boston: Beacon, 1969). Also see the useful review of these and other theories by Andrew Mack, "Comparing Theories of Economic Imperialism," in Rosen and Kurth, eds., op. cit. Some of this may also be found in Gunnar Myrdal, *Theory and Underdeveloped Regions* (London: Duckworth, 1957).

42

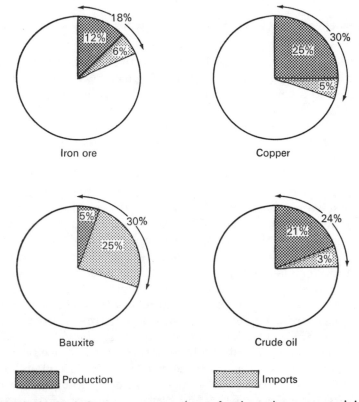

Iron ore

Copper

Bauxite

Crude oil

▓▓▓ Production   ░░░ Imports

Figure 2.2. United States consumption of selected raw materials: percentage of world total in 1970. [Source: Peter G. Peterson, *The United States in the Changing World Economy*, vol. 2, *Statistical Background Material*. Washington, D.C.: Government Printing Office, 1971, chart 65.]

be expected to explain every case. *Sensitivity* to particular needs ought to be a major element in any theory, rather than merely a mechanical percentaging. The value of some products may be relatively slight, but they may be very hard to do without. One author tellingly notes that even many American investments in developed countries in fact are heavily dependent on raw-material supplies; for instance, he alleges that 25 percent of the great total of American direct investment in Europe is in petroleum processing and distribution.[27]

One other "radical" argument about the importance of under-

[27]Jonathan Galloway, "Multinational Corporations and Military-Industrial Linkages," in Rosen, ed., op. cit., p. 278.

developed countries concerns the essential unity of the international capitalist economy, and the danger to it of a cumulating, snowballing withdrawal of revolutionary socialist states from that system. The following sort of statement is fairly common:

As a general rule, the American government's attitude to governments in the Third World, or for that matter in the whole non-socialist world, depends very largely on the degree to which these governments favour American free enterprise in their countries or are likely to favour it in the future. . . .[28]

More pointedly,

For the United States to defend its empire today means to fight socialism, not only in the empire but wherever it exists, for socialism is by its very nature an international movement which gains strength everywhere from a success anywhere. Hence all revolutions must be opposed, since every source which gives them material or moral aid must be weakened and if possible destroyed.[29]

We certainly know that multinational corporations have intervened against nationalist, socializing regimes in less developed countries, and that they have attempted to gain the active support of the United States government in their efforts. The affair of ITT in Chile is the most blatant example (though it appears that other firms with operations in Chile were reluctant to second ITT's efforts, and the corporation's interest seems not to have been the prime influence behind the actions of the American government).

Potential as well as actual economic interests must be protected, and as much of the world as possible kept open for United States trade, investment, and utilization of resources. According to this view, communist revolutionary movements, and other nationalist movements that would restrict or hamper American capitalist enterprise abroad, must be resisted. The immediate interests of the investors in the threatened country must, of course, be protected. But since existing interests in Vietnam, for example, are slight, it is the potential that counts. Banning Garrett has argued that the Indochina war was intended to create economic opportunity rather than merely to seize existing resources, and that this led to the need for a military protection force of this "compulsive capital development."[30]

---

[28]Miliband, op. cit.; see also the previous quotation from Miliband (cited in footnote 17).

[29]Baran and Sweezy, op. cit., p. 205.

[30]"The Strange Economics of the Vietnam War," *Ramparts* 10, No. 5 (November 1971): 34.

Because the costs of protection are so disproportionate to any gains that can be envisaged in Indochina itself, the potential availability argument is often expanded. Competing multinational corporations with conflicting interests are seen as united in wanting "the world of nations in which they operate to be as large as possible."[31] Moreover, the United States "requires the option to expand to regions it has not yet penetrated."[32] For these opportunities to remain profitable as well as available, it is necessary that the "political and economic principles of capitalism should prevail and that the door be fully open for foreign capital at all times."[33] Thus it is necessary to forestall that particular kind of domino effect that might result from another communist or nationalist takeover. This would seem to apply most strongly to firms with specific interests in Southeast Asia or in less developed countries elsewhere, but even other firms will share a general concern for perpetuating the "rules of the game" that "guarantee the sanctity of private property and other essentials of capitalism."[34] Because of Vietnam's modest economic value, military intervention is all the more significant "as an example of America's determination to hold the line as a matter of principle against revolutionary movements.[35] Indeed, the very fact that the United States was willing to fight in order to hold an area of such marginal economic value served as an especially powerful demonstration of its readiness to defend bigger or nearer areas where the economic stakes were larger.

Some of the derivable hypotheses are not very different from those deriving from "surplus capital" or other economic explanations that led to hypotheses like 1.2 and 1.5. To them we could add one specifically relevant to Vietnam:

---

[31]Paul A. Baran and Paul M. Sweezy, "Notes on the Theory of Imperialism," in K. T. Fann and Donald C. Hodges, eds., *Readings in U.S. Imperialism* (Boston: Porter Sargent, 1971), p. 81.

[32]Gabriel Kolko, op. cit.

[33]Magdoff, op. cit., p. 85. See also Joyce and Gabriel Kolko, *The Limits of Power: The World and United States Foreign Policy, 1945–1954* (New York: Harper & Row, 1972), p. 23: "The question of foreign economic policy was not the containment of Communism, but more directly the extension and expansion of American capitalism."

[34]Ad Hoc Committee on the Economy and the War, "Economic Interests and American Foreign Policy," *Review of Radical Political Economics* (August 1970), p. 26.

[35]Gabriel Kolko, op. cit., p. 85.

1.7 *Businessmen will be less likely to regard the American interven-tion in Vietnam as a mistake, less likely to think the war was bad for the American economy in general, and less likely to think they personally are worse off as a result of the war, than will other elites.*

More focused hypotheses also are derivable, however; namely, concerning differential motivations *within* the business community:

2.1 *Executives from corporations with substantial foreign sales or investments, or with expectations of substantially increasing foreign activi-ties, or with expectations of increasing activities specifically in less developed countries, will look more favorably upon the effects of the war (as specified in 1.7) than will executives from other corporations.*

2.2 *Executives from the corporations (specified in 2.1) will be more hawkish on a variety of foreign policy issues than will executives from other corporations.*

2.3 *Executives from such corporations will be more favorable toward United States government activities to protect American business interests abroad, and toward the promotion of governments in less developed countries that are well disposed to the activities of foreign investors and maintenance of the free enterprise system; similarly, they will be more hostile toward socialist and communist governments in less developed countries than will executives from other corporations.*

"Merchants of Death" versus Multinational Corporations

Another rather different set of theories stressing the particular interests of certain kinds of firms is represented in the "military-industrial complex" literature. We noted earlier the neo-Marxist argument that military spending is required to maintain an ade-quate level of demand in the economy. A more widely accepted view is that any diminution in aggregate demand resulting from a cut in arms spending could readily be made up by stimulating private spending through tax cuts and/or by expanding public spending for civilian purposes. (The latter would be somewhat more effective, dollar for dollar, for reasons identified in the technical economics literature, but might be somewhat less palatable to conservatives.) Nevertheless, some industries, and some geographical areas, would suffer severe short- or medium-term damage from any reduction of military expenditures. Controversy surrounds the question whether profits in the defense industries are higher than in comparable nondefense industries; overall, there seems to be no conclusive evidence that this is so.[36] Nevertheless a cutback, disrupting production and marketing in these industries and forcing their firms to make and find buyers for alternative products, would cause sharp losses for a while, concentrated in five industrial categories: aircraft, ordinance, electronics, nonferrous metals, and research and development. Workers as well as capitalists would be hurt.

Certainly *someone* stands to benefit from every dollar of the national product that is spent; some industries do benefit from military spending and would suffer from its reduction. The important question concerns the breadth and depth of that "suffering" as contrasted with the benefits to other industries of the diversion of resources away from military ends. As one author perceptively points out, the "disarmament" damage to each of the industries just mentioned (and probably to certain geographically defined labor markets as well) would likely exceed the gains accruing to any other *single* sector of industry. That is, military spending does not necessarily benefit the economy as a whole; rather, *most* firms would benefit *modestly* from a shift to other kinds of government or private spending—but the gains from defense spending to a few industries are proportionately greater to those industries than are the costs to any one sector when spread among all the sectors of the civilian economy. He then links this conclusion to a generally accepted description of political behavior in pluralist democracies: groups will concentrate their political activities on those issues that promise them the greatest gains, and will not deeply resist efforts of other groups pursuing their most important special interests when those efforts involve modest costs (so long as the prospective costs remain modest). Thus by a principle of "compensating strategies," a pork-barrel-like situation can be maintained where each looks out for getting something for himself and tolerates similar activities by others.[37]

---

[36]This is the conclusion of Robert J. Art, "Why We Overspend and Underaccomplish: Weapons Procurement and the Military-Industrial Complex," in Rosen, ed., op. cit., pp. 263–264, after reviewing four studies. Other relevant works in this large literature include Stanley Lieberson, "An Empirical Study of Military-Industrial Linkages," in Sam Sarkesian, ed., *The Military-Industrial Complex: A Reassessment* (Beverly Hills: Sage, 1972), who concludes that if anything, the returns to investment in defense industries are relatively low; and Richard Kaufman, *The War Profiteers* (Indianapolis: Bobbs-Merrill, 1970), who indicates, as the title suggests, that the opposite is true.

[37]Lieberson, op. cit. For an early view that the economic benefits are diffused among many firms only very distantly engaged in war production, see Richard Lewinsohn, *The Profits of War Through the Ages* (London: George Routledge and Sons, 1936).

This essentially political explanation would account for continuing excessive levels of military spending (and perhaps even maintenance of an ideological climate of fear and hostility necessary to support such a defense posture), despite the fact that economic gains were limited to but a small segment of the economy. This view is entirely consistent with the findings of a major study of American businessmen's attitudes toward tariff issues. According to those authors, "The men who feared loss from a tariff cut were more in favor of raising tariffs than were those who explicitly asserted that they would gain by the increase. We see that fear of loss is a more powerful stimulus than prospect of gain."[38]

From this perspective we can derive several more hypotheses concerning businessmen's attitudes toward military expenditures in particular, and more generally, levels of threat perception, hawkishness, and support for the Vietnam war (as a source of demand for military products):

3.1 *Executives from corporations making substantial sales to the Department of Defense will be more favorable toward military preparedness than will executives from other corporations.*

3.2 *Executives from such corporations will be more hawkish on a variety of foreign policy issues than will executives from other corporations.*

3.3 *Executives from such corporations will look more favorably on the effects of the Vietnam war (as specified in hypothesis 1.7) than will executives from other corporations.*

There is, of course, quite a different theoretical perspective, which postulates international commerce as a force for peace and restraining conflict. The nineteenth-century English liberal advocates of free trade, such as Richard Cobden and John Stuart Mill, developed this view, as did Saint-Simon and many other French liberals and socialists.[39] Writing in this tradition in 1909, Sir Norman Angell pleaded that a major European war would rupture the economies of all the participants, winners as well as losers, and that the economic losses to Great Britain in particular would far exceed any foreseeable gains.[40]

Many businessmen themselves seem to have accepted such an assessment. In his classic study of American military officers,

---

[38]Raymond A. Bauer, Ithiel de Sola Pool, and Anthony Dexter, *American Business and Public Policy: The Politics of Foreign Trade* (New York, Atherton, 1963), p. 142. See also E. E. Schattschneider, *Politics, Pressures, and the Tariff* (New York: Prentice-Hall, 1935).

[39]See Silberner, op. cit.

[40]*The Great Illusion* (London: William Heinemann, 1909), esp. ch. 9.

Samuel Huntington drew a basic distinction between the values
he saw as prevailing among military officers and those prevailing
in the business world, both in the twentieth century and earlier
in American history. For example, he contrasted the military ethic
with exponents of the "business pacifism" common in the late
nineteenth century. According to him, "business pacifism" manifested beliefs that "military forces in peace were passively destructive, pure consumers, parasites living off the fruit of other men's
labors"; "an optimistic belief in human nature, reason, and progress"; and a belief that "international free trade by multiplying
contacts among nations and creating mutual interests would eventually render war unthinkable." Moreover, he stressed the influence
of Herbert Spencer and William Graham Sumner on businessmen:
"Both argued that while war had served useful purposes in previous
eras, its utility was now over."[41] We earlier noted the view of
Polanyi that the merchants of international finance had been responsible for avoiding major conflict among the great powers
(though they were responsible also for many minor wars). Certainly
a fear of the consequences of European conflagration was mirrored
in the very high correlation observed between perceptions of international hostility and the outflow of gold from London in the 1914
crisis. Prices on the security markets of all the major powers
collapsed at the same time.[42]

A related position holds that businessmen engaged in large-
scale international commerce, or, in modern terms, executives of
the multinational corporations, will be a force for peace even if
businessmen as a class are not. We mentioned the belief of Kautsky
that international cartels might, in their "super-imperialism,"
impose a pacific order. A prominent modern writer, though frequently critical of multinational corporations, holds out somewhat
the same hope:

The growing power and internationalist ideology of the corporations
means that the number one nation no longer has the discretion traditionally associated with national sovereignty. Schumpeter's analysis
of the modern capitalist is vindicated. The interest of the leading corporations is indeed in peace, and, increasingly, the corporate managers

---

[41]*The Soldier and the State* (Cambridge, Mass.: Harvard University Press,
1957), pp. 223, 225–226.
[42]Ole R. Holsti and Robert C. North, "Comparative Data from Content
Analysis: Perceptions of Hostility and Economic Variables in the 1914
Crisis," in Merritt and Rokkan, eds., *Comparing Nations* (New Haven, Conn.:
Yale University Press, 1966).

are coming to see it. That being so, the power of the corporations will serve as a restraining influence on military adventurism.[43]

This statement is also common in various contemporary writings sympathetic to the multinational corporation. Another writer, from a somewhat different radical perspective, asserts that the international sector of the capitalist class (as contrasted with the national sector) is less chauvinist, less supportive of an aggressive foreign policy, and, with its wider horizons, is ultimately more critical of the Vietnam intervention.[44] From yet another angle, a view that is a commonplace in the literature of international political integration, and supported by fairly good evidence, is that business executives whose firms are heavily engaged in international trade or are otherwise in special contact with the international community are more favorably disposed toward integration and to accommodation with other nations' views.[45]

We can draw a number of hypotheses from these statements:

1.8 *Businessmen will be less favorable toward military preparedness than will other elites.*

1.9 *Businessmen will be less hawkish on a variety of foreign policy issues than will other elites.*

1.10 *Businessmen will be more likely to regard the American intervention in Vietnam as a mistake, more likely to think the war was bad for the American economy in general, and more likely to think they personally are worse off as a result of the war, than will other elites.*

2.4 *Executives from corporations with substantial foreign sales or investments, or with expectations of substantially increasing foreign activities, will look less favorably upon the effects of the Vietnam war (as specified in 1.10) than will executives from other corporations.*

2.5 *Executives from such corporations (as specified in 2.4) will be less hawkish on a variety of foreign policy issues than will executives from other corporations.*

2.6 *Executives from corporations with expectations of substantially increasing sales or investments in the Soviet Union and/or China will be less hawkish on a variety of foreign policy issues than will executives from other corporations.*

---

[43]Richard Barnet, *Roots of War* (New York: Atheneum, 1972), p. 236.

[44]Thomas F. Mayer, "Imperialism and American Class Structure," Institute of Behavioral Science, University of Colorado, Boulder, Colorado, 1973, mimeo.

[45]See Bruce M. Russett, *Power and Community in World Politics* (San Francisco: W. H. Freeman, 1974), pp. 331–332; also Bernard Mennis and Karl P. Sauvant, "Multinational Corporations, Managers, and the Development of Regional Identifications in Western Europe," *Annals of the American Academy of Political and Social Science* 403 (September 1972): 22–33.

It would be wrong, however, to expect the differences between executives from different kinds of firms to be overwhelming. Given the content of so many people's beliefs on foreign policy, various hawkish as well as "dovish" attitudes will be widespread throughout the business community, and among other elites, even now. The most casual perceptions make it obvious that ideologies of anticommunism, interventionism, or national preparedness have many advocates who themselves stand to gain little materially from them. More important, individuals' perceptions of their self-interest vary even within groups where objectively each individual may have the same material stake in an outcome. The definition of one's self-interest is a very complex matter, subject to a variety of influences from colleagues, friends, the media, pressure groups, and of course one's whole set of experiences and political socialization. Bauer, Pool, and Dexter are very explicit about this at repeated points in their book:

A pressure group's function is, in large part, to define the interests of its partisans. Interests may not be self-evident, and a pressure group may define interests in such a way as to gain supporters it would not otherwise have; a firm or businessman may go to either side depending on how the definition is set up for him.

Unlike our friends who told us, "Tell me a man's interest and I will tell you his stand," we would say, "Tell us where a man stands and we will tell you what perceptions of his interests will serve to make that stand a self-consistent and stable one." There are perceptions of self-interest available to bolster any stand by any individual.

Noting aptly that the idea of personal self-interest is as vague a concept as is that of national interest, they conclude it is especially hard to predict the views of executives from big corporations merely from their apparent economic interests. Men from larger firms are more informed about issues, participate more in discussions, are more politically active, and have a wider frame of reference than men from small firms.

Any single criterion of self-interest which we employed as a predictor of activity produced proportionately more increase in activity among the men from the smaller firms.

In general, . . . the larger a firm is, the more concern its chief officers must have for the interaction of their own behavior and that of the economic, social, and political environment in which they operate.[46]

---

[46]Bauer, Pool, and Dexter, op. cit.; quotations respectively from pages 398, 142–143, 229, 487. Note also the comment by Stephen Krasner: "Governmental actors can manipulate the perceptions of self-interest held by pri-

The businessmen whose views we will be discussing in this book are from very large corporations indeed, so this point should be very important. Not that we should not expect to identify associations between apparent economic interest and views on foreign policy issues, but simply that we should expect the effect frequently to be blurred, and in any case often not to be drawn overtly by the individual concerned.

Ideology and Values

Particular policy preferences can indeed be variously motivated; although direct economic interests will doubtless play a significant role in many instances, there is surely more to it. We have repeatedly mentioned the complexity of trying to sort them out, and the need to recognize the likelihood of a convergence of interests, "overdetermining" any particular policy. A critic of recent American foreign policy puts the argument this way:

The threatening behavior of hawkish groups in rival countries becomes the most potent bargaining counter in domestic politics. It provides the most telling justification for large defense budgets and relaxation of controls over how military appropriations are spent. At the same time it legitimizes reduced concern for civil rights and for welfare programs, keeps the economy buoyant, minimizes unemployment problems and the political threat they pose for the incumbent office-holder, and justifies increased controls over dissenting and protest activities. There is something for almost everybody and corresponding status benefits for those high in the political, industrial, military, and labor hierarchies.[47]

A similar convergence of interests has been noted in the Soviet Union, where the military, managers of heavy industry, and the conservative wing of the Party apparatus all benefit from a high level of real or apparent international tension—with the party apparatus gaining from a greater demand for ideological orthodoxy.[48]

---

vate groups; and particularly some business groups. Large complex firms, dealing with a multiplicity of products in many countries, may find it hard to define, in any given case, what policy would best further their economic aims. The managers of such firms usually have considerable discretion. They can allow their role as citizen to intrude upon their role as corporate managers." Stephen D. Krasner, "American Coffee Policy: Public Goals and Business Interests," in Abraham Lowenthal and Ernest May, eds., *United States Policy Making toward Latin America* (New York: Council on Foreign Relations, forthcoming, 1975).

[47]Murray Edelman, *Politics as Symbolic Action* (Chicago: Markham, 1971), p. 161.

[48]Vernon V. Aspaturian, "The Soviet Military-Industrial Complex: Does It Exist?" in Rosen, ed., op. cit.

Economic interest and ideology—whether of the "liberal messianist" variety or of a conservative anticommunist sort—might therefore combine, in the American case, to produce a more powerful impetus to an assertive, activist foreign policy than either could produce alone. If *perceptions* rather than "objective" interests determine behavior, then surely ideology is a key contributor to perception. William Appleman Williams, one of the first prominent revisionist historians, discusses the power of what he calls the ideology of the open door:

As they devoted more of their attention and energy to the challenge of extending the new American frontier, many economic leaders became enthusiastic converts to the mission to reform the world. The convergence of a sense of economic necessity and a moral calling transformed the traditional concept of open door expansion into a vision of an American century. In this fashion the United States entered and fought World War II. Americans . . . had come firmly to believe that their own prosperity and democracy depended upon the continued expansion of their economic system under the strategy of the open door.[49]

In a sense we are back to our position, stated in the previous chapter, of recognizing the probable element of truth in each of several theories—but still requiring some judgment as to the relative importance of each. For many analysts it is the ideological factor that matters most. An example is the work of two critics of the arms industry's alleged role in the United States' entry into World War I, who nevertheless conclude,

The root of the trouble . . . goes far deeper than the arms industry. It lies in the prevailing temper of peoples toward nationalism, militarism, and war, in the civilization which forms this temper and prevents any radical change. . . . If the arms industry is a cancer on the body of modern civilization, it is not an extraneous growth, it is the result of the unhealthy condition of the body itself.[50]

Men frequently pursue economic interests, and governments may pursue the economic interests of their citizens. Sometimes, however, government officials act for their own reasons—personal

---

[49]William Appleman Williams, *The Tragedy of American Diplomacy* (rev. ed.; New York: Dell, 1972), p. 201. An early statement of the role of what J. A. Hobson termed the "justificatory ideologies of imperialism," and their sometimes independent influence, is found in his *The Psychology of Jingoism* (London: G. Richards, 1901).

[50]H. C. Engelbrecht and F. C. Harrighen, *Merchants of Death* (New York: Dodd, Mead, 1939), pp. 8–10, as quoted in Jerome Slater and Terry Nardin, "The Concept of a Military-Industrial Complex," in Rosen, ed., op. cit., p. 56.

interests, or ideological or strategic considerations perhaps—while clothing their actions in the language of economic interests so as to broaden the base of their support. They may attempt to enlist the support of appropriate economic interests for policies on which they have already decided, for quite other reasons. Viewing only the policy output, it may be virtually impossible to decide which is the driving motivation, who is initiating a policy, and who is being used to lend support and legitimacy. We noted one aspect of this in Staley's discussion of the role of private investors in overseas diplomatic intervention. Another manifestation appears in a discussion of a famous statement by Assistant Secretary of State Dean Acheson to a congressional committee in 1944. Acheson declared that America must for economic reasons follow a much more internationalist political policy, because the economy required expanding markets abroad to absorb its "unlimited creative energy" and avoid stagnation of the domestic economy.[51] This statement, and others like it, are frequently referred to by radical and/or neo-Marxist opponents of American foreign policy. But to quote Robert W. Tucker,

Why may we not argue that such statements as the one above [i.e., Acheson's] obscure far more than they reveal the true sources of policy, that their purpose is largely to elicit support for a policy that is pursued primarily for quite different reasons?[52]

One executive (of a major oil company) interviewed for this project declared that "never again" would his firm "be used as an instrument of United States foreign policy." That statement may bring a smile to some readers, but the general theoretical question— which are the "real" motivations of government, and which are merely ex post facto justifications?—remains a pertinent one.

Neo-Marxist writers themselves do not contend that there is any "straight-line relationship between certain interests and appetites and a system of ideas or dogmas." It is, according to one, a vulgarization and an error "to suppose that the materialist interpretation of history is an 'economic interpretation' of a simple mechanical kind. Thus in considering a political struggle or the emergence of a new theory it is [erroneously, by the vulgarizers] supposed that Marxists trace a direct line to some economic interest, or see them [actors] as working out some blatant economic

[51]Williams, op. cit., p. 235.
[52]*The Radical Left and American Foreign Policy* (Baltimore: The Johns Hopkins University Press, 1971), p. 61.

motive. . . . Soldiers, administrators, missionaries, and others actively engaged in the development of modern colonialism did not necessarily have direct economic or material interests in this work."[53] The point is a good one. No modern social scientific theory is expected to explain *all* variations of a phenomenon, merely to identify forces accounting for substantial parts of the variance. If some neo-Marxist writers wax overenthusiastic over the explanatory power of their theories, others are more temperate, and anyway excessive theoretical enthusiasm is not a fault limited to radicals. It is contentious, intentionally or not, for the radicals' critics to attribute to them an effort to explain everything in economic terms. On the other hand, we do need a more rigorous effort, on all sides, to specify much more carefully the frequency and circumstances under which economic motivations would be expected to apply. Otherwise we are back in the realm of citing examples and counterexamples, asserting on the basis of an unspecified sample from an unspecified universe that the one is more common than the other. In fact the writer just cited, despite the cautions and qualifications, holds most tenaciously to his economic interpretation as being by far the most powerful one, and fails to present the sort of systematization that would enable us satisfactorily to confirm or refute his generalizations.

The basic problem with an economic interpretation is still more fundamental. Eventually one encounters the argument that ideology is a "false consciousness," a superstructure manufactured, deliberately or otherwise, to justify international conflict in the interest of particular groups. "Historical materialism does not take at face value the reasons which men give for their actions."[54] The capitalist economic system in the United States generates an ideological superstructure of anticommunism "that lends political legitimacy and moral energy to the system's foreign policies." According to a nineteenth-century Marxist historian,

Everywhere the first impulse to social action is given as a rule by real interest, i.e., by political and economic interests. But ideal interests lend wings to these real interests, give them a spiritual meaning, and serve to justify them. . . . Interests without such "spiritual wings" are lame; but on the other hand, ideas can win out in history only if and inasfar as they are associated with real interests. . . . Wherever interests are vigorously pursued, an ideology tends to be developed also to give meaning, re-enforcement, and justification to these interests.[55]

[53]Kemp, op. cit., pp. 10–13.
[54]Ibid., p. 11.
[55]Otto Hintze, quoted by James Kurth, "Testing Theories of Economic Imperialism," in Rosen and Kurth, eds., op. cit., p. 12. The preceding phrase

At one level there can be no solution to the problem as posed this way. How can we possibly sort out the "real" motivations from the "manufactured" ones, when both are expressed? If we cannot get inside a man's head we cannot know why he does what he does; even he may not know, and even psychoanalysts disagree about unconscious motivations. Nor would it help much to look at temporal priority, for it is widely recognized that in a democracy, elites and attentive segments of the public are likely to articulate beliefs and policy preferences before the public at large does so, but that is no proof that such beliefs and preferences are "imposed," whether to serve narrow material interests or not.

At another level, however, we can suggest some relevant evidence. If an economic interpretation is to have validity, we should expect that those whose interests allegedly are served by such beliefs will express them most frequently and/or most strongly. That is, if an assertive, aggressive, or vigorously anticommunist foreign policy does indeed serve the interests of the capitalist class, then we should expect capitalists to support that policy even more than do other groups or classes. Doubtless writers, politicians, administrative officials, labor union leaders, and others will also, with substantial strength or frequency, support the policy. But speaking in broad generalizations, there ought to be *some* diminution in that support as we move further away from the interests of capitalist entrepreneurs themselves. We are thus driven back to our earlier hypotheses about particular attitudes of business executives as contrasted with those of other elites about foreign policy, namely, hypotheses 1.1, 1.2, 1.5, and 1.7, covering attitudes toward military expenditures, less developed countries, the Vietnam war, and foreign policy hawkishness in general.

Additionally, it seems appropriate to add hypotheses about the kind of motivations expressed. Frequently businessmen, like other

---

is Kurth's characterization of economic interest arguments, though he does not necessarily accept it as an accurate description of reality. Related statements about anticommunist ideology as a deliberate misrepresentation foisted upon the gullible in order to cloak capitalist interests can be found in widely read and by no means always Marxist writers, such as David Horowitz, Sidney Lens, Fred J. Cook, Seymour Melman, and sometimes Richard Barnet, as noted by Slater and Nardin in Rosen, ed., op. cit., p. 38. One of the best-known arguments is that by Marc Pilisuk and Thomas Hayden, that the cold war anticommunist consensus was hardly spontaneous, but imposed, and manipulated by the elites by their control over education and the mass media; it was a "false consciousness" made to serve the parochial interests. See their "Is There a Military-Industrial Complex Which Prevents Peace?," *Journal of Social Issues* 21, No. 3 (July 1965): 67–117. See also Bukharin, op. cit., p. 109.

elites, may be expected to clothe their preferences in terms of ideology, strategic considerations, or other national interest arguments. They may do so deliberately to hide their real motives, unconsciously because the other motives are their conscious ones, or possibly because by some objective criterion, however hard to apply, the economic motivations are not important. Nevertheless since it is they, in terms of economic theories, who stand to gain most, it is reasonable to expect economic motivations to come peeping through more often for them than for other groups. Therefore, we add two general hypotheses:

4.1 *Economic motivations will be more closely associated with the foreign policy preferences expressed by businessmen than with the preferences expressed by other elites.*

4.2 *Economic motivations and interests will be more closely associated with the foreign policy preferences expressed by businessmen than will domestic ideology or strategic motivations.*

This second hypothesis is difficult to investigate, and we should not attach too much weight to the crude quantitative results. One part of the difficulty is simply in finding adequate tests for identifying ideological, strategic, or economic motivations. Some are harder to tap than others, or we might not include the most appropriate tests. A good job of devising tests for ideological motivations and a poor one of devising tests for economic motivations would inevitably bias the results toward finding the former more important. We thus could probably attach some real significance to very gross differences in the explanatory power of one or the other, but we should be extremely tentative about results that were not very clear-cut.

Another problem, however, is a theoretical one. If the *ideology concerning domestic politics* really is one that serves capitalists' interests, then they are likely also to hold it strongly. And those particular businessmen (from firms with large investments in LDCs, or large defense contracts) whose economic interests were best served by military preparedness or cold war anticommunist policies might be expected also to hold that ideology most strongly. Recall the argument, for example, by Baran and Sweezy, that high military spending is ideologically attractive to capitalists on the grounds that it maintains adequate aggregate demand in the economy *without* interfering with work incentives or competing with private enterprise, as most government spending for domestic needs would do. In this case, in addition to a high correlation of economic interest directly with foreign policy preference, we would find a high correlation of economic interest with domestic ideology, and of domestic ideology in turn with foreign policy preference. That is, the causal arrow might run equally well economic interest → domestic conservative → foreign policy hawk as directly from economic interest → hawk, and we would have to carry out careful probes to see which set of correlations was more important. Nevertheless, the distinction becomes important *only* if the individual links from economic interest to domestic ideology, and especially from economic interest to foreign policy preference, are themselves strong.

We can add one last hypothesis designed to determine which aspects of a conservative view on domestic politics are most closely related to foreign policy; that is, whether businessmen's concerns with their economic position have special impact on foreign policy hawkishness. It is a key addition to hypothesis 1.6 about businessmen's attitudes toward income redistribution:

4.3 *Among businessmen, foreign policy hawkishness will be more closely associated with a conservative position on income redistribution than with conservative attitudes on civil rights or civil liberties.*

Finally, we should acknowledge that there is a version of economic determinist theories to which all our discussion of businessmen's attitudes is basically irrelevant. It asserts that the attitudes of businessmen are not the cause of governmental behavior; rather, government officials are sensitive to the needs of the capitalist system they serve, and frequently they anticipate any particular demands from the business and financial community. Such officials would recognize the symptoms of capitalism in crisis and, on their own initiative and responsibility for the system, would take up and pursue the aggressive, expansionist policy needed to sustain that system. By this explanation government officials or political leaders might well be *more* hawkish than the businessmen; certainly they might impute to businessmen a set of hawkish perspectives not in fact held or yet fully crystallized by the businessmen.

Although some evidence can occasionally be found to support such a theory,[56] it is an extraordinarily difficult one to test adequately. In light of the previous arguments about why, from an

---

[56]Some illustrations of government officials attributing to businessmen protectionist views they did not in fact hold can be found in Bauer, Pool, and Dexter, op. cit. Also see the description of the degree to which American officials—apparently without prompting—felt it important to preserve, for Japanese commerce, access to Southeast Asia, in *The Pentagon Papers: Senator Gravel Edition* (Boston: Beacon, 1971), e.g., vol. 1, p. 84.

economic interest perspective, businessmen would be expected to be more hawkish, we do not find this version especially plausible, though we surely cannot dismiss it. We can use it as a guide in examining some of our data in the following chapter—for example, in comparing the attitudes of businessmen with those of government officials—but the results cannot be in any way determinative. Although the finding that officials or politicians are more hawkish than businessmen would be consistent with such a perspective, such a finding would in no way discriminate that theory from others. Too many anti-economic determinist theories would hypothesize precisely the same results, and we would have no basis for choosing. That kind of discrimination will have to await another research project, using very different kinds of data.

We will be testing the preceding hypotheses (and others more fully developed later in the exposition) at various points throughout the book, but especially in the next two chapters, where we examine survey data on the policy preferences of military officers and corporate executives. Analysts of every ideological persuasion must face the evidence openly.

CHAPTER THREE

Political Contraction
and
Economic Expansion

*Spartans, in the course of my life I have
taken part in many wars, and I see among
you people of the same age as I am. They
and I have had experience, and so are not
likely to share in what may be a general
enthusiasm for war, nor to think that war
is a good thing or a safe thing.*

King Archidamus to the Spartans,
in Thucydides, History of the
Peloponnesian War

Businessmen do not now, and doubtless never did, see the world
with a single eye. Like other human beings they differ among themselves in what they fear, what they hold dear, and what they
expect. They begin with varying assumptions and thus, even in
good logic, reach varying conclusions. Corporate executives cannot
all be characterized as possessing "the business mind" any more
than factory workers, military officers, blacks, or other groups can
be treated as being mentally homogeneous. At the same time, this
fact should not prevent us from trying to see if broad agreement
exists among most businessmen on certain important topics, or at
least if the range of disagreement among businessmen occupies a
different point on a broader spectrum than it does for other groups.

In this chapter we ask whether the central tendency of belief or preference among corporate executives is markedly different from that existing among other groups—that is, whether the "average" business leader can be distinguished from the average member of other elite groups. Specifically, how, if at all, do businessmen differ in their political beliefs and values?

We will be exploring various facets of that question, and various implications of our answers, throughout this book. In this chapter, however, we shall conduct a basic mapping operation to identify key aspects as they appeared in 1973. We think our results have important implications for earlier as well as later periods, but the source of our data is a survey of a large sample of business executives that we conducted in the spring of 1973. We asked our sample a variety of questions about how they viewed foreign and domestic policy; we also asked for some information about themselves and the firms for which they worked. The questionnaire certainly did not query everything we or others might have liked to know about these topics; it could hardly do so within a length that would be tolerable to its recipients. We wanted to get some responses from many businessmen, and therefore we restricted our scope to questions that an executive could answer within thirty minutes. We nevertheless did focus on what we believe are some of the central issues that are necessary to understanding not only what businessmen believe about foreign policy but why they do so. Many of the questions had already been included in similar or identical versions of other investigators' questionnaires, so we were able to make some close comparisons of our businessmen with members of other groups. And as we shall discuss shortly, we carried out our own further survey, in which we asked senior military officers to answer similar questions. That questionnaire, with the percentage breakdown of results, appears in the Appendix of the book. But we did not limit ourselves, even in this phase of the project, to the survey. Some of the main questions asked in the survey, as well as some additional questions based on certain ambiguities and fascinating sidelines of the survey, were used in the interviews we conducted of about a score of senior corporate executives in New York City and Western Europe during the year following the survey. Although they were not intended, by number or selection, to be a scientific sample, these interviews provided essential depth for interpreting the survey results, and we shall frequently draw on them for purposes of illustration.

The Survey of Business Executives and Military Officers

A digression about our survey methods is necessary to establish the utility and limitations of our basic data. The business sample initially was composed of 1,059 high-level vice presidents selected from the *Fortune* 500 industrial corporations[1] and leading financial firms. We divided the firms into four subcategories, and they were so coded on each questionnaire:

1. "Defense related" corporations from the *Fortune* 500 industrials (40 such firms) and the *Fortune* listing of major transportation firms (one firm). "Defense related" was defined as those firms having 10 percent or more of their total sales for 1971 in contracts with the Department of Defense.[2] We double-sampled these firms, choosing two executives from each.

2. All other *Fortune* 500 industrial corporations—a total of 460. We surveyed one executive from each. These and the firms just mentioned earn 79 percent of all corporate profits in manufacturing; in 1973 they employed 15.5 million workers, or 76 percent of all people employed in manufacturing.

3. Banks—the 150 largest commercial banks and the 25 largest mutual savings banks as listed in *Moody's Bank and Finance Manual*.[3] The top 50 commercial banks were double-sampled; we chose one executive from each of the others (225 total).

4. Other financial institutions—the largest diversified financial companies listed in *Fortune*[4] and the largest savings and loan associations, insurance companies, and investment companies listed in *Moody's Bank and Finance Manual*.[5] Inclusion of each company was determined roughly by the size of that company's assets. After deleting a few Canadian firms we were left with the following numbers of firms, each sampled once: 33 diversified financial companies, 18 savings and loan associations, 107 investment companies, and 134 insurance firms (a total of 292).

We focused on high-level vice presidents in order to get individuals who presumably make decisions affecting a variety of

[1]"The 500 Largest Industrial Corporations (Ranked by Sales)," *Fortune* 85, No. 5 (May 1972): 190–206.
[2]As listed in *Economic Priorities Report* 3, No. 5 (November–December 1972): 34–35.
[3]*Moody's Bank and Finance Manual* (New York: Moody's Investment Service, 1972), pp. a45–a47.
[4]May 1972, p. 214.
[5]Op. cit., listed separately and respectively on pp. a50, a54, and a59.

important policy areas in their firms. We did not attempt to reach chief executives for two reasons. First, these individuals had been the subject of several political surveys in recent years, notably those conducted by Daniel Yankelovich and reported by Arthur Louis in *Fortune* magazine, and by Allen Barton and his associates at Columbia University's Bureau of Applied Social Research.[6] We felt that many of them might therefore be unwilling to participate in yet another survey.

Second, we wanted to maintain the complete anonymity of our sources, not just from anyone reading our published reports, but from anyone using our punched cards (which we are making publicly available)[7] and even from ourselves. It was possible that if the entire universe of chief executives were chosen, enough biographical information could be gleaned from the questionnaire responses to identify many of the men in question. But by taking a sample from the large universe (well over 10,000) of vice presidents of these firms, we could effectively make it impossible for anyone to match questionnaires with specific individuals. Perhaps such care was excessive. Had we done otherwise, and especially had we asked questions that pinpointed biographical details or data about the respondents' firms more closely, we would have gained valuable information. This last decision was a painful and sometimes intellectually costly renunciation. But we conducted this survey at a time when many social scientists had become concerned about their ability to protect the anonymity of their sources. Professor Samuel Popkin (then of Harvard) had been briefly imprisoned in November 1972 for refusing to divulge his confidential sources to a federal grand jury. Nothing similar had yet happened to a scholar conducting large-scale survey research (Popkin's material was from selected personal interviews with government officials), and it seemed unlikely that any government agency would be that interested in the kind of information we were seeking. Nevertheless, we wanted to be able to give our respondents an absolute guarantee that their anonymity would be respected, and devising our sample and questionnaire this way seemed to be the surest way to do so.

Specifically, the sample was chosen by drawing randomly from the list of executive vice presidents for each firm, as enumerated in Standard and Poor's *Register of Corporations, Directors, and Execu-*

---

[6]See references and discussion that follow.
[7]From the Inter-university Consortium for Political Research, Ann Arbor, Michigan, 48106.

tives.[8] When there were not at least two people designated as executive vice presidents of a given corporation, we expanded the list to include senior and/or group vice presidents. When the list contained no officers with such designations, we chose a name randomly from the entire list of vice presidents. For the double-sampled firms (subcategories 1 and 3), we chose from a list including not fewer than four vice presidents of one rank or another. The sample was predominantly but by no means exclusively composed of men living in the Northeastern states (48 percent); 29 percent were from the Midwest and the remaining 23 percent from the South and West.

We pretested the questionnaire in January 1973 on a group of executives from Connecticut securities firms. After making some changes, we sent the first mailing to our chosen sample on March 13, 1973. Each recipient received a questionnaire (coded by type of firm as previously noted) and a personalized, individually signed covering letter explaining the nature of the study, its relation to other studies of American leadership groups, and our intention to provide strict anonymity. We also tried to indicate our intention to be fair-minded, and to make clear that despite the sensitive nature of some of the questions, we had no wish to exploit the answers for ideological advantage.[9] The envelope included a business reply postcard that the respondent could return, with his name and address, in order to receive a report on the results. This card was to be returned separately from the questionnaire itself, for which we provided a stamped, self-addressed envelope. A follow-up mailing went out on April 5. This mailing was essentially identical with the first except, of course, for the covering letter.

Some intended recipients of the first mailing had died, retired, or otherwise left their firms. When our materials were returned for these reasons, either unopened or with a covering letter from a secretary, we replaced the departed executive in our sample with another from the same firm, selected according to the same

---

[8]*Register of Corporations, Directors, and Executives* (New York: Standard and Poor's Corporation, 1972). Standard and Poor's list varied by firm. Sometimes it listed executive vice presidents, senior vice presidents, and all other vice presidents; sometimes it listed only executive *or* senior vice presidents and all other vice presidents; sometimes it listed all vice presidents without distinguishing among them.

[9]We were ourselves especially sensitive to this danger. One of us, for example, had a few months earlier dutifully filled out a questionnaire on international politics sent by *Finance* magazine—only to discover later that the results were being used as part of a public relations promotion for the effort to secure the Nobel Peace Prize for President Nixon.

procedure. There were 36 such replacements; each was also sent a follow-up, the last mailing of which went out on April 17.[10] Late in the mailing sequence, 13 additional instances of nonreceipt came to our attention and were not replaced. Thus the total number of questionnaires sent out and perhaps received by their intended recipients did not exceed 1,046 (1,059 in the original mailing, minus a total of 49 known nonreceipts, plus 36 replacements). With 567 returned questionnaires, the response rate figured on the latter base was 54 percent for our survey, a very high percentage as mail surveys go. This response rate did not vary significantly among the four subgroups previously identified, ranging from 50 percent for the defense-related firms to 56 percent among "other financial institutions." About 44 percent were returned in reply to the first mailing; the other 10 percent were in response to the follow-up. To our knowledge, the rate of response to only one survey of comparable individuals has exceeded that rate, and there the circumstances were exceptional.[11] Even if the total number of questionnaires we *mailed*, including the replacements, were used, the response rate on this base of 1,095 would be 52 percent.

With regard to executives, however, one question about the responses must still be answered: Did they delegate the job to a secretary, another subordinate, or the firm's public relations officer? If the task was delegated in many instances, then our data would be worthless. But we are confident, from a variety of pieces of information, that it was not. Most significant perhaps is the large number (over 25 percent) of questionnaires that were marked with various handwritten comments either about the questions or about the subject of the questions. Often these comments were extensive, and clearly written by someone who cared about the topic—not by

---

[10] One case was rather poignant. The secretary reported that Mr. Jones had received our questionnaire, but suffered a fatal heart attack before he could answer it. We trust the relationship was not causal.

[11] The higher rate was the 61 percent achieved by James N. Rosenau in his survey, *National Leadership and Foreign Policy* (Princeton, N.J.: Princeton University Press, 1963). Rosenau's case is exceptional because his sample was composed of executives who had already shown considerable personal interest in the topic at issue by attending a conference, and his questionnaire was explicitly a follow-up to that conference. He reports (pp. 367–368) that a 25 percent return is typically considered a high response rate to a mail questionnaire, and that the rate often falls to 5–10 percent. Occasionally other professional groups (not businessmen) have evidenced very high response rates when the topic was of professional interest and the sponsorship "respectable." See Charles Glock et al., *To Comfort and to Challenge* (Berkeley: University of California Press, 1966).

someone merely going through the motions on order. A second clue is the postcards we included to give the respondent a chance to receive a copy of our report on the project. We explicitly adopted this as a device to increase respondents' interest in the study: to demonstrate to them our good faith by showing them the uses to which we put their replies, and thus to raise the response rate. A total of 383 of these cards were returned to us, and when we checked the senders' names against our mailing list, we found that all but 20 (5 percent) were signed by intended recipients of our questionnaire. Of the 20, 17 were signed by other executives of comparable rank in the same corporation, presumably successors to our addressees. Although it is conceivable that an executive might have someone else fill out his questionnaire but ask that the report be sent to himself, this seems unlikely. Also, in response to the follow-up (which went to all members of the sample) we received quite a number of notes, signed by the addressee, saying that he had already returned his questionnaire from the first mailing. Finally, in three cases where the addressee had left the firm, we received a specific communication telling us that another executive of at least equivalent rank would answer the questionnaire.[12] Thus we feel sure that the vast majority of respondents took the effort seriously, and took seriously our admonition, in the initial covering letter, that "It is important that I have *your* views, not those of one of your subordinates or those of your company."

It was necessary to compare the responses of these executives with those of other American leadership groups. We had access to data about the responses of various civilian groups to many of the same questions (see the following discussion), but we also wanted to compare our results with military officers' values and beliefs. Since no comparable public survey of senior military officers had ever been taken, to our knowledge, we realized we would have to do our own. We decided that the only feasible population available to us was that of all United States military officers enrolled in the five war colleges (Air, Army, Navy, National, and the Industrial College of the Armed Forces). These institutions are commonly characterized as being "at the peak of the military educational system." Their goals are "to prepare carefully selected officers for the highest level command and staff positions within their own services

---

[12]In one case we were notified by telephone, forty-eight hours after we mailed our questionnaires, that the addressee had retired but that his questionnaire would be filled out by the firm's president.

and with national and international forces and headquarters."[13]

Virtually all officers enrolled hold the rank of Lieutenant Colonel (or Commander in the Navy) or Colonel (Navy Captain). Nearly one-fourth are graduates of one of the service academies, and about 30 percent have already served in a staff post at the Office of the Secretary of Defense, the Joint Chiefs of Staff, NATO, or Combined Staff Europe or Far East. Thus these are experienced upper-middle-range officers who are, on the whole, destined for important positions within the next few years. They are somewhat younger than our vice presidents (their mean age is about 42 years, whereas that of the vice presidents is about 52 years), but otherwise are not a bad match for them.

Because this was a civilian survey of active-duty military officers, we were required to notify the Director for Manpower Research in the Office of the Assistant Secretary of Defense of our intent. He replied, citing Department of Defense Instruction 1100.13, Section V.D., and informing us that "we cannot encourage nor discourage participation, and similarly we cannot approve nor disapprove your survey." This notification was all we needed in order to ask the responsible officials of the War Colleges to distribute questionnaire materials to the students. We in no way asked or expected these officials to endorse the survey, but merely requested that they put into each student's mailbox an envelope containing a questionnaire, form covering letter, and stamped self-addressed envelope. Unlike the materials used in the businessmen's survey, neither the outer envelope nor the letter was personally addressed, as we had no list of the officers by name. The covering letter stressed essentially the same points as did that addressed to the businessmen: the role of this particular survey in a larger study of American leadership groups, the importance we attached to receiving the respondent's material, and our preservation of complete anonymity. Although the questionnaires were sent in bulk to the Commandant of each War College and distributed through the college's mail system, the stamped self-addressed reply envelope ensured that the returns would come directly to us. This mailing was usually followed approximately two weeks later by distribution of a follow-up letter, another copy of the questionnaire, a return envelope, and a postcard to be returned separately from the

---

[13]Amos H. Jordan and William J. Taylor, Jr., "The Military Man in Academia," *Annals of the American Academy of Political and Social Science* 104 (March 1973): 138.

questionnaire by those who wished to have a report on the results.[14] (Unlike our procedure in the businessmen's survey, we did not include such an opportunity in the initial distribution.) The follow-up letter stressed our objectivity and attempted to explain the need for closed-ended questions on certain matters, especially of strategy and national security policy, that obviously were complex and would seem so to our sophisticated respondents. After a pretest on active duty officers then enrolled as students at Yale, all materials were distributed during the first three weeks of April 1973.

Conversations with others, who knew how widespread survey research is as an information-gathering tool within the armed services, led us to expect a favorable response rate from these officers. Nevertheless, we lacked some of the conditions that may have contributed to our success with the businessmen, notably the personally addressed letter and, in the initial mailing, the postcard invitation to receive a report on the study. As a result we were very pleased with the high response rate we did achieve: usable questionnaires from 621 officers, or 69 percent of the population contacted—a rate that was 15 percentage points higher than that achieved with the business sample.

With two exceptions this result was quite uniform among the War Colleges. Our response from the Air War College in Maxwell, Alabama, was low (only 47 percent), probably as a result of the limited cooperation we received there. Our questionnaires were distributed at the Air War College only after a three-week delay during which special acquiescence was sought from Air Force Headquarters in Washington and a special covering letter was prepared by the college for distribution with our materials. The letter noted that "Though the survey instruments have been placed in the student distribution boxes, this does not imply a position on the part of AU [Air University] that the surveys must be completed and returned. The questions are undeniably controversial; the responses are wholly voluntary." Also unlike the situation at the other War Colleges, the follow-up material was never placed in the students' mailboxes. Under these circumstances we think we did well to achieve a 47 percent return. This low return is nevertheless balanced by a 90 percent return from the Army War College at Carlisle Barracks, Pennsylvania, where the officers seem to have

---

[14]To preserve *complete* anonymity we destroyed the cards received from both businessmen and military officers immediately after mailing copies of our reports to the businessmen and officers who requested them.

been encouraged to complete the questionnaire. If, as is quite possible, there is some bias in the pattern of returned questionnaires from the Air War College, it should be balanced by the opposite more-than-normal return from the Army War College.[15]

A Comparison of Elites' Beliefs

We first want to know whether the beliefs of the business executives differ significantly from those of the military officers, and indeed those of other civilian elites. Are businessmen more conservative on domestic policy, or more hawkish on foreign policy, and if so, on what specific issues?[16] If there were no significant differences, it would be difficult to support the argument that corporate economic interests, in general, promote distinctive political views. If differences do occur, are they concentrated on issues directly and obviously related to economic matters, or do they also (instead?) embrace matters only more distantly related to economics? Discovery of differences on economics-related foreign policy issues (for example, relations with nationalist and socialist regimes in the third world) would give some support to economics-oriented theories about the roots of American foreign policy, just as failure to find any significant differences would cast grave doubt on such theories. Doubts about such theories would also arise from finding that businessmen differ from other elites on issues of domestic policy, but not on foreign policy questions.

We begin by comparing the responses to twelve questions on the business survey with responses to the same questions on the military survey, and also with responses of other American elite groups. In designing the questionnaire we took these questions from a questionnaire used by Dr. Allen H. Barton and his associates at Columbia University in a 1971–1972 survey of American elites

---

[15]Unless, that is, Air Force officers generally differ from Army officers. (Most, though by no means all, officers attending the Air War College are from the Air Force, and those attending the Army War College are from the Army.) But we checked for service-specific differences, and found only a few that are statistically significant. See Bruce M. Russett, "Political Perspectives of U.S. Military and Business Elites," *Armed Forces and Society* 1, No. 1 (Fall 1974): 99, footnote 14.

[16]We apologize for using such emotive labels as hawk and dove to characterize foreign policy differences, but there is no ready alternative. "Liberal-conservative" has little meaning except in the area of domestic policy (and needs to be carefully qualified even there); "activist-passive" is hardly accurate; "internationalist-isolationist" is as pejorative and is still more inaccurate, again unless carefully qualified, than is hawk-dove.

(business, political, top civil servants, media executives and professionals, labor leaders, and voluntary organization leaders).[17] Barton's sample is a bit more elite than ours (he reached essentially the pinnacle of most of the organizations listed), and was surveyed 15–18 months earlier, but neither of these differences should invalidate careful comparisons. The questions were as follows. (Item numbers refer to the order in the Yale questionnaire, which is given in full, along with the responses of the Yale military and business samples, in the Appendix.)

25. In the next 5 years should the level of U.S. defense spending be:
    a. Raised substantially, by 25% or more
    b. Raised somewhat, less than 25%
    c. Kept about the same
    d. Reduced somewhat, less than 25%
    e. Reduced substantially, by 25% or more
    f. Other

In each of the following questions, the respondent is asked whether he would "agree strongly, agree with qualifications, disagree with qualifications, or disagree strongly" with the statement given.

9. The United States should seek agreement to mutually dismantle alliances such as NATO and the Warsaw Pact.
10. The United States must always keep ahead of the Russians in strategic nuclear weapons.
11. The United States has sometimes contributed to the escalation of the cold war by overreacting to Soviet moves or military developments.
12. The revolutionary forces in the "third world" are now basically nationalistic rather than controlled by the U.S.S.R. or China.
13. The U.S. should be prepared to accept socialist governments in Latin America even if the communists play an important role in them.
15. Poverty in the United States is now mainly due to cultural and psychological problems of the poor.
16. Differences in income between people in this country should be reduced.

---

[17]Allen H. Barton, "Conflict and Consensus Among American Leaders," *Public Opinion Quarterly* 38, No. 4 (Winter 1974–1975): 507–530; supplemented by further data very graciously provided by Dr. Barton. Individuals interviewed in the Columbia sample are identified as follows: Businessmen who were owners of $100 million or more in assets or who were chief executives of large industrial corporations (*Fortune* 500); Republican party officials, senators, ranking House committee members, administration officials; Democratic senators, House committee chairmen, party officials; labor union presidents (unions of 50,000 or more members); career civil servants (GS 17 and 18); voluntary organization leaders; mass media executives and professionals.

17. Marijuana should be legalized.
18. Supreme Court decisions of the 1960's have imposed excessive restrictions on the police.
19. Practices of the FBI and military intelligence in recent years pose a threat to civil liberties.
20. The main cause of Negro riots in the cities is white racism.

Table 3.1 presents the responses and compares our results not only with the average for the entire Columbia elite sample, but with each of the latter's subgroups as well. It is much more interesting to know which particular groups the businessmen most (or least) resemble than to compare them with such an amorphous lot as leaders chosen from the American population as a whole. For simplicity, the figures in the table refer to the percentage of each group giving the dovish or liberal answer (agree strongly or with qualifications, or disagree strongly or with qualifications) to each of the statements.[18] For item 25, answers d and e (reduce somewhat, or reduce substantially) are considered dovish. Our military and business samples, hereafter referred to as Yale military and Yale business, appear in the first two columns, the Columbia business sample appears next, and the other Columbia subsamples appear in the following six columns. The percentage for the entire Columbia elite sample is in the final column, on the extreme right.

On every item the Yale business sample is somewhat more hawkish or conservative than is the total Columbia elite sample, although in two instances the difference is not statistically significant (item 12 about whether revolutionary forces in the "third world" are basically nationalistic or controlled by China or the U.S.S.R., and item 17 about legalizing marijuana).[19]

---

[18]Percentages always exclude those who did not respond, but except for open-ended item 36, this rate was always well under 5 percent.

[19]Unless otherwise noted we will require that differences be statistically significant at the .01 level using analysis of variance. That is, under the assumptions of random sampling the odds are less than 1 in 100 that the differences in the total population are not in the same direction as found in our sample. In fact, we do not of course have true random samples, but this usage is nevertheless a common and generally accepted convention if applied cautiously. By setting our criterion at the .01 level, we are deliberately applying a rather rigorous criterion compared with that sometimes employed (the .05 or .02 levels).

Generally, differences between two groups of at least 4 percent will be significant at the .01 probability level, though as the break approaches 50–50, roughly a 5 percent level is required for samples of the size of the Yale military and business samples and the total Columbia elite sample. In comparisons involving the smaller Columbia subsamples, larger differences are required

Table 3.1 *Percentage of Various Elite Groups Holding Dovish or Liberal Positions, Strongly or with Qualifications, on Questions of Foreign and Domestic Policy*

Questionnaire Item	Yale Sample		Columbia Elite Sample							
	Military	Business	Business	Republican Politicians	Democratic Politicians	Labor	Civil Servants	Voluntary Organizations	Media	Total Columbia Sample
25. Reduce defense spending	12	51	63	43	71	76	74	78	79	66
9. Dismantle alliances	22	34	47	32	52	55	53	51	62	48
10. U.S. keep ahead in nuclear—disagree	26	22	30	28	38	31	40	57	63	39
11. U.S. contributed to cold war	58	52	65	37	77	81	70	74	82	67
12. Third-world nationalistic	84	74	70	77	72	60	84	83	91	77
13. Accept socialist governments	78	78	81	78	83	83	88	87	93	84
15. Poverty cultural and psych.—disagree	47	43	49	60	65	78	64	75	67	62
16. Reduce income differences	38	36	18	35	58	71	56	70	56	46
17. Legalize marijuana	29	31	26	16	19	27	40	56	57	32
18. Excessive restrictions on police—disagree	16	15	18	38	53	61	45	65	69	45
19. FBI and milit. intell. threat to civil libs.	18	31	28	24	54	54	52	64	67	44
20. White racism	17	18	26	18	32	33	26	54	40	31
N =	621	567	132	105	99	48	54	52	63	593

The difference between the two samples is slightly greater on the six domestic policy items (the businessmen's score averages about 13 percentage points more conservative than does that for the average civilian leader) than on foreign policy (the businessmen are 11 percent more hawkish). Much the same is true for differences between the Columbia business subsample and the entire Columbia elite group, though the Columbia business sample of corporation presidents tends to be less hawkish on foreign policy items than does the Yale group of vice presidents. Overall, the Columbia business sample is much more conservative than is the score for all elites (16 percentage points difference), but only a little more hawkish (a difference of 4 percent). On the whole, this is of course really not surprising; we should be astonished if the business executives turned out to be more liberal or dovish than the average American leader. For economic interest theories of *foreign policy*, however, it is not very encouraging to find that the *businessmen are nearer to the elite consensus on foreign policy items than on domestic policy items*. Their particular economic interests cannot be said to have moved them very far to the right on foreign policy matters.

More important is the comparison of businessmen with other subgroups in the elite population. Businessmen, for example, are sometimes to the left and sometimes, but less often, to the right of the average senior military officer. The Yale businessmen are significantly more dovish than the military on defense expenditures (25) and alliances (9), but markedly more conservative in their views about the balance of nuclear weapons (10) and third-world governments (12). The latter finding is certainly relevant to our central concerns, but a seemingly related question about readiness to accept socialist governments in Latin America (13) produced no difference at all between the two groups. The Columbia group is a bit more dovish overall, and significantly more dovish than the military on item 11 (United States contribution to the cold war), as well as on items 25 and 9. There is no significant difference between the two groups on item 10, but the Yale businessmen were more hawkish in their answers to this question. Of the six domestic policy items (15–20) only one question, number 19 about intelligence activities, shows that a statistically significant difference exists between the Yale business and military. (The

---

for statistical significance. Since the analysis of variance compares differences across the entire distribution (distinguishing between agreements "strongly" and "with qualifications"), however, the comparisons we note as significantly different do not always correspond precisely to these percentage differences in the table.

businessmen are more liberal.) The answers of the two Yale groups
to the others—notably including number 16 about income differences, where presumably the businessmen would stand to lose
more than the military from redistribution—are about the same.
The Columbia businessmen are much more conservative than the
military on this issue, but the reverse is true on item 20 (white
racism).

A comparison of the business executives with the other important civilian elite groups within the Columbia sample shows that
businessmen are *always* to the right of the average Democratic
politician, civil servant, voluntary organization leader, and major
media figure. They usually are to the right also of labor leaders, but
the Yale businessmen take a more liberal view on two issues:
legalizing marijuana (17) and third-world nationalism (12); the
Columbia business sample is more liberal than the labor leaders
only on item 12. But both *business samples are often more liberal or
dovish than are the Republican politicians*: party officials, administration officials, and legislators. For instance, the Yale business group
is more liberal or dovish on six items and is tied with the Republican leaders on two others; similarly, the Columbia business group
is more liberal or dovish than the Republican leaders on eight of the
twelve questions. The difference is most remarkable on foreign and
defense policy items: readiness to reduce defense spending (25),
dismantle alliances (9), and acknowledge a significant United States
contribution to the hostilities of the cold war (11). On these issues
the business executives are markedly less hawkish than are leaders
of the so-called party of business. These findings certainly are not
in line with some simplistic ideas about the military-industrial
complex. At the end of Chapter 2 we noted a theory that postulates
that political officials are sometimes more hawkish than businessmen. Our material on Republican leaders tends to support that
view, but the material on Democratic leaders and civil servants
definitely does not.

We can briefly sum up the evidence for some of our hypotheses
so far. First, the three concerning attitudes toward military expenditures:

1.1 *Businessmen will be more favorable toward military preparedness
than will other elites.*
1.3 *Military men will be more favorable toward military preparedness
than will civilian elites, including businessmen.*
1.8 *Businessmen will be less favorable toward military preparedness
than will other elites.*

Hypothesis 1.3 is clearly confirmed. The differences are not so clear-cut as to allow a sharp choice between 1.1 and its converse, 1.8. The businessmen are significantly less favorable toward military preparedness than are military men or Republican party officials, but they are more favorable than are other elites.

We have evidence concerning a part of hypothesis 1.2:

1.2 *Businessmen will be . . . more hostile [than other elites] toward socialist and communist governments in less developed countries.*

Again the results are ambiguous, depending on the question and on the group with whom the comparison is being made. In partial confirmation of the hypothesis, the businessmen are less ready than military elites, and somewhat less ready than many but *not* all of the other civilian elites, to see revolutionary forces in the third world as "basically nationalistic rather than controlled by the U.S.S.R. or China" (12). But on the probably more relevant item, "The U.S. should be prepared to accept socialist governments in Latin America even if the communists play an important role in them" (13), they hold essentially the same position as military men and Republican politicians, though they are somewhat to the right of all other elite groups. On balance, this is no more than very modest evidence in support of the hypothesis.

The next hypothesis concerns attitudes toward income distribution.

1.6 *Businessmen will be more opposed to income redistribution (in an egalitarian direction) than will other elites.*

We find strong support for this hypothesis among Columbia businessmen, who were to the right of all other elite groups. Support for the hypothesis is much less obvious among the Yale businessmen, who are less egalitarian than the average of civilian elites but not different from military men or Republican politicians.

We also have three hypotheses about attitudes on the range of foreign policy issues.

1.4 *Military men will be more "hawkish" on a variety of foreign policy issues than will civilian elites, including businessmen.*
1.5 *Businessmen will be more hawkish . . . than will other elites.*
1.9 *Businessmen will be less hawkish . . . than will other elites.*

The answers to questions 9–11 provide evidence in support of hypothesis 1.4, in comparing military men with all civilian elites, but strong only on question 9 (dismantle alliances) and very mixed on questions 10 and 11 when the comparison is specifically with businessmen. As for the two hypotheses directed toward businessmen, 1.5 is supported, and its converse 1.9 rejected, when the comparison is with most civilian elites. But the opposite is more nearly true—1.5 is rejected and 1.9 is supported—when businessmen are compared with military men or Republican politicians, who tend to be equally hawkish or even a little more so.

In summary, we have three hypotheses postulating that businessmen's economic interests will lead to aggressive foreign policy (1.1, 1.2, and 1.5) and one postulating that these interests will lead to a conservative domestic policy with some implications for military and foreign policy (1.6). On balance the evidence shows slight, but only slight, confirmation of these hypotheses. With regard to the contrary hypotheses, that their economic interests will lead businessmen to espouse a more pacific foreign policy (1.8 and 1.9), the evidence indicates disconfirmation. Perhaps importantly, the frequent position of Republican politicians at the same point or to the right of the businessmen suggests that other factors (for example, the relatively independent influence of ideology) are as powerful as economic interests.

Businessmen and Soldiers

We can pursue our inquiry by comparing the Yale military and business samples on a variety of other questions, including some about fairly basic matters of political philosophy.[20] Items 1 and 2 in the questionnaire, and item 8 about the continued utility of ground combat, tell us something about "business pacifism." Several questions, among them item 28 about what action the government should take to protect American investments in less developed countries and item 23 about the relative importance of various policy objectives of the United States in underdeveloped countries (including rapid economic development, and governments in less developed countries that retain the free enterprise system or allow broad opportunities for American investment), obviously are of interest in estimating economic motivations.

---

[20]Our focus here is largely on the military as a control group for the business sample. For an analysis of this material that is directed much more toward key problems of military sociology and civil-military relations, see Russett, "Political Perspectives of U.S. Military and Business Elites," op. cit., pp. 79–108.

To flesh out our image of possible business-military differences we added some questions on the probability of war (3, 4, and 5), a question about the relative importance of various kinds of problems, domestic and foreign, facing the United States (6), a question about perceptions of change in the communist threat (7a, b), another question about perceptions of communist nations' foreign policy aims (14), another question about race relations in America (21), a question about readiness to defend American allies and neutrals in case of communist invasion or insurgency (22), a question about attitude toward foreign aid and troops abroad (24), and several questions about national defense and American activities in Vietnam (25–27, 29–32), sometimes with special reference to the economic implications thereof. We thought that this would give us, in the first instance, a wide spectrum of issues to analyze for differences on domestic and foreign policy.

By making a simple comparison of the two groups and applying the technique known as analysis of variance, we can determine in what ways the Yale sample of business executives differs from the military officers.[21] In the next chapter we shall look at the results that are obtained when a variety of variables are controlled (to see how economic interests, for instance, seem to affect perceptions on issues not immediately related to economics). Here we shall discuss the analysis of variance results in rather summary fashion. Usually we will not give full statements of the questionnaire items or a detailed listing of the numerical differences, since that is found in the Appendix, where the questions are given in full with the responses (percentages or means, as appropriate) for both groups, business to the left and military to the right. Statistically significant (at the .01 level) differences are identified by asterisks.

Again, on matters of domestic policy the businessmen are just about as conservative as are their military counterparts. In both groups those who think the "internal threat of communism" has decreased outnumber by about two to one those who think the threat has grown (question 7b).[22] The business executives tend to rate "social and economic disparities within the U.S." (6e) as the

---

[21]We also analyzed these data by multiple regression methods, using business/military as one independent dummy variable along with others, but the results do not differ in any notable way from those reported here.

[22]Probably this marks some relaxation in their sense of threat. A survey of 300 chief executives of the *Fortune* 500 firms in 1969 found that 31 percent believed the threat of communism had increased, and only 26 percent perceived a decrease. Nearly two-thirds of those seeing an increase described it as a rise in communist strength within the United States. See Arthur M. Louis, "What Business Thinks," *Fortune* 80, No. 4 (September 1969): 207.

second most important problem facing the country, whereas the military men usually rate it a fairly distant third. On the other hand, the businessmen also are relatively more worried about that conservative problem, "domestic order and stability" (6d). They are significantly less sympathetic to blacks on the question of school integration (21). There is little difference between the two groups on the other domestic policy items (15–20).

The Businessmen's Retreat from World Power

On foreign policy matters, however, it is very clearly the military officers who have the greater expectation of war, and take the more hawkish view. In addition to their responses to the items mentioned in Table 3.1, they tend to regard war as more likely in the next decade (question 3), to see counterinsurgency war as the most likely type of war (5d), to consider "military and technological advances of China and Russia" as the most important rather than the least important of five problems facing the country (6a), to think that the external threat of communism has increased or at least has not diminished (7a), and to consider ground combat still "an effective means of settling disputes" (8)—though the last response especially is hardly a surprise. Less sanguine about the beneficent effects of trade than are the businessmen, the military are less likely to consider economic interdependence a force for peace (1a) and more ready to view it as a major cause of war (2d). They are very much more likely to consider power-oriented methods as necessary to maintaining peace: military superiority of the United States, collective security through alliance, and efforts to achieve a balance of power (1d–f).[23]

---

[23]Although the comparison is beyond our concern here, it would be important to discover the degree to which the business and military samples agree in a distinctively American way, by contrasting their opinions with beliefs held in other nations. One suggestive bit of evidence comes from a recent set of mass surveys in ten European (East and West) and Asian countries. Those surveyed agreed with our samples (especially the businessmen) in rating military means quite low on the scale of important means to peace, and in rating trade ("increased trade, exchange, and co-operation") quite high. By contrast, they listed international institutions high ("improve the United Nations so as to make it more efficient than it is today" was rated third out of twenty-five proposals) and, most distinctively, two "poverty gap" peace proposals were rated first and fourth, respectively ("hunger and poverty must be abolished all over the world," "the gap between poor and rich countries must disappear"). Despite obvious incomparabilities in method, the low rating of "narrowing the gap" (1b) on our survey surely represents a very different world view. See J. Galtung, H. Ornauer, A. Sicinski, and W. Wiberg, *Images of the World in the Year 2000* (Paris: Mouton, 1974), p. 81.

In line with this, the military also are more prepared than are the businessmen to use armed force to defend allies and neutrals against communism invasion and insurgency in every instance we posed. We asked (question 22): "In the event that one of the following nations is attacked by foreign communist forces . . . *and* requests U.S. help, there are 3 courses of action the U.S. might take: (1) Use military force to extend all needed help; (2) Provide help, but short of U.S. military involvement; (3) Stay out. Please *indicate the . . . course of action . . .* you think the U.S. should take for each nation." Of the seven countries we listed, a majority of the businessmen were prepared to recommend United States military action for only two—Mexico and West Germany, and the majority was a bare one for West Germany. The average business executive would send some help, but no military forces, to Brazil, Japan, and Thailand, in that order of preference. For India and Yugoslavia a majority checked the "stay out" option, and we encountered comments like "Are you kidding?" scrawled on the questionnaire. By contrast, the average military officer would use troops to defend Brazil, Japan, and Thailand, as well as Mexico and West Germany.

This businessmen's skepticism about military action on behalf of allies and neutrals becomes even more extreme when we substitute, in place of the hypothetical attack by foreign communist forces, "a serious insurgency problem led by an indigenous communist movement." Then there is no longer a majority of executives prepared to use military force on behalf of the governments of *any* of these countries; moreover, Thailand joins India and Yugoslavia as nations that a clear majority of the executives would stay out of entirely. All this despite the fact that in our questions we deliberately labeled the attacking or insurgent forces "communist."[24]

Of course, these are highly abstract, hypothetical situations, and the choice among these three options is hardly more than a parody of the enormously complex set of options that would in fact be at the disposal of a policy maker in a real world situation. And faced with the reality of an attack or insurgency against an im-

---

[24]A survey of 300 chief executives of the *Fortune* 500 firms in 1969 offered them seven potential *casus belli* and asked which ones were worth fighting for. Not one was cited by a majority. Ranked highest (by 40 percent) was "protecting our national interest"; only 19 percent selected "containing the communists." See Arthur M. Louis, "What Business Thinks," *Fortune* 80, No. 5 (October 1969): 139–140. Since this was probably near the peak of disillusionment over Vietnam, our finding of continued great reluctance, even in 1973, after the conclusion of American involvement, is of special interest.

Table 3.2 *Average Scores on Question of Intervention in Response to Communist Attack*

Country	Business	Military	National Sample
Brazil	1.7	1.3	2.2
India	2.5	2.4	2.4
Japan	1.8	1.2	2.2
Mexico	1.3	1.1	1.7
Thailand	2.4	1.7	2.3
West Germany	1.6	1.1	1.9
Yugoslavia	2.5	2.3	2.5

portant United States ally, the executives might be much more prepared to sanction the use of force. Their statements in the abstract ought not to be considered predictive.[25] Furthermore, the businessmen at least are readier to use force than is the average citizen. For example, a 1971 national survey asked essentially the same question about reaction to an attack.[26] Table 3.2 compares the responses obtained in that survey with those of the Yale businessmen. Remember that a high score represents a reluctance to intervene.

Note that though the businessmen look more favorably on military action to defend Mexico and the developed countries than does the general public, they actually are slightly (and not statistically significantly) *less* well disposed toward military action when less developed Thailand and India are at issue.

The apparent resistance of the businessmen to being drawn into an overseas war is very striking, especially when their answers are compared with those of the military men.[27] Once burned on

---

[25]This is just one aspect of a general warning that the marginals should be treated with the greatest care when examined in isolation. The contrast between the low expectation of "major domestic civil disturbance in the United States that would involve the Armed Forces" (5e) and the high rating of "domestic order and stability" as a major problem (6d) illustrates the sort of pitfall awaiting the overenthusiastic user of a single response. The proper use of these figures remains that of comparison within and between groups.

[26]Albert H. Cantril and Charles W. Roll, Jr., *Hopes and Fears of the American People* (New York: Universe, 1971), p. 47.

[27]One commentator pointed out to us that businessmen's readiness to intervene was directly proportional to the value of United States foreign investment in each country—Mexico, West Germany, Brazil, Japan, and then the last three bringing up the rear. This is true, but except for statistically insignificant reversals of the scores of the general public and the military

Vietnam, they are wary of a second wound. Other bits of evidence support this interpretation. Compared with the military, the corporation executives look very unfavorably on economic and military assistance to foreign countries, and want a reduction of United States armed forces abroad (24a–c). Approximately 54 percent wanted a decrease in economic aid, and 71 percent wanted a reduction in military aid. As many as 91 percent wanted a cut of some sort in the number of American troops in Europe.[28] Most (59 percent) preferred to make that cut contingent on a Mutual Balanced Force Reduction accord with the Soviet Union, but as many as 12 percent chose "total withdrawal" as the option that best described their views. These answers, from what once was thought to be a rather "internationalist" corporate elite, are very striking.[29]

---

for Brazil-Japan, and of the military for India-Yugoslavia, the businessmen seem no different from others. They cannot therefore be singled out for transforming economic interest into political intent. The rather intriguing match of intervention readiness with investment patterns evidenced by all respondents should not be ignored, but a mixture of geographical distance and sociopolitical "distance" seems at least as plausible in accounting for the rankings. See Charles Doran, "A Theory of Bounded Deterrence," *Journal of Conflict Resolution* 17, No. 2 (June 1973): 243–269.

[28]Due to a printing error we are unable to make a proper comparison between the business and military samples on the matter of troops in Asia, but there is every reason to believe the same pattern would apply.

[29]Many readers may not be very surprised to find businessmen less hawkish than *military officers*. Nevertheless, the degree of surprise depends on a person's perspective, and such an expectation is frequently found among radical writers. For example, according to Joyce and Gabriel Kolko, "In the spring of 1950, NSC-68 revealed that the civilians were far more martial than the generals when containment doctrine was failing to turn the political tide in Asia and sustain military mastery in Europe. The desire also to spend money as a tool of foreign economic policy as well was scarcely comprehensible to the docile military men." Joyce Kolko and Gabriel Kolko, *The Limits of Power: The World and United States Foreign Policy* (New York: Harper & Row, 1972), p. 508. See also Gabriel Kolko, *The Roots of American Foreign Policy: An Analysis of Power and Purpose* (Boston: Beacon, 1969), pp. 27–47; and Gar Alperovitz, *Cold War Essays* (Garden City, N.Y.: Anchor, 1969), p. 76. We owe these references to the useful article by Ole Holsti, "The Study of International Politics Makes Strange Bedfellows: Theories of the Radical Right and the Radical Left," *American Political Science Review* 68, No. 1 (March 1974): 229.

On the approval that formerly existed among many businessmen for foreign aid (especially the Marshall Plan), see David W. Eakins, "Business Planners and America's Postwar Expansion," in David Horowitz, ed., *Corporations and the Cold War* (New York: Monthly Review Press, 1969). Eakins attributes this to a desire to use foreign aid as a means of providing sufficient aggregate demand to keep the economy going. For two divergent views in the business community, see David S. McLellan and Charles E. Woodhouse, "The Business Elite and Foreign Policy," *Western Political Quarterly* 13, No. 1 (March 1960): 172–190.

The same impression emerges from looking at the questions about defense spending, where again there is marked skepticism about the value of military force. As noted earlier, over half the business sample would reduce American defense spending (item 25). That percentage is lower than the percentage we found for the elite at large, but far higher than the percentage for the military (of course) and, more interestingly, higher than the percentage for the *public at large*. In the Gallup poll asking basically the same question at the same time (American Institute of Public Opinion, February 1973), "just" 43 percent of the general populace wanted defense spending cut. (Even that represents, as does every other poll on the matter since 1969, a very high point compared with the polls taken during the earlier cold war years. See the next chapter.)

Moreover, even those who would resist substantial cuts in the defense budget seem *unconvinced that such cuts really would have important deleterious effects* on the country. We offered several options as to possible increases or decreases in United States defense spending; only 15 percent chose the rather extreme "Reduced substantially, by 25 percent or more" option. But when we then asked, "Do you think a 25 percent reduction in defense spending would have an adverse effect on American security vis-à-vis other nations?," only 52 percent (as compared with 85 percent who favored smaller cuts, or none) answered "yes." Just 33 percent thought such a large cut "would have an adverse effect upon the American *economy*," and only 38 percent thought "a retrenchment of U.S. foreign policy commitments would have a negative effect on U.S. *economic expansion abroad*" (items 26, 27, 29). All of these figures, markedly lower than those for the military, provide no evidence for theories that business executives advocate heavy military spending either to prop up the economy or to provide an essential military-political insurance for overseas commercial enterprise.[30] In fact, the military prove to be much more vigorous in their allegiance to economic determinism, as more than 60 percent of them do expect a reduction in military preparedness to have deleterious economic effects both at home and abroad. Or perhaps simply their interest in maintaining what they consider adequate military forces very readily leads them to see all kinds of damage, including economic, flowing from a failure to do so. But we find

---

[30]All this implies much greater skepticism about military needs than did simply the 1969 report that almost two-thirds of the chief executives of major corporations thought defense expenditures were "unduly high because of waste and inefficiency." Reported in Louis, *Fortune* (September 1969), p. 207.

that the businessmen evidence substantial readiness to see the United States retreat from many of the military and political commitments of world power.

We can again sum up our findings to this point relative to the hypotheses.

Hypotheses 1.1, 1.3, and 1.8 regarding attitudes toward military preparedness: The evidence clearly supports 1.3 and 1.8 and disconfirms 1.1 when businessmen are compared with military officers; the latter are much more favorable. In some ways this is not surprising, but the fact that military men see a cut in military spending as much more damaging to the *economy*, at home and abroad, is important evidence against the tenability of many economic interest theories.

Hypotheses 1.4, 1.5, and 1.9, regarding foreign policy hawkishness: In general, the evidence clearly supports 1.4 and 1.9, and disconfirms 1.5 when businessmen are compared with military officers; the latter are more hawkish.

Hypothesis 1.6, that businessmen will be more opposed to income redistribution (in an egalitarian direction) than will other elites: Evidence against the hypothesis is that the businessmen identified "social and racial disparities within the U.S." as a more serious problem than did the military. Coupled with the evidence on question 16 discussed previously, we perhaps still have some confirmation of the hypothesis, but the support for it certainly is not strong.

So far, the evidence is running generally *against* theories postulating that businessmen advocate a high level of military expenditures as an acceptable means of maintaining a high aggregate level of economic demand. (Measures that would have the effect of somewhat reducing income inequalities would not be acceptable.) The evidence also is running *against* theories that trace an assertive or aggressive foreign policy to an anticommunist ideology attributable specifically to the *articulated class interests* of capitalists. The ideology may be adhered to by some businessmen, but it is not unusually common among them. We have yet, however, to consider the key hypotheses about the role of government in promoting business interests abroad, particularly in the less developed countries, and about the Vietnam experience.

Policy in the Less Developed Areas

Every use or overt threat of use of armed force by the United States since the end of World War II has been in the underdeveloped parts of the world: Central America and the Caribbean,

Table 3.3 *Mean Ratings of Seven Objectives of Governments in LDCs*

Objective	Business	Military
A stable government capable of preserving internal order*	2.3	1.9
A government which will not engage in unprovoked aggression against other nations*	3.3	3.0
A government which maintains civil liberties	3.7	3.8
A government which is neutral or pro-American in its foreign policy*	4.0	3.6
Rapid economic development*	4.4	4.8
A government which retains the free enterprise system*	4.5	5.1
A government which allows broad opportunities for American business investment	5.7	5.7

*Difference between business and military is statistically significant, $p \leq .01$.

the Middle East, the Far East, and Southeast Asia. Many of these actions arose only gradually, as a result of conflict between the United States government and a third-world government. Frequently, though by no means always, the economic policy of the third-world government, or its treatment of American private business investments, had some role as cause or contributor to the dispute, a dispute that sometimes (as in Cuba at the Bay of Pigs) escalated from situations that did not initially seem likely to lead to military force. In the process the escalation also meant that the dispute was expanded to encompass a broad range of political and strategic questions extending far beyond the original economic issues. Without in the least implying that such escalation and expansion must always occur, it nevertheless is necessary to look at some responses bearing on the issues frequently in dispute, especially to judge the strength of possible economic motivations among businessmen in particular.

We asked respondents to rank in order (from 1 to 7 with 1 the most important) seven possible objectives for American foreign policy in less developed countries; specifically, we asked them to indicate what kinds of policies pursued by the governments in those countries would best coincide with the interests of the United States (question 23). We did not in this context ask them what, if any, influence the United States should bring to bear in order to ensure that such policies were pursued, but merely which policies they would prefer. The choices among the seven options were as shown in Table 3.3.

The overall rankings of these objectives by the two groups are virtually identical. In rating American investment opportunities as least important, the two groups even produced the same scores. We tapped no peculiarly business-oriented perspectives with this question, asked in this rather bald-faced way, at least. Also, military and executives on the average showed no significant difference with regard to the importance of civil liberties; they agreed on a roughly middle position well below "law and order" and a nonaggressive foreign policy. On the remaining items, however, they did disagree significantly in their rating scores if not in their rank order. Although stable government and nonaggressive foreign policy topped both lists on the average, the military men were much more unanimous, and this accounted for their higher scores. The executives, on the other hand, rated the remaining two economic criteria, rapid economic development and maintenance of the free enterprise system, significantly more favorably than did the military. The greatest single divergence is, in fact, about the importance of the free enterprise system. The businessmen gave it an average ranking of 4.5, whereas the military awarded it but a 5.1.

Like many of our results, this can be interpreted in more than a single way. From one perspective, it is notable that *both* groups ranked all three economic criteria *below* the foreign policy or internal political criteria. Taking the answers at face value, economic motivations would seem unimportant in determining policy toward the LDCs. From another point of view, the somewhat greater *relative* preference of the businessmen for economic criteria (or, more precisely, the less complete unanimity on ranking these criteria at the bottom) should also be noted.

We asked both groups (question 28) what kinds of actions the United States government should take to protect the investments of American businesses in less developed countries, and offered four possibilities, of which they could choose one or more. The results are shown in Table 3.4. Totals add to more than 100 percent because of multiple responses.

We see an overwhelming consensus that some kind of action is appropriate; less than 10 percent of either group chose "nothing." Moreover, the great majority wanted something more than (or at least in addition to) government insurance against expropriation losses. Virtually all who checked "military action" also checked "diplomatic or economic action," so those two totals should not be added. Even so, almost 4 businessmen in 5, and almost 7 military

Table 3.4 *Rating of Appropriateness of United States Government Actions to Protect United States Foreign Investments in Less Developed Countries (percent)*

Action	Business	Military
Nothing	9.2	9.8
Government insurance*	44.7	23.2
Diplomatic or economic action to prevent expropriation or ensure just compensation*	78.3	85.7
Military action to prevent expropriation or ensure just compensation	4.1	6.3

*Difference is statistically significant, p ≤ .01.

officers out of 8, believed that diplomatic or economic action of some sort was appropriate. Military officers were still more favorably disposed toward "diplomatic or economic action" than were the businessmen, but they were less given to approval of government insurance. This might imply that businessmen were less prepared to seek actual United States government sanctions against nationalizing foreign states, but we doubt that the evidence for that conclusion is sufficiently strong. The items enumerated in Table 3.4 do not form a neat scale. Obviously "nothing" is at one end of the spectrum and "military action" is at the other, but between them the choice between insurance and diplomatic or economic action is not so predictable.

Furthermore, as Theodore Moran, among others, has pointed out, government insurance may serve as a means of involving the United States government in the fate of a firm's commercial disputes and thus lead to the subsequent economic or diplomatic sanctions. He notes the importance some firms have attached to obtaining an AID guarantee (insurance) against expropriation, and then taking other measures, such as securing a loan from the Export-Import Bank, that will make sure that any nationalization will be widely felt by various agencies and political actors in the United States government. The need to pay out the insurance might therefore trigger government diplomatic or economic sanctions that would not otherwise be applied.[31] It is entirely possible

---

[31]Theodore Moran, "Transnational Strategies of Protection and Defense by Multinational Corporations: Spreading the Risk and Raising the Cost for Nationalization in Natural Resources," *International Organization* 27, No. 2 (Spring 1973): 274–287.

that some of our sophisticated executives, seeing this, thus felt it unnecessary (and perhaps also compromising) to check "diplomatic or economic action" in addition to insurance. In any event, the readiness of corporate executives to endorse government insurance reflects a willingness sometimes to relax the principles of free enterprise to permit government action on their behalf.

We should not make too much of these results. Asked in such a straightforward fashion it was unlikely that many businessmen or military officers would check the "military action" option; that was bound to bring out a good deal of hesitation. Also the categories are very broad, and given to various interpretations. The absolute percentages have only limited meaning, though we hope to make better use of them in the following chapter where we ask *what kinds* of executives checked one answer rather than another. Our probes in the interviews, however, were a bit enlightening; they allowed for the sensitivity of this particular question and the inhibitions that we would expect to prevent an executive from explicitly endorsing forceful action—whether or not his private feelings agreed with his statement. Most did reject military moves:

I see almost no circumstance under which the United States would or should intervene to protect American investments; the chances of United States military involvement in the near future are minimal.

It will be a cold day in hell before we send more troops.

One executive, when pressed (August 1973), thought he could imagine a military intervention in the Middle East if the United States domestic economy should be greatly squeezed. A vice president of an international oil company (a vice president for public relations, to be sure) nevertheless explicitly rejected this possibility on pragmatic grounds when we raised it:

I can't imagine using military force in the Middle East to insure oil— it would be too difficult. Think of the probable Russian reaction, or how easy it would be to sabotage the wells.

Overall there was little evidence that businessmen were, especially and explicitly in light of the Vietnam fiasco, thinking very much in terms of gunboat diplomacy. Our intuitions—and they are no more than that—were to take them more or less at their word, with the important caveat that we were ignorant about how permanent this conviction might be, and what kinds of strains it could resist. But as Moran declared, there are means other than gunboats. Businessmen on average list "national and socialist

movements in less developed countries" as the least serious of the
five problems suggested (item 6), and, as we noted, see counterinsurgency war as less *likely* than do the military officers. Nevertheless, because disputes can expand and escalate to require the use of
force even though military methods were not initially contemplated,
we must look more closely at businessmen's attitudes toward the
Vietnam experience to gain a better sense of how great their reluctance to use armed force might really be.

Vietnam and Its Lessons

We earlier said that many of these executives had been burned by
the Vietnam experience, and turned away from global political involvement for that reason. We will further document and explore
this statement in the next chapter, but some aspects are relevant
here. When we asked (question 30), "Do you personally think it was
correct for the U.S. to send ground combat troops to Vietnam?,"
only 37 percent replied "yes," while 53 percent said "no" and
another 10 percent still could not decide. This is a *far* more negative evaluation than that of the military (whose comparable
figures were 70, 28, and 2 percent), although it still is less negative
than that of the general public early in 1973 (29 percent said the
action was not a mistake, 60 percent said it was, and 11 percent
did not answer).[32] Of the total number of businessmen who said it
was not correct, only 40 percent indicated they had held that view
since the beginning of the war. Allowing for an occasional bit of
perfectly human "foresight in hindsight" as they recalled their
views almost ten years previously, at least one-third, and possibly
two-fifths, of all executives changed from hawk to dove during the
course of the war.

Table 3.5 shows the reasons given by those who now disapprove of the war (question 32) and compares the businessmen with
the military. The great majority in both groups answered in rather
pragmatic cost-benefit terms, citing either damage to the United
States itself or a situation that offered poor prospects of a victory
(with or without the added proviso that a still larger commitment
would be required). "Consequences for the U.S. economy" are
listed fairly rarely by either group, though more often (but not
statistically significantly) by the businessmen than by the military.
And of those businessmen who approved of American participation

---

[32]American Institute of Public Opinion survey, January 1973.

Table 3.5 *Reasons Given by Businessmen and Military Officers Who Disapprove of U.S. Sending Ground Combat Troops to Vietnam*

Reason	Businessmen		Military	
	N	%	N	%
Consequences for U.S. economy	22	7	6	4
Consequences for U.S. social and political institutions*	114	38	48	28
Poor prospects of victory/poor prospects without larger commitment*	113	38	98	56
Consequences for Vietnamese people	37	12	12	7
All other reasons	13	5	7	5
Total	299	100	171	100

*Difference is statistically significant, p ≤ .01.

in the war, only a single one gave "consequences for the U.S. economy" as his reason, and none gave consequences for himself personally. If corporate executives thought that the war benefited their economic interests, there is certainly *no* evidence of it here. Including "consequences for U.S. social and political institutions" with "consequences for the U.S. economy" indicates that the businessmen are much more likely than the military to feel that the country was badly damaged by the experience. This is confirmed by comparing the reasons for disapproval given by those who were against the war from the beginning with those given by the hawk-to-dove converts (see Table 3.6).

Among both military officers and businessmen, "consequences for U.S. social and political institutions" are cited far more often by those who turned against the war during its course than by those who report themselves as always having been against it; in fact, almost half of the business converts give this as their major reason. At the same time, the fact that nearly two-fifths of the business "doves" and over half of the military "doves" disapprove of the war primarily because victory could not be achieved suggests that their "dovishness" runs a bit thin. Many of these people might support a war in another place and time if the circumstances looked more auspicious.

Businessmen's evaluations of the Vietnam experience are so central to our concerns that we asked them several other questions

Table 3.6 *Reasons Given by Businessmen and Military Officers Who Thought U.S. Intervention in Vietnam Was Incorrect from the Beginning, and by Those Who Later Turned against It*

Reason	No. of Businessmen		No. of Military	
	Against War from Beginning	Turned against War	Against War from Beginning	Turned against War
Consequences for U.S. economy	11	11	0	6
Consequences for U.S. social and political institutions	33	80	7	40
Poor prospects of victory/ poor prospects without larger commitment	57	54	27	69
All other reasons	14	27	6	10
Total	115	172	40	125

that we did not address to the military officers. We inquired directly whether they thought the effect of the war on the economy was beneficial, whether they thought it would have been beneficial (or at least not detrimental) if inflation had been controlled, whether they thought it had damaged American social and political institutions, and whether, and why, they considered themselves to be personally better or worse off as a result of the war (questions 33–37).

On the matters of the economy and American social and political institutions there was near unanimity on a judgment of ill effect, among hawks and doves alike. More than 86 percent declared the war had been bad for American social and political institutions, and 77 percent felt the war had been bad for the economy in general; only 9 percent thought the economy as a whole had benefited. More interestingly, most (55 percent) of those who thought the effect was bad declared this would have been true *even if* inflation had been controlled. Although it is impossible to know precisely how their thoughts developed on this point, it seems that most of them were thinking in terms of distorted priorities and production patterns, and neglect of capital and social investment in the civilian sector. The consensus on economic harm is slightly less broad than that on social and political harm.

Table 3.7 *Principal Reasons Given Why Businessmen Felt Themselves Better or Worse Off as a Result of the Vietnam War*

Reason	No. of Businessmen
Worse	
Economic damage to country or themselves directly	96
Domestic politics and society	91
Misallocation of resources	20
International politics considerations	12
Failure of United States to win	11
Personal loss, alienation	9
Total giving reasons	239
No reason given	40
Better	
International politics considerations	25
"Learned a lesson"	15
Economic benefits	7
Total giving reasons	47
No reason given	2
Neither better nor worse	229

Certainly inflation was blamed for much of the damage, and certainly a smaller war would have had fewer ill economic effects. But certainly too there is much sentiment here, at least in retrospect with regard to this war, that belligerency brings few gains to the economy, and imposes many costs that go well beyond merely the costs incurred from inflation.

The responses of these businessmen to question 36 (how they 'felt *they personally* had fared as a result of the war) are shown in Table 3.7. Whereas the majority had judged the war bad for both the economy and social and political institutions, we found a large proportion (41 percent) answering that they were essentially neither better nor worse—that the war had no substantial effect on their own lives. Considering the virtual unanimity regarding damage to the United States as a whole, this sense of immunity is curious. Surely it reflects the fact that these are indeed elite and privileged Americans, domiciled far from the ghettoes of discontent, with a living standard safe from really serious disruption by inflation or higher taxes, and too old to be drafted into fighting in the jungles of Asia. Even when we asked them *why* they felt themselves better or worse off (question 37), less than a literal two handfuls (9, less than 2 percent) answered in directly *personal* terms such as family loss or alienation. Statistically, as part of the total American male population of this age group, we might have expected about 1 percent, that is 5 or 6, of these men to have had a son killed or wounded in the Vietnam war. Not one of them, however, mentioned such a misfortune. Probably most of their sons, with college or other deferments, did not in fact serve in the military at that time, or if they did, certainly not as combat personnel. The few purely personal statements referred to morale and morality— for instance, saying they were worse off because they were "more cynical, distrustful, disillusioned," or "because, as a Christian, I was unable to do anything about what I considered a very immoral war."

A very large proportion (91 out of 239 giving a reason why they were worse off, or 38 percent) in one way or another mentioned harm to the social and political fabric of the country, frequently referring to popular morale. For example:

The impact of the war has caused divisions within the country, both socially and politically, which will affect us all.

Because the "American Way of Life and Ideals" which people in my age group accepted as a truism have proven to be illusory.

Our country has never been so divided on any subject since the Civil War. As a loyal American this has hurt me.

The haphazard erosion and destruction of social values as well as institutions was caused by the complete frustration *all* aspects of American life suffered because of the futility of the war.

Resultant public's distrust of the establishment in all forms; i.e., government, business, and all institutions.

Values are all but gone; young people disillusioned; politicians lie.

Others referred more specifically to racial and social tensions, neglect of social priorities, and the provocation of political division; some (20, or 8 percent) combined these reasons with resource wastage and detriment to the economy in general:

Technology expenditures were reduced in favor of munitions, war machinery, and so on.

The war was bad when combined with failure to retrench other expenditures. The attempt to maintain a normal domestic policy and substantially increase military outlays produced the bad result.

We diverted our resources to war with no possible economic benefit while our investment in plant and modern machinery fell behind Germany and Japan, thus losing much of our cost-production advantage.

We should have *stayed out* and strengthened ourselves at home (both militarily and social and economy-wise).

Only 12 or about 5 percent of those considering themselves damaged on the whole by the war mentioned considerations of international politics. The most articulate comments of this sort were obtained during one of our subsequent interviews with an executive from a major multinational oil company. Speaking in August 1973 (before the Yom Kippur war), he said he had felt from the beginning that the Vietnam war was a mistake; in fact, he had felt since 1955 that American involvement in Southeast Asia was a mistake, because it diverted the government from the *real* problem of foreign policy, the Middle East. The Southeast Asia embroglio had, he fervently believed, distracted attention away from resolving the major oil crisis that would come.

The largest single group of executives mentioned explicitly economic reasons. Actually, 96 (42 percent of those giving reasons why they were worse off) gave this response—a far greater number than when we asked (question 32) for the single most important reason why they regarded United States intervention in the war as correct or not. The proportion of hawk-to-dove converts who mentioned damage to the economy was almost twice as large as the proportion mentioning the economy among those who had opposed the war from the beginning (44 percent versus 23 percent). The latter mentioned inflation, taxes, balance of payment problems that had hurt the economy in general, and thus had hurt them indirectly, or had hurt their firms, incomes, or investments in particular and thus had hurt them directly. Common comments included:

Inflation resulting from mismanagement of the war economy has reduced the purchasing power of my discretionary income, relatively.

President Johnson tried to run a guns and butter economy and wasted resources resulting in an unstable long-run economy.

Because the future prospects for the United States economy may have been adversely affected for all time to come.

We built a large military business for this firm—cut to zero in 1969. The time would have been better spend on building civilian business.

Again we have large-scale evidence, illustrated with some occasionally vivid examples, that American corporate executives did not see themselves, their firms, or the economy as a whole benefiting from the war—far from it. Only a total of 7 out of the entire 567 mentioned personal economic gain of any sort. Two supporters of the war declared:

Troubled times accelerate the opening of opportunities for economists and foreign specialists.

Our part of the electronics industry has prospered more than the other industries.

A man who was employed in a defense-dependent industry mentioned simply "higher salary"; another man said, "Economically inflation has not hurt; expansion of the economy has broadened my financial horizons." Importantly, however, both these men list themselves as *opponents* of the war, since its beginning.

Sentiment that the most damaging aspect of the war was the failure to pursue it aggressively enough is quite rare. Only eleven men answered in terms like, "The idea was right but the management was horrible"; "We fought the war in a miserably ineffective fashion which undermined the free world's position"; or "This war should have been fought to win and win quick!" Every bit as illuminating are comments by 15 men who listed themselves as better off as a result of the war—better off in the sense that they had "learned a lesson" that seems best expressed simply as "never again." Three of them remarked:

We are wiser. America learned of its limitations.

I realized the general absurdity of man killing man, and realized the general futility of war.

Better, in the sense that I now have a greater appreciation for human life values, plus an understanding that the United States must not always become involved or impose our "ways" on other countries.

Since these 15 men represent almost one-third of the mere 47 who in any way felt themselves "better off" because of the war, even that number needs to be reduced if benefit is to be construed in any material way. Against all this criticism, soul-searching, and sense of loss, the 25 men (over half of those "better off," but only 4 percent of the entire sample) who answered in terms of anticommunism or cold war containment look like a very isolated minority. (Virtually all of these 25 expressed themselves in terms of ideological anticommunism or strategic containment; none referred to economic considerations such as maintaining investment prospects or access to markets.) We feel that the weight of evidence indicates a great reluctance to see the United States again become militarily involved in a far-off land, even under seemingly more favorable conditions. We will nevertheless keep returning to this question throughout the book, especially to consider how permanent this attitude may be.

To sum up our findings thus far, we have a picture of the average corporate executive as looking somewhat more favorably on a continued world-wide political and military role for the United States than do many other American leaders, but certainly not to the point implied by the classic image of the "internationalist," "activist," "interventionist" American of the cold war era, out to build a world safe from a threatening communism. The executives are markedly less true to this image than are the military elite, and we find an absolute majority of business executives expressing such dovish or isolationist sentiments as:

Ground combat is no longer an effective means of settling disputes (59 percent).

The United States has sometimes contributed to the cold war by over-reacting to Soviet moves or military developments (52 percent).

The revolutionary forces of the third world are now basically nationalistic rather than controlled by the U.S.S.R. or China (74 percent).

The U.S. should be prepared to accept socialist governments in Latin America even if the communists play an important role in them (78 percent).

Economic aid appropriations should be decreased (54 percent).

Military aid appropriations should be decreased (71 percent).

U.S. troops in Europe should be reduced, in some way (91 percent).

In the next five years the level of U.S. defense spending should be reduced (51 percent).

A 25% reduction in defense spending would not have an adverse effect upon the American economy (59 percent).

It was not correct for the U.S. to send ground combat troops to Vietnam (53 percent).

We could also, of course, point to views on some other questions that would dilute this impression, notably:

The United States should not seek agreement to mutually dismantle alliances such as NATO and the Warsaw Pact (66 percent).

At present, communist nations are generally expansionist rather than defensive in their foreign policy aims (65 percent).

A 25% reduction in defense spending would have an adverse effect on American security vis-à-vis other nations (53 percent).

These men are not, certainly, full-fledged doves, and some of the inconsistencies among these views could produce quite unpredictable results in terms of particular policy options. For example, there is very great potential tension between the desire to reduce the level of defense spending and the insistence that the United States should keep ahead of the Soviet Union in strategic nuclear weapons. Those two goals might be compatible with certain kinds of arms control agreements with the Soviet Union, but not with the more probable kind that would accord parity to the two superpowers. We simply cannot tell which way these men might go; even deep probing in our interviews would have been unlikely to resolve the ambivalence. This duality is very reminiscent of the stance of many Americans during the Korean war and for a long time during the Vietnam war—the simultaneous acceptance by them of somewhat contradictory positions, and a basic willingness to follow the lead of the Executive. A potential majority could then be mobilized for either moderately hawkish or moderately dovish policies, and the nation's leaders, whose capacity to lead was generally accepted especially by the relatively elite and affluent segments of the populace, were depended on to point the direction. This reminds us too of the attitudes of many Americans concerning the appropriate level of military preparedness during the cold war years.[33] This flexibility persists, except that the range of generally acceptable policies has been shifted. Its midpoint, formerly moderately on the "internationalist" or "hawkish" side of the spectrum, is now moderately toward the "isolationist" or "dovish" end (again, with the usual reservations about the precise significance of these labels). Surely there is little sign of the existence of widely held, strong beliefs among business executives that would push any American executive into a hawkish or interventionist policy in the near future. We shall return to the theme of change in elite opinion, and its likely permanence, in the next chapter.

Of the remaining key hypotheses testable in this chapter, we found some moderate support for the following:

1.2 *Businessmen will be more favorable than other elites toward United States government activities to protect American business interests*

[33]See Andre Modigliani, "Hawks and Doves, Isolationism and Political Distrust: An Analysis of Public Opinion on Military Policy," *American Political Science Review* 66, No. 3 (September 1972): 960–978; Sidney Verba et al., "Public Opinion and the War in Vietnam," *American Political Science Review* 61, No. 2 (June 1967): 317–333; Samuel P. Huntington, *The Common Defense* (New York: Columbia University Press, 1961).

abroad, and toward the promotion of governments in less developed countries that are well disposed to the activities of foreign investors and maintenance of the free enterprise system; similarly, they will be more hostile toward socialist and communist governments in less developed countries.

In comparing business and military elites, we found absolutely no evidence for 1.7, its converse:

1.7 *Businessmen will be less likely to regard the American intervention in Vietnam as a mistake, less likely to think the war was bad for the American economy in general, and less likely to think they personally are worse off as a result of the war, than will other elites.*

Rather the business-military comparison provides very strong evidence in support of the converse of 1.7:

1.10 *Businessmen will be more likely to regard the American intervention in Vietnam as a mistake . . . than will other elites.*

There is reason to think, however, that this is in substantial part a post hoc phenomenon, and that the differences between the two groups may have been much less marked at the beginning of the war. Since Vietnam as a key event may have restructured businessmen's perceptions of their economic interests, as well as other elements of their world view, we must remain alert to the possibility that economic theories about the sources of an aggressive foreign policy were formerly correct even though little evidence emerges in a 1973 survey. We will address this in subsequent chapters, with different data.

Economic Expansion

Despite all their reservations about an active world political role for the United States, these businessmen fully expect America's economic interdependence with the rest of the world to increase. In looking at American business prospects in general, 83 percent of our respondents expected that "American business involvement in foreign markets and foreign investment will increase substantially in the next decade" (question 38). There was a consensus (98 percent) that "American business transactions with Russia and/or China will increase substantially over the next decade" (question 40), and a smaller but still very impressive 62 percent expected that "American sales and investments in less developed countries will increase relative to American sales and investments in developed countries" (question 39). When we asked them the same questions specifically about expectations for *their own firms* they were a little more restrained, but in general they still anticipated expansion: 72 percent expected that their own firms would increase the proportion of activities carried on abroad, 44 percent looked for substantial increase in their firm's activities with the Soviet Union and/or China, and 37 percent anticipated an increase in their firm's activities in less developed countries relative to the developed ones (questions 41–43). Corresponding percentages for executives from *Fortune* 500 firms (that is, excluding the banks and financial institutions) were 85, 60, and 54, respectively—not too much less than the number who made expansive projections for American foreign business activities as a whole. Both sets of figures portend continued and wide-ranging growth in the American overseas presence.

As we probed for the reasons in our interviews it became apparent that the bases for these projections varied widely. Comments about the vastly increased need for raw-material imports were common, but so too were those about the likelihood of expanded markets in Europe, the communist states, and the third world; different companies were optimistic about different areas. We often uncovered enormous enthusiasm—sometimes a positive licking of chops—about the large "untapped" markets and raw-material sources of the Soviet Union, Eastern Europe, and China. Men who probably only a few months before had used the then-standard term "Red China" to refer to the country ruled from Peking quickly became careful, by summer 1973, to call it "the P.R.C." Hopes to establish or expand licensing agreements with Eastern Europe and the Soviet Union were expressed most frequently, and much interest was also shown in the Soviet Union as a source of petroleum and critical nonferrous metals for American industry. With some exceptions China seemed a little less interesting, in recognition of its very low level of per capita income. Some of this enthusiasm is likely to have faded since the winter of 1973–1974 as the détente suffered strains and the effort to accord the Soviet Union most-favored-nation trading status was thwarted in Congress. In the fall of 1973 one executive specifically criticized "excessive euphoria in the business community" in light of what still remained an insufficiently favorable East-West political environment.[34]

---

[34]There is precedent for great sweeps of business enthusiasm for East-West trade that were later dashed. In September 1945, *Fortune* sampled a

Overall, expectations were probably most restrained for the less developed countries, described by one executive as "a hit and miss proposition." Brazil, Indonesia, and Southeast Asia generally elicited the most interest; Africa and India often were considered too poor and/or politically unstable to be of much interest for investment, though perhaps appropriate markets for certain exports. We did not encounter the kind of widespread interest that would presage a reversal of the existing pattern of American export and foreign investment, directed primarily to developed rather than to less developed countries. The interview statements were thus broadly consistent with the survey answers by 63 percent of all executives, that they did *not* expect their firms to increase activities in LDCs relative to developed countries. Most interest was focused on the large sophisticated markets of Western Europe and Japan. One executive told us that his firm had done very well within the United States, but had reached the point where further domestic expansion ran into firm opposition from the Antitrust Division of the Justice Department. To find promising markets for products within the firm's general field of expertise, therefore, the firm was forced to look for foreign markets and the acquisition of foreign companies—almost a classic example of the outward flow of surplus capital, though he did not use the term. (Other firms also seem to have been impelled by domestic antitrust considerations to seek investments abroad where antitrust forces are weaker or nonexistent.) Western Europe was the appropriate target for his company's rather sophisticated product.

With some exceptions, therefore, American overseas economic expansion was thought likely to be concentrated on those politically stable and "friendly" areas where foreign investment is generally accepted if not welcomed, or at least where expropriation is not to be feared. In this respect the Soviet Union was considered, by those interested in the possibilities, as safer than the LDCs; the Russians were "tough bargainers," but could be depended on to keep their bargains. There is little here to suggest much *proportionate increase* in the sort of investment that gives rise to political

---

group of executives in its "Management Poll," and found that 91 percent thought it was to the long-term advantage of the United States to promote trade relations with the Soviet Union; 84 percent were prepared to approve a Soviet request for $6 billion in credits, either through government or private banking channels; and 33 percent saw the Soviet Union as one of those parts of the world where the largest increase in American foreign business would occur (second only to South America, and far more important than Europe). "U.S. Opinion on Russia," *Fortune* 32, No. 3 (September 1945): 238.

frictions resulting from attempted nationalization. All the same, there is a curious tension or even paradox between the political and the economic evaluations expressed by our sample. They intend to expand their investments and markets, especially in Western Europe and Japan. At the same time they want American troops withdrawn, and would be most reluctant to endorse the use of American military forces to defend those countries from communist attack or insurgency. This definitely is not consistent with the standard image of the "internationalist" executive of the 1950s and 1960s. Evaluations of the likelihood and severity of communist military threats have doubtless been relaxed, but so too has the readiness to meet those threats if they do occur. In what they regard as an increasingly interdependent world economy, there is nevertheless a widespread and very conscious retreat from what used to be called the political "responsibilities" of world power. Business executives' views of foreign policy in this changed world are still unsettled; in common with many Americans they have yet to bring all the threads together into a fully integrated and organized perspective.

CHAPTER FOUR

Economic Man, Ideology, and Realpolitik

*All public facts are to be individualized,
all private facts are to be generalized.*

Ralph Waldo Emerson,
Essay on History

Three Kinds of Theories

Why do business executives believe as they do about foreign policy? Having established an overview of the content of their beliefs on a variety of issues, we must try to discover the sources of those beliefs, and to explain the manifest differences that exist among executives. In doing so we can draw on the review in Chapter 1 of perspectives about why nations behave as they do, and especially on attempted explanations of the motivations behind American foreign policy in recent years.

One of the widely held points of view, discussed in detail in Chapter 2, assumes that nations, or at least various elites attempting to influence foreign policy, promote their particular actual or perceived *economic interests*. This view is essentially an extension of the rational actor or economic man model from classical economics. One version asserts that military expenditures (and a conflictive international environment to justify them) is essential to the prosperity of capitalist economies. Many other contemporary versions involve the various economic interpretations of imperialism. A quite opposite view incorporating economic influences regards international trade and commerce as a force for *peace*, building linkages of interdependence to mitigate national parochialism, providing bonds of communication, and promoting common interests in the avoidance of destructive conflicts. It is often hoped specifically that increased East-West trade will have this effect, burying the cold war rather than one or both of its protagonists.

Quite a different explanation stresses the *ideological* determinants of foreign policy. By this view recent American foreign policy has been primarily motivated by militant anticommunism; American support, political and military, of governments like that in Saigon stemmed from fears of a monolithic (at least until recently) communist enemy of the American political, economic, and social system—an enemy that had to be resisted lest its influence spread widely in the world at large and undermine American institutions at home. Those who were militant anticommunists on foreign policy issues often (though certainly not always) were ideological conservatives on domestic policy. They frequently viewed civil rights advocates as subversive of the existing order, feared "communist-inspired levelers" who sought greater equality between races and between classes, and wanted to use the police power of the state to restrict the civil liberties of critics they thought to be subversive. Resistance to communists abroad and resistance to radicals at home were part of the same world view.

Neither foreign policy anticommunism nor domestic conservatism needs to be motivated by the defense of economic interests in particular, and we must not simply assume that either is. Nevertheless, in some sense a militant anticommunist might find the ideology congenial just because communism threatened his economic interests, and for that reason would both adopt it and promote its adoption by others whose stakes were not as direct as his. We shall be alert to the possibility. In what we termed the "democratic variant," American involvement in Vietnam was the result of the existence of militant anticommunism not so much among sophisticated American political leaders as among the electorate, who constrained the leaders to adopt a rigid stance even though they might have thought it unlikely to achieve the desired international results.

A final explanation is related to the second, but worth analyzing as distinct. According to it, American military and other support of anticommunist regimes like the one in South Vietnam is motivated less by economics or ideology than by seemingly "hard-headed" *strategic* considerations. Policy makers fear communist powers not as communists, but simply as major centers of power whose expansion would have to be vigilantly contained whatever the ideology of their leaders. Various balance of power theories would come under this heading, as would concerns for specific elements of rival power such as economic strength or, especially, strategic and other forms of military power. Here we have the view that the driving force of international politics is power and the pursuit of "national interest" (much broader than mere parochial economic interests). Such a view is often associated with a kind of Burkean classical conservatism, stressing human nature as a prime cause of political violence and making pessimistic assumptions about the inevitability of war. By this view weakness must be avoided and force met with force if opponents are not ultimately to build up irresistible force. Ideology is relevant only as an instrument in the struggle for power, not as its motive. The Soviet Union and China would have to be opposed whatever their ideology. A refinement of this view pays special attention to the nature of contemporary strategic weapons and the need always to maintain a secure second-strike capability—and perhaps very much more—against any major power with similar capability or potential.

We have argued that all of these explanations hold some ring of truth; doubtless all of them have been in the minds of virtually all American elites and foreign policy analysts. It is as pointless to search for "the" explanation for recent United States foreign policy as it would be to adopt a unicausal explanation for any complex social phenomenon. But doubtless too the strength of these various motivations varies greatly from one individual to another, and overall some of them explain relatively minor aspects of the behavior of relatively few individuals, whereas others are more widespread as major motives. It is important, therefore, to assess their relative power among American elites, and especially to assess their relative power among American corporate executives as they look at foreign policy.

We can use the survey material to make an effort at such a relative assessment, however crude. The survey does not constitute the sole evidence that we have, and in many ways it is unsatisfactory and incomplete. Yet it represents one of the few pieces of systematic evidence available on the matter of motivation. Since the matter is an important one, both for understanding the roots of past policy and for building expectations of what the future may hold, it behooves us to make what we can of the survey material.

As dependent variables to be explained we have a variety of questions on specific foreign policy issues and perceptions—largely the questions we began to look at in the preceding chapter. In addition we can identify some more comprehensive dimensions of policy preference, sets of questions whose separate items seem closely associated in the minds of the businessmen who answered them. We took the responses to questions 8–14 (foreign policy items), 15–21 (domestic policy), the separate items comprising question 22 (defense against invasion and insurgency), and 24(a–d)–27, 29, and 30 (foreign aid and defense questions), and performed separate factor analyses on each of the four sets. Factor analysis is a procedure that allows us to see just how closely interrelated the answers to separate questions really are. It reveals the principal underlying dimension or dimensions of each set, and gives us the loading, or correlation, of each individual item with that dimension. All items with high loadings thus are closely related to that dimension, and usually to one another. The results of each of our factor analyses are shown in Table 4.1. The first figure in each column is the percentage of total variance in each set of items that is accounted for by each factor. All factor loadings of .50 or higher are underlined for emphasis.[1] Negative loadings in the first two sets indicate that those who *disagree* with the statement as phrased tend to *agree* with the positively loaded items.

In the foreign policy set of questions, five of the seven items show substantial correlations with the first factor, as do six of the seven items with the first factor in the domestic policy set. Such correlation indicates that the respondents generally perceived the

---

[1]The method used was principal components, with unities inserted in the diagonals. For the foreign policy questions two factors had eigenvalues greater than one and were orthogonally rotated, and for the country defense questions three factors had eigenvalues greater than one and were rotated. After rotation only the first foreign policy factor, and the first two country defense factors, were readily interpretable and accounted for large proportions of the total variance, so only they are presented. For the domestic ideology and defense policy ("hard-line") questions, only one factor in each case showed eigenvalues at the level of unity, so there was no point in proceeding beyond the unrotated factor solution. We have sometimes reversed signs to make the presentation clearer.

The factor structure in this table is, incidentally, virtually identical to the one that emerges when the same questions in the military officers' survey are similarly analyzed. See Bruce M. Russett, "Political Perspectives of U.S. Military and Business Elites," *Armed Forces and Society* 1, No. 1 (Autumn 1974): 79–108.

Table 4.1 *Factor Loadings for Sets of Policy Questions*

Foreign policy: hawk		Factor 1 34%
8.	Ground combat not effective	.03
9.	Dismantle alliances	—.23
10.	U.S. keep ahead of Soviets	.72
11.	U.S. sometimes overreacted	—.65
12.	Third world nationalist	—.61
13.	Accept socialists in Latin Am.	—.69
14.	Communists are expansionist	.57

Domestic policy: liberal		Factor 1 36%
15.	Poverty cultural and psychological	—.19
16.	Reduce income differences	.59
17.	Legalize marijuana	.66
18.	Supreme Court restricts police	—.71
19.	Civil liberties threatened	.70
20.	White racism	.58
21.	School integration too rapid	—.61

Defense policy: hard line		Factor 1 31%
24a.	Economic aid	.26
24b.	Military aid	.74
24c.	Troops in Europe	.59
24d.	Troops in Asia	.59
25.	Defense spending	.70
26.	Defense cut hurt security	.71
27.	Defense cut hurt economy	.26
29.	Retrenchment hurt econ. expan. abroad	.42
30.	Vietnam correct	.52

Defense against invasion	Factor 1 23%	Factor 2 21%
Brazil	.31	—.15
India	.04	—.66
Japan	.15	—.35
Mexico	.27	.06
Thailand	.12	—.66
West Germany	.19	—.21
Yugoslavia	—.06	—.71

Defense against insurgencies		
Brazil	.80	—.18
India	.38	—.65
Japan	.71	—.28
Mexico	.83	.06
Thailand	.54	—.59
West Germany	.77	—.16
Yugoslavia	.36	—.68

questions in the same way, and a scale can be constructed from the separate items giving an overall hawkish-dovish (or conservative-liberal for the domestic items) score for each respondent. For example, relatively few respondents disagreed with the assessment that revolutionary forces in the third world are basically nationalistic; those who did tend to be the most hawkish, and they are very unlikely to give dovish answers on any of the other questions associated with the factor—and especially unlikely to give a dovish answer to question 10 about strategic weapons (to which relatively few respondents gave a dovish answer). Thus we not only can characterize each business executive in terms of these scales (sets of factor scores, actually), but we can then try to see which other variables in our data can usefully explain or "predict" these general points of view. By the same procedure we can identify one major factor concerned with defense policy. The items about military aid and about troops in Europe, Asia, and Vietnam, and the first two questions about the appropriate level of defense spending all are correlated with it; only the economic items drop out.

Finally, question 22 about which countries should be defended how, and under what conditions, has two distinct and unrelated dimensions. One factor or dimension seems best labeled "defense against insurgencies." We know from the analysis of the preceding chapter that businessmen are much more ready to see the United States come to the defense of countries abroad when those countries are subject to foreign invasion; thus when this factor shows high loadings on the insurgency questions, we can readily identify those executives who would assist countries subject to insurgency, as well as, of course, protect them from invasion. These executives, then, would be most strongly oriented toward collective military defense around the world. Many of our respondents indeed saw this dimension (do we defend countries against insurgency, or only against invasion?) as the primary underlying consideration in these questions. Many others, however, perceived another kind of underlying, completely independent dimension: not so much what do we defend against, but *whom* do we defend? This dimension is revealed by the second factor, and we see that, for both invasion and insurgencies, high negative loadings result for particular countries: India, Yugoslavia, and to a somewhat lesser degree, Thailand. Here, then, we have a way of identifying those men who, though they are prepared to defend American allies in Western Europe, Latin America, and the major state of Japan, are not prepared to do anything, against any kind of military threat, for neutralist countries like India and Yugoslavia. This same attitude generally extends to Thailand, probably because of its vulnerability in Southeast Asia and despite the SEATO alliance commitment.

We shall consider each of the sets of factor scores as dependent variables to be explained. Some of them are related to one another. For example, individuals' scores on the foreign policy factor correlate .48 with hard line scores on the defense factor, as we would expect. A hawk on the general foreign policy scale is likely also to favor a strong defense policy. Nevertheless, the correlation is *only* .48, telling us that these two are seen as somewhat separate and distinct aspects of policy, and should be examined separately. By the same token the "defense against insurgencies" factor correlated but .33 with the foreign policy hawk position, and the correlation of the "do not defend neutrals" factor with the hawk position is an insignificant .09. Each of these dimensions deserves separate analytical treatment. In addition, we shall also single out many individual questions for particular attention, including all those that do not correlate well with the major foreign policy and defense policy factors in Table 4.1, as well as the defense spending (item 25) and Vietnam questions, which are especially important in their own right.

Three Kinds of Information

For independent variables we have used a number of questions designed to identify real or perceived economic interests of particular corporate executives. Question 44 tells us the approximate size of each executive's firm's stake in overseas business. Questions 41 and 42 ask the executive to project the activities of his firm during the next decade. Presumably a firm that currently has extensive operations overseas, or that plans to expand its activities either overseas in general or in the less developed countries particularly, could be said to have an economic interest in opposing the spread of socialist or communist nationalizing regimes. We also have our very general categorizations of firms by industry or type of business, the most important of which are manufacturing firms whose defense contracts make up more than 10 percent of their total sales. The apparent interest of these firms in heavy defense spending, a militant foreign policy to justify that spending, and perhaps even wars to stimulate it, has been the subject of many theories. On the other hand, firms with perceived prospects for substantially increased intercourse with Russia and/or China (question 43) presumably would have some stake in continued and strengthened détente. We should expect their executives to oppose any military or political acts by the United States government that might threaten détente, as another Vietnam would probably do.

Now we must recognize that the information we have on these firms is crude, coded according to rather gross categories, and frequently nothing more than nominal variables. Neatly calibrated information on firms' activities would have required the questionnaire to include a kind and degree of information sufficient to allow anyone using the data to identify precisely which firm the executive in question worked for. That would violate either of two conditions: our pledge of complete anonymity to our respondents, or the principle of making our data fully available to other researchers for secondary analysis. As a result we simply refrained from attempting to obtain some information we would like to have had. Nevertheless, even the crude categories we did use should be sufficient to give us some idea of the power of these variables. In addition to these data on the respondent's firm, we have some information about the personal characteristics of the executive himself: age and service in the armed forces. These variables do not deal with economic interest, but are components of commonly held theories about the existence of a "generation gap" in foreign policy assessment, and the effect of military service on promoting hawkish views.[2]

A second set of variables concerns the impact on foreign policy preferences of ideology regarding domestic political issues. The factor analysis results just reported showed that responses to questions 16–21, dealing with civil rights, civil liberties, and income distribution, were all closely interrelated. We used the factor scores to form an interval scale from conservative to liberal. In addition to trying to explain domestic policy preference, we can use that preference as an independent variable to predict foreign policy preference. An ideology is customarily defined as a structured or

---

[2]See, for example, Wayne Moyer, "House Voting on Defense: An Ideological Explanation," in Bruce M. Russett and Alfred Stepan, eds., *Military Force and American Society* (New York: Harper & Row, 1973); and Nancy Adelman Phillips, "Militarism and Grass-Roots Involvement in the Military-Industrial Complex," *Journal of Conflict Resolution* 17, No. 4 (December 1973): 625–655. Moyer found congressmen holding reserve officer commissions to be more hawkish than congressmen who had served previously but were not in the reserves. Phillips found workingmen who had served in the armed forces to be more hawkish than those who had not, when age was controlled. Moyer also found older congressmen to be more hawkish than younger ones, when other variables were controlled.

closely interrelated set of beliefs. Such a coherent and organized set of beliefs helps a person to make sense of new pieces of information or adopt an opinion on a new problem. Insofar as the set of beliefs on domestic issues proves to be closely related to several issues of foreign policy, the "ideological" explanation would be appropriate. It would gain further credence at the expense of an economic explanation if domestic political beliefs, as well as foreign policy beliefs, proved to be relatively independent of the economic variables.

It is impossible utterly to refute the ultimate argument offered by some exponents of an economic explanation—that economic interests have so dominated the entire political culture of the United States that they account for ideological anticommunism. In other words, a conservative ideology, rightist at home and hawkish on foreign affairs, is merely an overlay, a superstructure, promoted and maintained by economic interests operating through the educational system and the mass and elite media. Such an ideology presumably would be found in virtually all classes and social groups, even when direct economic interests might be harmed by policies based on the ideology. As a general statement it carries a certain amount of plausibility, but there is no way to assess its force accurately. If it were a very powerful explanation, however, we would expect to find the conservative-hawkish ideology existing most prominently among those individuals to whom we could plausibly impute *some* real economic interest. Thus we would expect it to be (1) stronger among corporation executives than among other members of the American elite; and (2) stronger among those corporation executives with particular identifiable economic interests.

Hypotheses relevant to the first of these two propositions were tested in the preceding chapter, and we found that the businessman in both the Yale and Columbia samples were more hawkish or conservative than the average member of the civilian elite, but that the differences were rather more marked on domestic than on foreign policy issues—only a moderately convincing argument in support of an economic-determinist view of foreign policy. Moreover, both business samples were significantly more dovish on most foreign policy issues, and more liberal on many domestic issues, than were senior Republican party officials and politicians. Finally, the businessmen were more dovish on many foreign policy issues than were the military officers, with the notable and relevant exceptions about nationalism and socialism in third-world countries. The results, then, were partially consistent with an economic interpretation, but not so strong as to be very striking. We shall test hypotheses concerning the second proposition in the following paragraphs.

The final set of variables concerns strategic considerations, and realpolitik philosophies about power, national interest, and the inevitability of war. If important, these variables should make an independent contribution beyond that of a conservative ideology on domestic political issues. Various aspects of questions 1–5 are relevant here, as is, to some degree, question 6 identifying which problems, domestic and foreign, seem most salient to respondents. It is important to note that, with a few exceptions, we will not be attempting to explain the origins of either domestic policy preference or realpolitik international views. These must largely be taken as given at this stage.

The basic procedure for testing the relative importance of the three types of variables was to introduce them into regression equations with foreign policy preference as the dependent variable in each instance, using the technique of stepwise multiple regression.[3] Items 1, 2, and 4–5 were coded as dummy variables; that is, each of the options for each question was coded on a yes-no basis depending on whether the respondent chose that option. For example, item 2 became five separate nominal variables according to whether the respondent did or did not identify human nature, nationalism, and so on as the most important cause of war. We also included item 23, coded as separate dummy variables; this reveals some economic as well as some strategic *motivations* (rather than imputable economic *interests*, such as are indicated by items 41–44). A few of the items, such as 6 and 23, are sometimes dependent variables we want to explain, and these, of course, do not then also appear as independent variables.

---

[3]Item 49 was omitted because it showed virtually no variance; item 47, about time of service in the armed forces, was omitted because it was so highly correlated with item 45, about age. Several of the items about overseas activity of the firm (71–73 and 74) showed lower but nontrivial intercorrelations (between .45 and .52). This multicollinearity may demand some caution when the separate effects of these variables are considered, though we have carefully established that it did *not* cause any economic interest variables to fail to appear in Table 4.2, or notably to reduce their apparent effect. Multicollinearity among virtually all other variables (for example, between economic interest variables and domestic ideology) is nil: intercorrelations are .25 or lower.

Table 4.2 presents some of the results. The dependent variables are listed, by item number and name, down the left-hand side of the table. The middle column lists each of the independent variables that made a statistically significant contribution to explaining a particular dependent variable. To the right appear, in order, the regression coefficient (b), the standard error of that coefficient, and the F test for each independent variable. Most readers will want to concentrate their attention on the F tests, which give a reasonable measure of the relative contribution of each variable. We shall focus our discussion on that measure, but the other statistics are included for those who will find them useful. We also give the cumulative r^2 for the significant variables, as a measure of the total contribution they make to explaining the dependent variable.[4] We begin with the various composite scales from the factor analyses, and then look at many of the individual items in the order they appear on the questionnaire. Items are phrased in the direction of explanation by the independent variables. To help clarify the meaning of what is unavoidably a rather complicated presentation, the economic variables, interest and motivation, are identified with an asterisk.

Economic Interest and Motivation

This table shows some very complex results; take time to look at it carefully. We can quickly clear away a bit of the underbrush. For example, the noneconomic background variables prove to be utterly trivial. Prior military service is of no relevance whatever to the results. Age is only of marginally more importance, appearing in the results for only three of the thirty-three equations. Age is quite irrelevant to the three major policy dimensions listed under

---

[4]Since we are dealing with a rather large sample (567), only variables statistically significant at the .01 level are shown. (In other words, the probability that sampling error would make them seem to make a contribution if they did not do so in the entire population is less than one in 100.) This significance level still allows us to identify virtually all variables accounting for 1 percent or more of the variance, and frequently picks up some even below that percentage—so we are not missing much of substantive importance. Our real interest in the analysis is the *relative* impact of different variables, not whether they meet some minimum test of significance. Some readers may prefer virtually to ignore all independent variables with F tests below 10.0, when the coefficients tend to be a bit unstable and only about 1 percent of additional variance is typically at issue. The regression equation always proceeded down to much lower F test levels, typically about 2.5, before cutting off.

Table 4.2 Contribution of Various Influences to Policy Preferences and Salience

Dependent Variable	Independent Variable	Regression Coefficient	Standard Error	F Test
15–21 Domestic conservative $r^2 = .31$	Aim *not* civil liberties (23d)	.086	.027	9.97
	Problem *not* racial disparity (6e)	.190	.033	33.88
	Problem domestic order (6d)	.111	.034	11.06
	*Aim free enterprise (23e)	.114	.026	19.88
	Aim stable government (23a)	.130	.029	20.59
	Problem *not* world ecology (6c)	.098	.031	10.21
	*Banker	.268	.106	7.37
8–14 Foreign policy hawk $r^2 = .42$	Conservative	.415	.038	121.49
	Peace from military superiority (1d)	.730	.133	30.30
	Problem advance China and Russia (6a)	.119	.029	17.07
	War *not* counterinsurgency (5d)	.300	.083	12.92
	*Aim free enterprise (23e)	.064	.022	8.25
	Peace *not* economic cooperation (1a)	.025	.084	7.28
24–27, 29, 30 Defense scale— hard line $r^2 = .26$	Conservative	.330	.039	70.72
	Peace from military superiority (1d)	.539	.128	17.79
	Problem advance China and Russia (6a)	.116	.032	12.85
	*Firm will increase abroad (41)	.169	.050	11.15
	War *not* civil disturbance (5e)	.348	.130	7.16
22 Defense vs. insurgencies (1st factor) $r^2 = .13$	Conservative	.220	.048	20.99
	Peace from military superiority (1a)	.502	.143	12.28
	War cause economics (2d)	.411	.118	12.17
	Age—young (45)	.151	.054	7.81

(Continued)

Table 4.2 *Contribution of Various Influences to Policy Preferences and Salience (continued)*

Dependent Variable	Independent Variable	Regression Coefficient	Standard Error	F Test
22 Defend neutrals (2nd factor) $r^2 = .03$	Peace from military superiority (1d)	.432	.143	9.06
3 High probability U.S. in war $r^2 = .12$	War major non-nuclear	.826	.152	29.39
	Age—young (45)	.219	.052	17.77
	Conflict superpower-LDC (4b)	.410	.127	10.51
	War tactical nuclear (5b)	.527	.182	8.35
6 Problems facing U.S.				
a Advance China and Russia $r^2 = .11$	Peace from military superiority (1d)	.967	.223	18.20
	War *not* civil disturbance (5e)	.716	.159	20.22
	Conflict superpowers (4a)	1.376	.345	15.88
	Peace from balance of power (1f)	.739	.243	9.23
b Nationalism in LDCs $r^2 = .03$	Peace from narrow poverty gap (1b)	.639	.213	8.98
	*Aim free enterprise (23e)	.109	.035	9.50
c World ecology $r^2 = .05$	Liberal	.286	.062	21.54
	War cause human nature (2a)	.436	.145	9.09
	*Not defense industry	.724	.249	8.45
d Domestic order $r^2 = .09$	Conservative	.280	.053	27.80
	War civil disturbance (5e)	.578	.161	12.88
	*Not financial institution	.351	.127	7.62
	War cause *not* human nature (2a)	.354	.129	7.62
e Racial disparity $r^2 = .15$	Liberal	.295	.060	24.44
	War civil disturbance (5e)	.872	.162	28.98
	Peace from narrow poverty gap (1b)	.560	.205	7.47

7	Change in communist threat				
	a Internal threat increased $r^2 = .13$	Problem advance China and Russia (6a)	.126	.024	26.98
		War *not* counterinsurgency (5d)	.198	.075	7.00
		Peace from military superiority (1d)	.292	.104	7.86
		Fortune 500	.187	.068	7.62
	b Internal threat increased $r^2 = .16$	Conservative	.154	.039	15.74
		War *not* counterinsurgency (5d)	.215	.071	9.22
		Problem *not* racial disparity (6e)	.076	.028	7.56
		Problem domestic order (6d)	.079	.028	7.90
		Age—young (45)	.110	.042	7.08
		*Aim free enterprise (23e)	.080	.025	10.57
8	Ground combat still effective $r^2 = .01$	*Firm will increase abroad (41)	.117	.044	7.06
9	Mutually dismantle alliances $r^2 = .09$	Liberal	.173	.039	19.63
		War cause *not* ideology (2c)	.327	.103	10.09
		Peace from economic cooperation (1a)	.238	.075	9.97
23	Policy aims in LDCs				
	a Stable internal order $r^2 = .05$	Conservative	.301	.071	17.78
		*Firm will *not* increase China and Russia (43)	.258	.095	7.37
	b Neutral or pro-American $r^2 = .04$	Conservative	.254	.075	11.38
		Peace military superiority (1d)	.778	.258	9.10
	c Rapid economic development $r^2 = .01$	Peace from economic cooperation (1a)	.541	.190	8.13
	d Maintain certain liberties $r^2 = .11$	Liberal	.499	.082	37.41
		*Firm will *not* increase abroad (41)	.253	.096	6.93
	e Free enterprise system $r^2 = .06$	Conservative	.381	.071	28.88

(*Continued*)

Table 4.2 *Contribution of Various Influences to Policy Preferences and Salience (continued)*

Dependent Variable	Independent Variable	Regression Coefficient	Standard Error	F Test
23 f No aggression $r^2 = .06$	Liberal	.377	.078	23.46
	War cause human nature (2a)	.511	.188	7.39
g U.S. business investment $r^2 = .04$	Problem advance China and Russia (6a)	.138	.052	7.13
	Conservative	.193	.068	8.01
	*Firm will increase China and Russia (43)	.233	.082	8.03
24 a Keep economic aid high $r^2 = .09$	Conservative	.089	.732	7.67
	War between LDCs (5c)	.237	.083	8.13
	Peace *not* from arms control (1g)	.050	.173	8.30
	Aim rapid economic development (23c)	.047	.017	7.38
	War cause *not* human nature (2a)	.194	.073	7.01
25 Do *not* reduce defense spending $r^2 = .24$	Conservative	.337	.044	57.36
	Problem advance China and Russia (6a)	.116	.033	12.27
	Peace from military superiority (1d)	.662	.140	22.22
	*Firm will increase abroad (41)	.162	.054	9.02
27 Defense cut hurt economy $r^2 = .02$	*Defense industry	.503	.161	9.75
28 Protect business in LDCs a With government insurance $r^2 = .14$	*Firm will increase in LDCs (42)	.094	.023	16.15
	Liberal	.077	.022	11.88
	*High foreign sale ratio (44)	.096	.028	12.02
	War between LDCs (5c)	.174	.056	9.77
	War cause nationalism (2b)	.152	.053	8.33
b With economic or diplomatic action $r^2 = .02$	Peace *not* from narrow poverty gap (1b)	.022	.068	10.32

29	Retrenchment hurt economic activity abroad	Nothing significant in equation			
30	Correct to send troops to Vietnam	Conservative	.282	.040	49.87
	$r^2 = .15$	Peace from military supriority (1d)	.417	.145	8.26
		War civil disturbance (5e)	.336	.113	8.75
33	Vietnam *not* bad for U.S. economy	Aim government not aggressive (23f)	.051	.052	11.63
	$r^2 = .02$				
33/34	Vietnam *not* bad for U.S. economy, or if inflation controlled	Aim government not aggressive (23f)	.065	.018	13.80
	$r^2 = .03$				
35	Vietnam *not* bad for U.S. social and political institutions	Conservative	.070	.024	8.38
	$r^2 = .05$	Problem *not* domestic order (6d)	.059	.020	8.62
		*Not financial institution	.139	.053	6.85
36	Personal effect of Vietnam *not* bad	Conservative	.126	.029	18.16
	$r^2 = .07$	Problem *not* domestic order (6d)	.109	.024	20.17

Table 4.3 *Businessmen from Defense Contracting Firms Think a Cut in Defense Spending Would Hurt the American Economy*

Question/Answer	Firm with More Than 10% Defense Contracts (percent)	Firm with Less Than 10% Defense Contracts (percent)
Defense Cut Would Hurt Economy		
Yes	60	31
Don't know	8	7
No	33	61
N =	40	524

"Dependent Variable" in Table 4.2. This is hardly much evidence of any generation gap, at least among such elite executives—even though the age spread, from men in their thirties to men in their sixties, is reasonably wide.[5]

More interesting is the general *unimportance* (though not so unimportant as age and military service) of the variables for *economic interest and motivation.* Characteristics of the firm, including its degree and direction of current and anticipated overseas activity, make a difference in twelve instances. The difference is usually in the direction predicted by those who see economic interests as impelling the United States on a course of heavy "defense" spending and frequent military intervention abroad, but it is rarely much of a difference.

Being a heavy defense contractor in the "military-industrial complex" is strongly related to perception or policy only twice: Executives from such firms are *less* likely than others to consider world ecological problems to be among the most important problems facing the country (6c). And, more immediately to their interest than any other item, such executives think that a 25 percent cut in defense spending would hurt the American economy (27). Table 4.3 shows the percentage distributions on this question when just the two variables are cross-tabulated.

---

[5]Analyses of elites, rather than mass publics, frequently find that such background variables are relatively unimportant in explaining attitudes and behavior. See, for example, Daniel Lerner, "French Business Leaders Look at EDC," *Public Opinion Quarterly* 20, No. 1 (1956): 212–221; and Allen Barton and Wayne Parsons, "Social Background and Policy Attitudes of American Leaders," paper presented to the annual meeting of the American Political Science Association, Chicago, September 1974.

Table 4.4 *Businessmen from Defense Contracting Firms Think Defense Spending Should Not Be Cut, and That a Cut Would Hurt American Security*

Question/Answer	Firm with More Than 10% Defense Contracts (percent)	Firm with Less Than 10% Defense Contracts (percent)
Defense Spending Should Be		
Raised	33	20
Kept same	36	27
Cut less than 25%	15	38
Cut 25% or more	15	16
N =	39	512
Defense Cut Would Hurt Security		
Yes	68	51
Don't know	13	12
No	20	37
N =	40	527

These are the only items for which defense spending enters into the regression equations at the .01 level of significance. But although it is appropriate to insist on that level of statistical significance for most of our items, such a test is too stringent when we have but forty executives from heavily defense-oriented firms. If we look, for this small group, at differences significant at the .05 level, we find other important bivariate relations. A high level of defense contracting is associated with a high perceived probability that the United States will be involved in war (3), disagreement with the statement that alliances ought to be dismantled (9), a belief that defense spending ought not to be cut (25), and a belief that a 25 percent cut in defense spending would harm American security (26). Table 4.4 shows the percentages for two of these questions.

Although they are not quite eye-popping, these differences are far from trivial. Very roughly, perhaps an extra one in six of the relatively small proportion of executives who work for defense-oriented firms has taken up a point of view more favorable toward military spending than is held by executives of firms that are less defense oriented. This estimate of the number of executives with different opinions has to be very rough given the small sample;

very possibly even greater differences are masked by our unavoidable but crude use of the 10 percent mark simply to divide firms into the two categories. Very real pressures of self-interest appear to be operating to justify heavy defense spending and probably to promote it. *We have some real confirmation of a key element of military-industrial complex theories.*

It is always possible, of course, that we have the causal relation backward: Hawkish executives may gravitate to defense-oriented firms, rather than adopt beliefs justifying defense spending as a result of their employment. But on the whole this explanation seems less plausible, especially because we do *not* find *generally* hawkish or conservative attitudes to be related to the degree of a firm's defense orientation. Returning to Table 4.2, there is no relation, even at the lower .05 level, between a firm's defense orientation and the general foreign or domestic policy scales or the various questions on Vietnam. There is not even any relation to position on the multi-item defense scale or to approval of foreign economic or military assistance (not reported in the table). The relation is limited to the items we have noted—largely directly related to the level of defense spending—and does not seem to spill over to a comprehensive view of world affairs.[6]

It probably is entirely correct to see these people as anxious to have the pork barrel rolled their way, and as rationalizing that anxiety in broader terms of the general interest (American security and the prosperity of the American economy). It probably is not correct to blame this comparatively small group for the prevalence of anticommunism and cold war hawkishness generally. (Here it is important to know that the explanatory contribution, r^2, for the

---

[6]The result is, incidentally, consistent with earlier findings that, although senators from states that are heavily dependent on Defense Department spending rarely voted against an appropriation designed to bring a major contract to their states, the relationship of defense dependence to their position on broader issues of foreign policy was very modest, and much weaker than to their ideological position on domestic issues. See Bruce M. Russett, *What Price Vigilance? The Burdens of National Defense* (New Haven, Conn.: Yale University Press, 1970), ch. 3; also Moyer, op cit.; and Robert A. Bernstein and William W. Anthony, "The ABM Issue in the Senate, 1967–70: The Importance of Ideology," *American Political Science Review* 68, No. 3 (September 1974): 198–120. A content analysis of business executives' speeches found that top executives of aerospace firms were more favorable toward military spending, and also—surprising in light of the previously mentioned findings—more "nationalistic" (including anticommunist) than were executives from other industries. Maynard S. Seider, "American Big Business Ideology: A Content Analysis of Executive Speeches," *American Sociological Review* 39 (December 1974): 802–815.

defense industry independent variable is always below .03.) Looking over the materials from our survey, we find the same proportion of executives from defense-dependent firms as of other executives to be critical of the Vietnam affair. Their criticism was expressed in terms like these: "The money spent would have made the United States a better place to live if expended to meet our domestic shortcomings and needs." Another executive remarked more pointedly,

We have been further barbarized by this war. Our society is distinctly less principled, partly as a result. I am less secure in this sort of environment, and so are you!

When asked whether the internal threat of communism to the United States had increased, decreased, or remained the same, this same man replied that it had remained the same: "Like zero. But ask me about the internal threat of Fascism!"

Let us refer to the relevant hypotheses:

3.1   *Executives from corporations making substantial sales to the Department of Defense will be more favorable toward military preparedness than will executives from other corporations.*

3.2   *Executives from such corporations will be more hawkish on a variety of foreign policy issues than will executives from other corporations.*

3.3   *Executives from such corporations will look more favorably upon the effects of the Vietnam war (as specified in hypothesis 1.7) than will executives from other corporations.*

Hypothesis 3.1 is definitely confirmed, at least for a fairly narrow range of military preparedness questions, but hypotheses 3.2 and 3.3 are just as definitely rejected.

Other kinds of "economic interest" theories of course focus less on the defense-oriented industries per se than on the role of foreign markets and investments. As noted, the fear that nationalist and socializing governments abroad would close off American access to markets, seize American-owned plants, and forbid the entry of new American investment is alleged to be a driving force toward American political and military intervention overseas, especially in the underdeveloped world. By this explanation a strongly anticommunist foreign policy in general, and the Vietnam affair in particular, was propelled by these motives. Again, Vietnam was alleged to be important to such interests only because Vietnam threatened to be the first in a row of economic dominoes, a place where a determined and dramatic resistance to leftist revolutionary regimes had to be made so as to discourage other economically more important countries from following in its path.

There is indeed some evidence in our survey data to support this interpretation. The relationships are not very strong, nor by any means do they appear in all the foreign policy items, but they do follow the predicted direction. We find a small relation between the foreign economic interests of the firm and a hard line on the defense scale. Similarly, an expectation that the respondent's firm will increase its activities abroad is associated with a belief that ground combat remains "an effective means of settling disputes" (8) and an opinion that defense spending should not be reduced (25). An expectation that the firm will *not* increase its activities in LDCs relative to developed countries is somewhat related to the conviction that it is important to maintain civil liberties in less developed countries (23d). Certainly there is little evidence here for the opposite hypothesis that global commercial interests will promote more pacific perspectives on world politics, either on classic cold war issues or on issues related to third-world regimes. Nor are executives from firms with substantial foreign sales particularly in favor of foreign aid, either military or economic.

Also relevant is the set of answers concerning proper United States government action to protect American business investments in less developed countries. Both a high foreign sales ratio (44) and an expectation of increased activity in less developed countries (42) are rather strongly associated with a desire for government insurance. (Because the two are fairly highly correlated with each other, it is impossible to tell which in fact makes the greater contribution to the dependent variable.) In a sense this represents a preference for a moderate and apparently nonpolitical kind of United States government assistance, as an alternative to economic, diplomatic, or military pressures on nationalizing governments. Thus by contrast, none of the economic interest variables is significantly associated with an expressed willingness to see "diplomatic or economic action to prevent expropriation or ensure just compensation" (28b). Since less than 10 percent of the sample said the American government should do "nothing," this seems to be a moderate choice, but deceptively so.[7] As we remarked in the preceding chapter, a substantial majority of those who marked "government insurance" *also* marked "diplomatic or economic

---

[7]So few chose the third or fourth options, "military action," and "nothing," as to make analysis of their proponents unprofitable.

action," and government-backed insurance is a means of directly involving the fate of United States government institutions in the fate of any nationalization. In this way it may be a prelude to, even a trigger for, subsequent diplomatic or economic action.

All these associations are in the direction predicted by a neo-imperialist economic interpretation of American policy, and should be recognized as such. At the same time, *the strength of the association is always quite weak*—it explains only approximately 1 percent of the variance. The associations with some other items, notably those about economic motivations, add to the evidence for the real if moderate operation of these forces. Four dependent policy variables are associated with a preference for governments in less developed countries that will retain "the free enterprise system," and here the association is sometimes stronger. These dependent variables are the scales for domestic conservatism, foreign policy hawkishness, a belief that nationalism in less developed countries is a major problem for the United States (6b), and fear of an internal communist threat (7b); two of them, however, are domestic rather than foreign policy variables. Note that it is the "free enterprise" option in question 23 that is so associated, not the one specifying "broad opportunities for American business investment," which was perhaps too blatant for many respondents to choose. On the other hand, there is a poignant aspect to the answers for question 35, which showed executives from financial institutions to be more likely to believe that the Vietnam experience had a *bad* effect on American social and political institutions—recall that the financial institutions most frequently represented in this group were insurance companies, which had to pay for the damages caused by much of the domestic strife during the 1960s. Executives from *Fortune* 500 firms (rather than from banks or other financial institutions) were more likely to think the external threat of communism had increased (7a), but it is hard to know quite what to make of that rather modest relationship.

Rather surprisingly, anticipation of closer economic relations with communist countries was not measurably related to "softer" foreign policy views toward them. Fully 44 percent of the sample expected their own firms to increase their business with China and the Soviet Union substantially during the next decade—appreciably more than the percentage that anticipated doing much more business with less developed countries. In our interviews, executives did seem to relate this expectation, as would be anticipated, to a very low expectation of major war with communist countries, and some did see the economic bonds as part of a deliberate policy to tie the communist superpowers to Western economies by bonds of common interest they could not readily break.[8] But even these rather obvious conclusions (whose interpretation is fraught with chicken-egg problems) do not appear statistically in the survey analysis, and we see no linkages between trade expectations and political positions toward Eastern countries. If strong commerical bonds between the United States and communist countries do become established they may have the desired effect of changing the attitudes of both Eastern and Western elites in favor of coexistence. Mere anticipation of those bonds, however, has done little to change the broad perspectives of American business executives. Thus we find no evidence here for the theory that the expectation of economic gains will overcome the foreign policy perspectives imposed by ideology.

To summarize this discussion, it is appropriate to refer to the relevant hypotheses:

2.1 *Executives from corporations with substantial foreign sales or investments, or with expectations of substantially increasing foreign activities, or with expectations of increasing activities specifically in less developed countries, will look more favorably upon the effects of the Vietnam war (as specified in 1.7) than will executives from other corporations.*

2.2 *Executives from the corporations specified in 2.1 will be more hawkish on a variety of foreign policy issues than will executives from other corporations.*

2.3 *Executives from such corporations will be more favorable toward United States government activities to protect American business interests abroad, and toward the promotion of governments in less developed countries that are well disposed to the activities of foreign investors and maintenance of the free enterprise system; similarly, they will be more hostile toward socialist and communist governments in less developed countries than will executives from other corporations.*

2.4 *Executives from corporations with substantial foreign sales or investments, or with expectations of substantially increasing foreign activities, will look less favorably upon the effects of the Vietnam war (as specified in 1.10) than will executives from other corporations.*

2.5 *Executives from such corporations (as specified in 2.4) will be less hawkish on a variety of foreign policy issues than will executives from other corporations.*

---

[8]A view expressed by George Ball, for example: "It should be perfectly evident that to press the Soviet Union toward autarky makes no sense . . . the Soviet Union would be less able to wage a protracted war if it had to depend on sources of supply on this side of the Iron Curtain." *The Discipline of Power* (Boston: Little, Brown, 1968), pp. 276–277.

2.6 *Executives from corporations with expectations of substantially increasing sales or investments in the Soviet Union and/or China will be less hawkish on a variety of foreign policy issues than will executives from other corporations.*

We found no support for the first hypothesis, rather modest support for the second, and quite a bit for the first part of hypothesis 2.3 dealing with the protection of American business abroad, but not for the remaining clauses of that hypothesis. (Similarly, no relationship emerged for the question about socialist and communist governments in Latin America, item 13, not reported in Table 4.2.) On the other hand, there is *no evidence whatever to support the opposite hypotheses* about the pacific effects of economic interest described in hypotheses 2.4 and 2.5. Nor is there any evidence to support hypothesis 2.6.

Overall, the results confirm only very moderately the hypotheses giving economic explanations of an aggressive or interventionist foreign policy. The statistical relationships sometimes do emerge, but they are almost always much less important than a number of other independent variables. This is consistent with the data on economic interest reported by Bauer, Pool, and Dexter, cited in Chapter 2. The most notable exception concerns the choice of government insurance as a means of protecting American private investments abroad. Here the economic influences seem strong (about 7 percent of the variance is explained), and the matter at issue surely has serious implications for government policy. There is a real possibility that this country could be drawn into military or political conflict with a foreign government that nationalized a large insured American firm. Also, the support base for an anti-Soviet and anti-Chinese foreign policy that is provided by large-scale defense contracting should not be minimized.

Ideologies and Realpolitik

These few, fairly strong, apparent influences of economic variables contrast sharply, however, with the power of domestic ideology in "explaining" foreign policy choice. The relationship is strongest between domestic conservatism and foreign policy hawkishness (fully 32 percent of the variance is accounted for by conservatism alone); but of major importance on the defense scale are readiness to fight communist insurgencies (22), and a large number of individual items—notably more than 10 percent of the variance is accounted for by conservatism both in favoring defense spending (25) and a conviction that American military intervention in Vietnam was correct (30). The F tests for the ideology scale sometimes exceed by as much as a factor of ten the corresponding tests for economic variables. In combination with the fact that foreign economic interests contribute nothing, and foreign economic motivations contribute little, to explaining domestic conservatism, it is clear that we are finding a powerful ideological influence that is substantially *independent of particular economic interests*, at least with the group of corporate executives as a whole. In other words, knowledge of businessmen's domestic policy perspectives is a far more valuable aid in predicting their foreign policy perspectives than knowledge of their firms' overseas economic interests; their domestic policy perspectives in turn are themselves independent of the economic interest variables. It may well be that the business community as a whole is impelled by its economic interests toward a hawkish or interventionist set of foreign policy preferences. In the preceding chapter we indeed found evidence, although not very surprising, that such preferences are more common among businessmen than among any other civilian elite group except Republican party officials and politicians. But whatever this effect on businessmen as a group—and the causes remain speculative— *within* the group domestic policy preference is by far the best discriminator of hawks and doves.[9] A broad-gauged ideological explanation, stressing the seeming coherence of beliefs on a wide variety of different political matters, appears to be very powerful.[10]

---

[9]Compare R. Joseph Monsen and Mark W. Cannon, *The Makers of Public Policy: American Power Groups and Their Ideologies* (New York: McGraw-Hill, 1965), p. 2: "The major occupational power groups in this country are held together not only by economic interest but also by common ideologies."

[10]"Very powerful" must be understood in the context of knowing that even in our most successful equation (for explaining the foreign policy hawk-dove scale), the combined r^2 is only .42, leaving 58 percent of the variance unexplained. Much of this unexplained variance is undoubtedly the result of measurement error, compounded by the rather gross categorization of many of the independent and dependent variables. But the size of it also suggests the importance of other variables we have not dealt with, such as personality, communications patterns, and life experience. A remotely adequate theory aiming at a comprehensive explanation of businessmen's attitudes—which is not the aim of this book—would have to include such variables. Explorations of the effect of personality characteristics on foreign policy beliefs include Herbert McClosky, "Personality and Attitude Correlates of Foreign Policy Orientation," in James N. Rosenau, ed., *Domestic Sources of Foreign Policy* (New York: Free Press, 1967); Paul M. Sniderman and Jack Citrin, "Psychological Sources of Political Belief: Self-Esteem and Isolationist Attitudes," *American Political Science Review* 65, No. 2 (June 1971): 401–417; and R. A. Brody and S. Verba, "Hawk and Dove: The Search for an Explanation of Vietnam Policy Preferences," *Acta Politica* 7, No. 3 (July 1972): 285–322.

Before considering this explanation more closely, however, we should complete examination of Table 4.2, looking now for the effects of strategic considerations and basic political philosophy. Very generally, these variables together are more important than the economic variables, but are substantially *less* so than the domestic liberal-conservative scale. By far the most important of these "strategic" independent variables are the conviction that peace is best obtained through military superiority (1d), and the belief that the "military and technological advances of China and Russia" are a major problem for the United States (6a). Reading down Table 4.2 to see which dependent variables the strategic variables affect, we see that the idea of peace through military superiority is associated with a hard line on the defense scale, the "defend neutrals" factor (22), fear of an external communist threat (7a), desire for governments in LDCs to be neutral or pro-American (23b), opposition to a reduction in defense spending (25), and approval of American involvement in Vietnam (30). All these associations make sense because the variables do indeed seem intuitively related to a strategic, geopolitical, "balance of power" view of world politics. Also much to be expected is the absence of "peace through military superiority" as an independent variable (that is, other "approaches to peace" answers to item 1 take its place) associated with dependent variables that overtly are much more concerned with economics than with geopolitics, such as a desire for rapid economic development in the LDCs (23c), a wish for mutually dismantling alliances like NATO and the Warsaw Pact (9), and the salience of national and socialist movements in the LDCs (6b) and social and racial disparities within the United States (6e).

We find the fear of military and technological advances of China and Russia almost as important an independent variable as "peace through military superiority," and again it largely affects the power-oriented items: the foreign policy and defense scales, fear of the external communist threat (7a), and preference for high levels of defense spending (25), as well as a desire for United States investment opportunities in LDCs (23g). By comparison, all the remaining items appear as significant independent variables only sporadically. (Two interesting exceptions occur when items 35 and 36 about Vietnam are the dependent variables. We previously saw that a *conservative* position on the domestic ideology scale is associated with perception of "domestic order and stability" as a major problem. But an evaluation of the effect of Vietnam as bad in these questions indicates that the respondents share a concern for domestic order and that they can be placed at the *liberal* end of the ideology scale. Obviously, we here are identifying men who wish to preserve the domestic tranquility of the United States and see Vietnam as causing a loss of that tranquility, rather than the reverse; i.e., the decline of order as causing the Vietnam venture to fail.)

Overall, the geopolitical concerns with relative military power do contribute significantly to foreign policy preferences when questions about interactions with other major powers are at stake, but not importantly when questions about relations with underdeveloped countries are primarily at issue. They therefore seem to be a force in promoting "hard-line," "keep your guard up" policies, but they perhaps exert less influence on most of the decisions that seem likely to lead to American military or political interventions in the third world.[11] Basic philosophical convictions, such as a belief that human nature is the primary cause of war (2a), almost never appear as important independent variables. (As to the earlier step in the apparent causal sequence—why some men initially adopt a strategic or power-oriented view of the world— we did not pose that question in the survey and really have no answer.)

Domestic political ideology is a far more powerful predictor of foreign policy preference than is either economic interest and motivation or strategic ideas. The difference seems strong enough to surmount most of the necessary reservations that the results could be an artifact merely of having better measures for ideology. This conclusion is supported by a set of regression analyses that we performed on the entire set of data for businessmen and military officers combined. If we treat the category of businessmen as itself denoting an economic interest in the capitalist system not shared by military officers, we can compare the relative effect of economic interest (the business/military dummy variable) and domestic ideology on foreign policy preference. The results are striking. When this analysis is performed on all the dependent variables listed in Table 4.2, in only two instances is business both significantly related to a hawkish position and more strongly so related than is domestic conservatism. The two instances are "aim free enterprise" in LDCs (23e) and the wish to protect American investments with government insurance (28a). Even in those two instances, the differences in the coefficients are very small. Surely these are the absolute minimum results that anyone could expect,

---

[11]A moderate exception is the factor about defending neutral countries against communist invasion or insurgency (22).

and as a whole they must be taken as an affirmation of the unimportance of economic as compared with ideological influences. The
finding that business/military differences are less important than
ideological ones on most issues also suggests the hurdles that ob-
struct efforts by businessmen to reach any consensus and act
politically as a united group.

We *divided* the entire business sample into conservatives and
liberals according to the domestic ideology scale, and performed
separate analyses of variance on each group for most of the foreign
policy preference questions in Table 4.2 to see if foreign policy
preferences seemed related to the foreign business activities of the
firms. No new significant relationships appeared, showing that
economic interest and ideology *do not interact* to produce a stronger
effect (e.g., economic interest does not become more powerful
among individuals who are conservative on domestic politics).

Another test needs to be made. It might reasonably be expected that even though economic motivations are relatively less
important than ideological ones, they will be more powerful with
businessmen than with representatives of other professions. For
example, the correlation of economic motivations with foreign policy
preference will be stronger among businessmen than among military men, even though it may be fairly weak for both. By contrast,
we might expect that other kinds of motivations, such as ideological
or especially strategic ones, would be more strongly associated with
foreign policy among the military than among the business executives. We can easily check this possibility. Table 4.5 shows in
summary form the results of applying a set of similar multiple
regression equations to both groups, using as dependent variables
the twenty-three foreign policy items listed in Table 4.2 that appeared in both the business and the military analyses.[12] The table
shows the number of items for which each type of motivation was
found to be statistically significant and *more important* in the
military sample than in the business sample, and vice versa.[13]
Some kinds of motivations (e.g., economic) enter significantly into

---

[12]That is, all but questions 33–36, which were not asked of the military
officers, and the second factor derived from question 22 about defending
neutral foreign nations. This factor did not appear in the military data.

[13]Economic motivations are here defined as answers e or g to question
23 about policy in underdeveloped countries (aims of free enterprise or opportunities for United States investment); ideological motivation is defined
by position on the liberal–conservative scale; strategic motivations are defined by answers to questions 1–5 plus answer b (pro-American foreign policy)
to question 23. Since we are comparing columns and not rows, the fact that
more variables are identified as "strategic" is unimportant.

Table 4.5 *Frequencies with Which Different Motivations Are More Closely Associated with Foreign Policy Preference among Businessmen and among Military Officers*

Motivation	Military	Business
All economic motivations	2	2
Ideological motivation	5	13
All strategic motivations	7	10

the equations only fairly rarely, and thus appear infrequently in either column of the table.

Again the expectations of an economic interest perspective are unsatisfied. Though they appear rarely for either group, economic motivations are the only type that appear as often on the military side as on the business side. Ideological and even strategic motivations, on the other hand, appear much more often on the business side than on the military side. On the whole, it is easier to "explain" businessmen's foreign policy attitudes than it is to explain those of military officers; the attitudes of the former are more structured. (We shall have more to say about that later.) But economic motivations, unlike the others, seem to make as great a difference to the military men's beliefs as to the businessmen's.

Two more major hypotheses about economic motivations are thus rejected by these data:

4.1 *Economic motivations will be more closely associated with the foreign policy preferences expressed by businessmen than with the preferences expressed by other elites.*

4.2 *Economic motivations and interests will be more closely associated with the foreign policy preferences expressed by businessmen than will domestic ideology or strategic motivations.*

(This hypothesis is not tested by Table 4.5, but was rejected in the preceding discussion.)

One further test is in order. Our domestic ideology scale is a composite of items tapping different substantive concerns. It has proved to be valuable as a summary measure of liberalism-conservatism, but we must now disaggregate it into several components. Two of the questions dealt primarily with inequalities of income in the economic system: poverty as the result of cultural and psychological problems of the poor (15), and reduction of

Table 4.6   *Correlation (r²) of Individual Domestic Policy Items with Foreign Policy*

Domestic Policy Item	Foreign Policy Scale Hawk	Defense and Vietnam (Items 25, 26, 30)
15. Poverty cultural and psychological	.01	.01
16. Reduce income differences—disagree	.02	.03
17. Legalize marijuana—disagree	.14	.04
18. Excessive restrictions on police	.16	.05
19. FBI and milit. intell. threat to civil libs.—disagree	.24	.11
20. White racism—disagree	.08	.04
21. School integration too rapid	.07	.03

differences in income in the United States (16). Three others in one way or another concerned civil liberties: legalization of marijuana (17), restrictions on the police (18), and practices of the FBI and military intelligence (19). The other two dealt with problems of civil rights and race relations: white racism (20), and school integration (21). We must find out *which* of these questions is most closely associated with hawkishness. An especially close association between hawkishness and conservatism on economic equality issues would support the view that foreign policy is determined by the same influences that promote a desire to maintain domestic economic privilege. Table 4.6 presents the squared correlation coefficients for each item with two kinds of foreign policy measures. The first column shows the correlation of each item with our basic hawk–dove scale; the second shows the average correlation of each with the three additional foreign policy items in the survey most closely correlated with domestic ideology—level of United States defense spending (25), the effect of a defense cut on American security (26), and correctness of United States intervention in Vietnam (30).

The results should be interpreted cautiously because of the intercorrelations among the domestic policy items. Nevertheless, the results seem clear-cut. The three civil liberties items are the most closely related to foreign policy preference, and of those three, the relationship is closest for the one that explicitly refers to civil liberties (19); this item accounts for almost one-fourth of the variance in the hawk–dove scale. The race relations or civil rights items are usually the second most closely related group, and the income equality questions are third and last.[14] The first of the equality items is perhaps not entirely apt. It carries some connotations that are relevant to race relations, and is perhaps too abstract or theoretical to tap attitudes very successfully. This is reflected in its low loading on the domestic ideology factor (see Table 4.1). The second equality item, however, is quite straightforward and does not suffer from these limitations. Allowing for the different usefulness of the two equality questions, it is probably safer to regard the equality questions (15 and 16) and the race relations items (20 and 21) as possibly being equally associated with foreign policy preference—but both are well behind the civil liberties items (17–19).

Thus it does not seem true that foreign policy hawks are concerned mainly with preserving their economic privileges at home. Although there is an association between the two attitudes, the relation between hawkishness and a restrictive view of civil liberties is much stronger. Hawks are most likely to be concerned with strengthening police powers to control dissent generally, rather than specifically to maintain economic differentials. Of course, it may be that their preoccupation with police powers is in fact directed chiefly against the "leveling" programs of domestic radicals, but the low correlations of foreign policy with items 15 and 16 make that appear unlikely.

We must now reject one more hypothesis:

4.3 *Among businessmen, foreign policy hawkishness will be more closely associated with a conservative position on income redistribution than with conservative attitudes on civil rights or civil liberties.*

Our conclusion remains that of the great *and independent* relevance of *ideological* influences to foreign policy preference, but we have not inquired deeply into the antecedents of domestic ideology, as we did not inquire into the antecedents of power-oriented views.

How Liberals Become Doves

The ideological explanation must be developed before it is acceptable as an explanation in any intellectual sense, beyond being merely a statistical explanation; it must be interpreted theoretically, to

---

[14]This finding is generally confirmed, in Congress, by Moyer, op. cit., p. 113.

produce a causal explanation from what is, strictly speaking, only a finding of correlation. Why should domestic conservatives be hawks on foreign policy? Or perhaps more interestingly, why do liberals on domestic matters turn out to be doves on foreign policy?

Most of the items of belief that now define a foreign policy hawk were in fact general items of belief, expressive of a near-consensus among Americans, not so many years ago. As just one example (though a major one), from the end of World War II to the 1960s, between 20 percent and 50 percent of all Americans wanted to spend more on defense, while the number who wanted defense spending cut was virtually always less than 30 percent and frequently was less than 10 percent. Highly educated, professional, and upper-income individuals were more pro-defense than were people of lower status.[15] The 20 percent of our businessmen who now want to raise military spending would then have been in much more numerous company. An explanation that takes into account shifts in foreign policy outlook by large parts of the population, and especially within the elites, is required.

Throughout the 1940s and 1950s, there was little association of domestic liberalism with the point of view we now term dovish. In fact, a large number of liberals took pride in being identified as liberal internationalists, a posture that, in its foreign policy component, included foreign aid, alliance commitments for the defense of other states in the free world, and high levels of military preparedness. Samuel Huntington reports that congressmen who were liberal on domestic issues in the 1950s were more likely to support higher defense expenditures than were domestic conservatives, and that Northern Democrats were as pro-defense as were either Republicans or Southern Democrats.[16] John Kennedy could in 1960

---

[15]See Bruce M. Russett, "The Revolt of the Masses: Public Opinion on Military Expenditures," in John Lovell and Phillip Kronenberg, eds., *New Civil-Military Relations* (New Brunswick, N.J.: Trans-action Books, 1974). Similar evidence that high socioeconomic status was associated with "internationalism" in the cold war period, and with support for administration policy in Korea and, at least initially, in Vietnam, can be found in Andre Modigliani, "Hawks and Doves, Isolationism and Political Distrust: An Analysis of Public Opinion on Military Policy," *American Political Science Review* 66, No. 3 (September 1972): 960–978; Richard F. Hamilton, "A Research Note on the Mass Support for 'Tough' Military Initiatives," *American Sociological Review* 33 (June 1968): 439–445; and Harlan Hahn, "Correlates of Public Sentiment About War: Local Referenda on the Vietnam Issue," *American Political Science Review* 64, No. 4 (December 1970): 1186–1198.

[16]Samuel P. Huntington, *The Common Defense* (New York: Columbia University Press, 1961), pp. 254–259.

campaign both as a liberal and against failures of the Republican administration to keep up the nation's military guard and prevent emergence of the alleged (and illusory) "missile gap." Many liberals today recall in rather embarrassed silence the "internationalist" rhetoric of Kennedy's purple Inaugural Address.

Liberals nevertheless saw themselves, and in large degree rightly so, as moderates on these foreign policy issues, desirous of an active American role in making the world safer, richer, and more democratic while avoiding what they termed hysterical anticommunism and military "pactomania" on the one hand and isolationist withdrawal on the other. Liberals were extremely prominent in the arms control movement, "realistically" dismissing the "utopian" hopes of general disarmament but working arduously for limited measures to tame and stabilize the balance of terror through negotiation with the Soviet Union and by placing lesser reliance on nuclear weapons, especially the threat of massive retaliation, to deter all kinds of attacks everywhere. This is the context in which the enthusiasm for built-up capabilities for waging conventional and counterinsurgency wars should be seen. In the same vein, Andre Modigliani found that foreign policy attitudes during the Korean war, rather than being given a single isolationist-interventionist dimension, could be better characterized as being divided into one of three quite distinct categories: supporters of the administration's limited war policy; those who wanted more vigorous military effort to bring victory, à la Douglas MacArthur; and those who wanted the United States to withdraw rapidly without much regard for the consequences.[17] The first generally fit the image of liberal internationalists, the second and third are different kinds of "conservatives."

This middle-of-the-road international image of the liberals fits with most of the quantitative evidence available for the period. For example, Leroy Rieselbach, and others before him, found essentially no systematic relation between congressmen's voting on

---

[17]Modigliani, op. cit. See also McClosky, op. cit., who attempts a distinction between "jingoist" isolationists who "would display a more bullying, sabre-rattling attitude toward other nations and would rely for protection on superior military force and the threat of using it unilaterally," and "pacific isolationists" who "would prefer to have the nation withdraw into its own shell, safeguarding itself by having as little to do as possible with other nations, and by avoiding the threat or use of force" (p. 103). The latter group, corresponding probably to Modigliani's third group, may now be showing up as doves in our data, and the former may be appearing as hawks. Pejorative labels, however, do not assist analysis.

domestic issues and on foreign policy issues.[18] As for the public at large, Norman Nie found really no correlation (actually an average of —.05) between foreign policy attitudes and a liberal position on several domestic policy items ("integration," "black welfare," and "social welfare" issues).[19]

All this is consistent with impressions of what happened in the United States during and after World War II. Before the war, nascent American participation was resisted by two broad types of isolationists. One was the Progressive-populist group composed of men like Senators Borah, Wheeler, Johnson, and LaFollette; President Robert Hutchins of the University of Chicago; *Nation* Editor Oswald Garrison Villard; Socialist leader Norman Thomas; historian Charles A. Beard; and economist Stuart Chase. Quite another group, in broad agreement with the first on what international policy should be if not on why it should be so, or on anything else, included President Herbert Hoover and Republican senators like Taft and Vandenberg, and then branched out to include such men as Charles Lindbergh and outright German or Nazi sympathizers. New Dealers and moderate, especially Eastern, Republicans supported President Roosevelt and his hesitant moves toward American involvement.

After the war both of its initial groups of opponents found themselves broadly in support of the new "internationalist" majority for an American role of world leadership. Many of the conservative isolationists could muster more enthusiasm for a campaign against communist Russia (and later China) than they were able, at least initially, to muster against Germany. Socialist and populist isolationists were appalled at the fate of their social democratic colleagues in communist-ruled states; even more to the point, they often had to fight a defensive battle for their political lives at home. In the face of the wave of anticommunism in the United States, which culminated in the Joseph McCarthy phenomenon, they often out-hawked the right on foreign policy, feeling obliged to prove that their progressive social views were fully

---

[18]Leroy N. Rieselbach, *The Roots of Isolationism* (Indianapolis: Bobbs-Merrill, 1966); and Duncan MacRae, *Dimensions of Congressional Voting* (Berkeley and Los Angeles: University of California Press, 1958).

[19]Norman Nie, "Mass Belief Systems Revisited: Political Change and Attitude Structure," *Journal of Politics* 36, No. 3 (August 1974): 540–591. However, McCloskey, op. cit., represents an exception in finding some association between isolationism and several aspects of domestic conservatism in his 1950s data.

compatible with loyalty to the United States in its new international struggle. A general consensus on foreign policy emerged. Insofar as that consensus was less than complete or allowed disagreement within a narrowed range of options, the traditional liberal-conservative distinctions on domestic issues seemed to have little relevance to it.

As we all know, however (having also found renewed evidence in this chapter), that situation has by now changed dramatically. A basic divergence of beliefs about the ends as well as the means of American foreign policy has emerged, and this divergence frequently coincides with divergences on domestic policy. The empirical evidence as to when, and especially why, this divergence emerged is less than complete, but there is enough to suggest that foreign policy views have changed greatly, probably much more than domestic policy views, and that shifts have come at *two* different points in time. The first clue emerges most clearly in the data on mass rather than elite opinion. This is at first surprising, but it may be simply because the data on mass opinion, gathered by the massive survey research efforts of recent decades, are particularly complete. Nie traced the relationship between domestic and foreign policy opinion through all the major pre-election polls in Presidential years from 1956 to 1968, with the addition of polls in 1958 and 1971. As noted earlier, the average correlation between liberal attitudes on domestic issues and dovish attitudes on cold war international issues was −.06 in 1956; it remained at −.07 in 1960. But in only four years the correlation jumped to .25 in 1964— a level at which it essentially remained in 1968 and 1971 (.24 in each year). We also have some national survey evidence that the foreign policy consensus of the mass public had begun very tentatively to crack by 1960. Russett found a mild increase, at that time, in the still very limited proportion of the population who wanted to spend less on defense, and Gerry Ruth Tyler discovered a similar growth between 1957 and early 1961 (which was subsequently reversed) in the proportion prepared to see "Red China" admitted to the United Nations.[20]

The data on elite opinion are less satisfactory because they have not been studied or gathered systematically over the years, with the same or similar questions applied at different time points.

[20]Nie, op. cit.; Russett, "Revolt of the Masses," op. cit.; and Gerry Ruth Sack Tyler, *A Contextual Analysis of Public Opinion Polls: The Question of the Admission of Communist China to the United Nations.* Ph.D. dissertation, Yale University, 1972, ch. 4.

Nevertheless, Bernard Mennis, interviewing in 1965, found a moderate relationship between liberal views on civil liberties and what we would now call moderately dovish foreign policy attitudes among senior foreign service officers and senior military officers at the Pentagon. Also, Russett found a sharp rise between 1961 and 1963 in the proportion of senators voting in favor of cuts in the Department of Defense budget as recommended by the Executive; this is further evidence for an erosion in the foreign policy consensus.[21]

An equally important shift among the elites, however, occurred sometime between 1967 and 1969. In his work on the Senate, for example, Russett found quite a substantial correlation in the 90th Congress (1967–1968) between voting on defense and foreign policy issues on the one hand, and voting on civil rights and urban affairs on the other. This is a new finding, one not present in Russett's analysis of the 87th Congress (1961–1962) or in earlier analyses by other scholars. More relevant still are Wayne Moyer's data on the House of Representatives.[22] He found a strong (.82) correlation in 1967–1968 between dovish votes on a cold war foreign policy scale and a liberal position on civil liberties, as well as weaker correlations between a cold war foreign policy scale and favorable attitudes toward government spending and also a generally liberal position on domestic politics. But votes specifically on defense or "preparedness" issues correlated much more weakly with all these other scales, including the foreign policy scale. Congressmen still only rarely voted against Defense Department appropriations; indeed there were only three such intrepid men in 1967. Most liberals had not yet come so far. But by 1970 the number of dissenting congressmen on the DOD appropriations bill had grown to 46, virtually all of them liberals. In the 91st Congress, voting on the preparedness scale correlated very highly with the general cold war foreign policy scale (.87) and almost as strongly with scales for urban and racial issues, government spending, and domestic liberalism in general. By 1969 and 1970 congressmen saw all these issues as closely interrelated, in a way that they had not only a very few years before. The reason seems obvious enough. Liberals saw the heavy costs, in terms of their preferred domestic policies, being imposed by an activist foreign policy in general and by the Vietnam

[21]Bernard Mennis, *American Foreign Policy Officials: Who They Are and What They Believe Regarding International Politics* (Columbus: Ohio State University Press, 1971), ch. 8; Russett, "Revolt of the Masses," op. cit.
[22]Russett, *What Price Vigilance?*, op. cit., ch. 3; and Moyer, op. cit.

experience in particular: alienation, police repression, and especially demotion of spending priorities for health, urban affairs, and education because of military commitments. This last demotion of spending priorities explains the ultimate, if delayed, turning against "preparedness," as well as the more specifically foreign affairs components of a hawkish policy. In the 1970s there are few liberal hawks displaying the kind of "liberal messianism" associated with such members of the Kennedy administration as W. W. Rostow.

Other evidence in the survey confirms this idea that foreign policy views were brought into line with domestic policy preferences rather than vice versa. Among the elites in our survey, almost one-fourth (22 percent) of the businessmen who thought the Vietnam war was a mistake report that they reached this conclusion during 1967 or 1968.[23] As noted in the preceding chapter, of those 299 men who considered the war a mistake, 38 percent cited damage to American social and political institutions as the reason: more cited this than any other single reason and far more (7 percent) cited this reason than damage to the American economy. When we asked our business executives whether they considered themselves better or worse off as a result of the war and why, 239 said worse and gave us a reason. Although economic reasons were frequently cited (by 42 percent) as most important, the number listing some version of damage to American political institutions or diversion of resources away from social priorities was still greater (more than 46 percent). Moreover, both strong foreign policy doves and vigorous domestic liberals (recall that the two dimensions are related but somewhat independent) agreed in rating "social and racial disparities within the United States" as the primary problem facing the country (question 6)—above foreign policy issues.

Further reason to identify Vietnam as the turning point will be given in the following chapter, where we show that a pattern emerged in 1967: conciliatory acts by both the United States and the communists in Vietnam caused prices on the Wall Street stock market to rise. As for the mass public, the big shift in opinion against the war occurred between February and October 1967, according to the *Gallup Opinion Index*. The Gallup survey indicated that roughly 15 percent of public opinion favored a cut in defense

---

[23]This is very likely an understatement. According to a survey of *Fortune* 500 presidents, "more than a quarter" of *all* of them said they had converted from hawks to doves during the year summer 1968–summer 1969 *alone*. See Arthur M. Louis, "What Business Thinks," *Fortune* 80, No. 4 (September 1969).

spending throughout the cold war years and as late as 1964, compared with roughly 50 percent in 1968 (according to the first survey taken on this topic after 1964).[24]

A sampling of some quotations from our survey demonstrates how executives linked these issues in their minds.[25] Among the war's opponents, the following statement was typical:

The most important ill effect of the Vietnam war on the United States has been on the level of morality, the becoming inured to "kill ratios," mass killing of civilians along with military disregard for human life. These have been accompanied by erosion of individual rights and privacy in the United States.

Another laments

the pain of conscience, the shame and guilt of a racist war, the setback to social and economic progress.

The emotional force of many reactions is expressed in these two comments:

It brought out the worst kind of actions on the part of our government officials—using any means, such as lying to the people and to Congress, that they thought justified by the end: trickery, sacrificing great virtue in our system.

Really, the Vietnam war was a disaster for everyone concerned with it. This includes the North and South Vietnamese, the soldiers, the civilians, the U.S. soldiers, and the U.S. as a whole. We are fools to permit U.S. Presidents to run such wars.

Hawks also linked domestic and foreign policy, though the conclusions they drew were very different; they saw domestic weakness as the cause of foreign failure rather than vice versa. For them the war coincided with an intensification of the domestic threat of communism, and they retained and sometimes strengthened their views on the need to be vigilant at home and abroad. One regretted the existence of "forces willing to denigrate our society—whether by design or idealism"; another saw the war as bringing

---

[24]Russett, "Revolt of the Masses," op. cit. Also note the following comment by a Florida toymaker on the state of the "war toy" market: "We could see a turning point about 1968, when the majority of public sentiment began to go against Vietnam. Today, I think we're seeing a continuation of the trend against war toys; there is just no feeling for them." In Judy Klemesrud, "And the War Toys Are Rolling Along," New York Times, December 22, 1974, Vol. 34, p. 6.

[25]We should also be alert to the likelihood, untestable with our data, that certain personality characteristics also predisposed individuals to shift from hawk to dove attitudes.

"disproportionate attention to, and action by, extremist minorities";
still another described the war as "a good scapegoat and a rallying
point for all of society's critics, but not the cause." The following
statement is part of one man's long tirade of bitterness:

> Our country has a vocal and unmolested communist party that is pro-
> tected by our form of government. Thus they [the party] divided
> America more than most realized until recently.

There were exceptions, though not many. Some men were doves
on foreign policy but remained relatively conservative on civil
liberties and racial and economic issues. The traditional business
opposition to "big government," high taxation, and greater equality
of income[26] remained fairly strong among many in our sample.

One man, for instance, was emphatically dovish on the issues
of troops abroad and foreign aid, and the minor damages he expected from a cut in defense spending, but he was just as emphatically conservative on the issues of civil rights and civil
liberties, and commented that "Our biggest domestic problem is our
huge and uncontrolled federal bureaucracy." This combination is
reminiscent of the views held by many Republican conservatives
in the early cold war years. Its appearance here—added to the
same man's early opposition to United States action in Vietnam—
suggests that conservative isolationism is not entirely dead, and
may even have been given a revival by the events of recent years.
But this example too is indicative of the self-consistent though
quite different way in which beliefs on foreign and domestic policy
are related in a person's mind.

Polarization and Salience

Although some readers may be surprised, as we were, to find
dovish and liberal attitudes consistently together on the one hand,
and conservative and hawkish attitudes regularly together on the
other, it is the pervasiveness of a particular ideological dimension
that is most surprising to us, not merely the fact that people impose
some such consistency. The literature on ideology, that is, how
people order their thoughts and information in order to interpret
new facts, is massive. Ole Holsti states the general view well when
he calls a "belief system"

---

[26]Among the many studies confirming this as the traditional business view,
see especially Francis X. Sutton et al., *The American Business Creed* (New
York: Schocken, 1962).

. . . a set of lenses through which information concerning the physical and social environment is received. It orients the individual to his environment, defining it for him and identifying for him its salient characteristics. . . . In addition to organizing perceptions into a meaningful guide for behavior, the belief system has the function of the establishment of goals and the ordering of preferences.[27]

More recently, many social scientists have turned with great interest to theories of "cognitive processing," stressing the deductive elements of an ideology—the "decision calculus" whereby new items are interpreted, usually in a way that makes sense of the new beliefs without importantly modifying the old. Analogizing from the past is also a common mechanism, as is overt deduction. Thus a person may evoke the memory of Munich as a "guide" to negotiation with an adversary, and he may just as effectively deduce an orderly set of propositions from general rules and apply them to the specific situation. The literature on cognitive dissonance, and its resolution, is in some degree also relevant here.[28]

Any way we look at the matter, repeated, and deep, shocks to the effectiveness of old beliefs are required before they shift markedly. The first reaction is typically one of denying that a new piece of information really is accurate, or denying its importance even if it is accurate. Or old views may be shifted temporarily, but may be realigned when the new piece of information is no longer salient. A major political event—major, that is, not just for what objectively it does to people but for its effect on how they think about their

[27]Ole R. Holsti, "The Belief System and National Images: A Case Study," *Journal of Conflict Resolution* 6, No. 3 (September 1962): 245.

[28]A sampling of the relevant literature, including some major works on foreign policy cognition, includes Robert P. Abelson, "Psychological Implication," in Abelson et al., eds., *Theories of Cognitive Consistency: A Source Book* (Chicago: Rand McNally, 1968); Abelson and Milton J. Rosenberg, "Symbolic Psychologic: A Model of Attitudinal Cognition," *Behavioral Science* 3, No. 1 (January 1958): 1–13; Robert Axelrod, "Psychoalgebra: A Mathematical Theory of Cognition and Choice with an Application to the British Eastern Committee in 1918," *Peace Research Society (International) Papers* 18 (1972): 113–131; Axelrod, "Schema Theory: An Information Processing Model of Perception and Cognition," *American Political Science Review* 67, No. 4 (December 1973): 1248–1266; K. E. Boulding, "National Images and International Systems," *Journal of Conflict Resolution* 3, No. 2 (June 1959): 120–131; Robert Jervis, *The Logic of Images in International Relations* (Princeton, N.J.: Princeton University Press, 1970); G. A. Kelly, *The Psychology of Personal Constructs* (New York: Norton, 1955); H. H. Kelley, *Attribution in Social Interaction* (New York: General Learning Press, 1971); Herbert C. Kelman and R. Baron, "Inconsistency as a Psychological Signal," in Abelson et al., eds., op. cit.; Michael J. Shapiro and G. Matthew Bonham, "Cognitive Process and Foreign Policy Decision-Making," *International Studies Quarterly* 17, No. 2 (June 1973): 147–174; and John Steinbrunner, *The Cybernetic Theory of Decision* (Princeton, N.J.: Princeton University Press, 1974).

world—can be defined as one that for many minds defies this normal pattern. Its consequences are so immediate, unavoidable, and serious that old beliefs must be modified to take it into account, and the modification remains even after the event and its objective consequences have faded into memory.

This, we feel, is what Vietnam has been to many of the elites we surveyed and interviewed. In some degree these men's minds had already been prepared for the shift in world view that Vietnam imposed. Almost 60 percent of them had fought in World War II, but the glorious memories of that great crusade for a just cause against a vicious enemy had faded after more than 25 years, and the rationale it provided for an internationalist, activist foreign policy diminished. The undeniable evidence of Soviet-Chinese conflict within the formerly monolithic-appearing "communist bloc" had some impact, as did the limited arms control measures and Soviet-American détente of the early and mid-1960s. The events of Vietnam do not alone account for the new foreign policy orientation. Many people's views had changed earlier; for others Vietnam was merely the catalyzing factor. But it did take the war to shift the views of many—and of course, many others did not change their fundamental beliefs even then. For those whose views did change, however, the effect is likely to last throughout most of their political lives, marking them off from those of another generation who will not have shared the trauma. Vietnam also may have profound consequences for the conduct of American foreign policy, by changing the boundaries of support among elites and the attentive public.[29]

The coalescence of domestic and foreign policy views in a single dimension is largely what most people mean by the "polarization" of political attitudes in the United States. In part they mean a widening of the extremes at the expense of the middle, but much of the phenomenon is simply a discovery that the people who agree

---

[29]An important and relevant article on long-term opinion changes is that by K. W. Deutsch and R. L. Merritt, "Effects of Events on National and International Images," in Herbert Kelman, ed., *International Behavior: A Social-Psychological Analysis* (New York: Holt, Rinehart and Winston, 1965). Also important are Davis Bobrow and Neal Cutler, "Time-Oriented Explanations of National Security Beliefs: Cohort, Life Style, and Situation," *Peace Research Society (International) Papers* 8 (1967): 31–57; Neal Cutler, "Generational Succession as a Source of Foreign Policy Attitudes," *Journal of Peace Research* 1 (1970): 33–47; the classic article by Karl Mannheim, "The Problem of Generation," in his *Essays on the Sociology of Knowledge* (London: Routledge and Kegan Paul, 1959); and an excellent review by Alan B. Spitzer, "The Historical Problem of Generations," *American Historical Review* 75, No. 5 (December 1973): 1353–1385.

with me on one issue are likely more or less to agree with me across the board, and my political opponents on one issue are likely to be against me on all. The pattern of "cross-cutting solidarities"— beloved by democratic theorists for its ability to mitigate conflict through the fact, and expectation, of fluidly shifting coalitions—is gravely weakened.

It is a phenomenon, moreover, that seems strongest among those for whom politics would be expected to be most salient: the closer people are to the levers of power, the more beliefs on domestic and foreign policy merge into a structured ideology. A variety of studies have established that interrelatedness of attitudes is closely associated with information level and with political interest: those who have a sizable amount of accurate information and a high degree of interest will relate various facts and principles to produce a coherent set of beliefs. Nie has reported the strongest and most recent evidence on this correlation.[30] He found only a moderate relationship between education and structuredness of political attitudes, but a much stronger one between political interest and attitude structuredness. Similarly, in Norway Helge Hveem found that attitudes were more structured among elites than among opinion makers, and more structured among opinion makers than among the general public.[31]

In our own data on elite opinion, coherence or structuredness is stronger among the businessmen than among the military officers.

---

[30]Nie, op. cit. See also Philip Converse, "The Nature of Belief Systems in Mass Publics," in David Apter, ed., *Ideology and Discontent* (New York: Free Press, 1964); William Gamson and Andre Modigliani, "Knowledge and Foreign Policy Opinions: Some Models for Consideration," *Public Opinion Quarterly* 30 (Summer 1966): 187–199; Herbert McCloskey, P. J. Hoffman, and R. O'Hara, "Issue Conflict and Consensus Among Party Leaders and Followers," *American Political Science Review* 54, No. 2 (June 1960): 406–427; Frederick D. Herzon, "Intensity of Opinion and the Organization of Political Attitudes," *Western Political Quarterly* 28, No. 1 (March 1975): 72–84; and Thomas Atkinson and Michael Ziegler, "The Scope of Preferences for Military Alternatives" (Toronto: York University, mimeo., 1973). But note the view of Eugene Litwak, Nancy Hooyman, and Donald Warren in "Ideological Complexity and Middle American Rationality," *Public Opinion Quarterly* 37, No. 3 (Fall 1973): 317–332. They argue, on the basis of some data, that middle-Americans show a complex multicausal belief system, frequently blaming poor *and* rich, or blacks *and* government, and so on. Such belief systems do not fit the usual measures of ideological consistency or show high correlation among the items, but, these authors contend, that is because the explanations of middle-Americans are quite different from those of upper-status people, not because of deficient cognitive skills or apathy. The matter requires investigation, but probably is not relevant to comparisons *among* different *upper-status* groups.

[31]Helge Hveem, *International Relations and World Images: A Study of Norwegian Foreign Policy Elites* (Oslo: Universitetsforlaget, 1972), pp. 233–234.

In the entire set of questions we used to identify foreign and domestic policy ideologies (items 8–21), the intercorrelations are higher for the business sample than for the military sample in 77 of the 91 instances, or 85 percent. Similarly, when we conducted each of the factor analyses on the military sample and on the business group, we found that the first factor always accounted for substantially more of the variance in the business sample than in the military group (for example, 34 percent versus 26 percent for foreign policy, 36 percent versus 29 percent for domestic policy, and 31 percent versus 26 percent for defense policy). And the scales themselves were more tightly intercorrelated for the business sample (.56, .37, and .48) than for the military (.37, .24, and .32).

Another way to analyze structuredness is to construct a special "unstructuredness" score for each group, and also for the various subgroups of the Columbia sample discussed in the preceding chapter. We can take the eleven agree-disagree questions common to all the surveys (items 9–13, 15–20) and ascertain the consistency of each individual's answers to them. We can score each person from 1 to 4 on each question, with 1 being the most conservative-hawkish position (strong agreement, or disagreement, whichever is appropriate) on the item, and 4 being the most liberal-dovish position. An individual who scored 4 on all 11 of the items, or all 3s, all 2s, or all 1s, would have the maximum possible degree of structuredness, whereas an individual who scored half 4s and half 1s would have maximum possible unstructuredness. In effect, by computing the variance of each individual's scores over the 11 items, we have a measure of the unstructuredness of his beliefs (high variance equals high unstructuredness). And by averaging this measure for all individuals within the group, we have a measure of the degree of unstructuredness that is typical for the group. The results are as follows:

Group	Unstructuredness Score
Labor leaders	.757
Military	.682
Yale businessmen	.675
Voluntary association leaders	.643
Republican politicians	.643
Columbia businessmen	.642
Senior civil servants	.630
Media leaders	.629
Democratic politicians	.621

These scores show that although these political questions fit together into a more interrelated world view for the businessmen than for the military, both groups show less structure than do most of the Columbia elite groups. The labor leaders show the least structuredness, but they are followed immediately by the military and then by the Yale business sample. The Columbia business sample is a bit lower down, but is effectively in a three-way tie with the voluntary association leaders and Republican politicians.[32]

The military and business elites surely must, on the average, have as much potential access to information on political matters as do most other American elites except perhaps for the politicians. If absence of an equally clear structure to their beliefs is traced to less complete information, then by inference they have less information not because they are kept in the dark against their will but simply because general political issues, outside their immediate professional concerns, matter less to them. Political issues seem less salient for military men than for businessmen and less for businessmen than for other civilian elites. *Politics just do not seem to be of as much interest for either of these subgroups as for other elites.* This applies to the whole range of domestic, foreign, and defense policy questions covered in the survey—though the difference between the military and business elites is, predictably, least on defense issues.

All this ties in with the wider evidence on ideological structure. The correlations between domestic and foreign policy issues for our elites ranged, as we noted, between the .20s and the .50s for military and business. This is midway between those for the least politicized group in America in the early 1970s (.24 as found by Nie for the mass public) and the most politicized group for which we have data (.63 and above for congressmen, as found by Moyer). Businessmen have traditionally had much greater access to the levers of American political power than have the military. Their greater politicization perhaps should thus concern us more, though for neither group is it high by elite standards. Of course, men in either group could be mobilized as a major force whenever their

---

[32]We owe this procedure for measuring unstructuredness to a suggestion in a personal communication from Professor Allen Barton, who offered it as a better alternative than a measure we initially employed.

In fact, the high score of the labor leaders is deceptive. Alone among the groups, the labor sample still retains many "liberal hawks"; thus for them their very low correlation of domestic policy items with foreign policy items produces an apparent unstructuredness that is only an artifact of the decision to lump foreign and domestic items together into the index.

professional expertise, or their economic or bureaucratic interests, seemed directly at issue.

As a last comment on this matter of salience, it would make a difference if foreign policy matters were more salient to hawks than to doves, or vice versa. If there were a clear tendency for one sort of person to care more about foreign policy than did the other, then we would expect his differential interest to carry over to foreign policy making. In fact, however, no such differential salience among business hawks and doves appears. On question 6 about major problems facing the United States, the most salient issue proved to be one of the two domestic issues: either domestic order and stability or domestic social and racial disparities. The three international issues followed, with military and technological advances of China and Russia trailing as last of the three. This same order holds for both doves and hawks. It is consistent with our conclusion in the preceding chapter that businessmen's concern with international politics is at a low ebb, and it generally holds true regardless of the businessman's particular ideological stripe. It contrasts with the situation among the military—those professionally concerned with international threats. China and Russia are the first concern, for the service hawks, and rank third even for those who are relatively dovish.

CHAPTER FIVE

Korea, Indochina, and the Stock Market

Use your heart to pray for peace and your head for investing.

Shearson, Hammill & Co. advertisement,
Wall Street Journal

How Investors May Look at War

By 1970 casual observers, as well as seasoned analysts, had begun to anticipate a rise in the stock market each time a major peace move was made in Southeast Asia. Such a market response would appear to challenge theories that capitalist economies profit by—indeed require—periodic wars. The available "evidence" on these matters, however, is merely anecdotal, and is sometimes contradicted by the market response to other events. Is there in fact a positive statistical relationship between de-escalatory moves in Indochina and stock market rises? Or does the memory of a few dramatic examples merely give this impression? If such a positive pattern of response could be systematically established, would this be a phenomenon of the later stages of the war? If it was, when did the shift occur and what kind of pattern, if any, emerges from the early period? Is the recent pattern similar to, or quite different from, earlier overseas United States wars?

Our effort to understand the causes of contemporary American military activity abroad must address itself to the perceptions and preferences of American investors. This study is concerned not with the effect of war on the economy, but with the attitudes prevalent in the financial community about the economic consequences of political and military intervention. In this chapter we examine two recent military involvements, in Korea and in Indochina—by far the longest and most costly of American military conflicts since 1945. We will try to ascertain the relationship between stock market fluctuations and important escalatory and de-escalatory events in the Indochina war, in order to test several hypotheses about these attitudes. For additional insight into these attitudes, we will investigate the relationship between these same events and the stocks of a selected group of corporations with substantial investment in less developed countries (LDC stocks), as well as a set of stocks of firms heavily dependent on sales to the Department of Defense. Finally, in order to provide some basis of comparison and historical perspective we analyze the relationship between important escalatory and de-escalatory events and stock market fluctuations during the Korean war.

The direction and magnitude of the net changes on the days the events are reported is used as an indicator of the financial community's attitudes. The primary concern is the immediate response of the financial community to dramatic and salient events indicating a widening or termination of military hostilities. Thus, the focus is not on the economy but on the investor. This is not an analysis of market trends nor an exercise in forecasting. Certainly it is not an investor's guide to future international crises, although a more comprehensive analysis of international crises for three decades might yield some insights regarding tendencies of the market to respond in particular ways at certain points in each crisis.[1]

The abrupt involvement of the United States in an international crisis is generally accompanied by a decline in stock prices, or at least a "dull" market, while buyers "wait and see" what course of action will be taken. After the uncertainties of the new situation have been removed and the nation is committed to military involvement, the chief reason for buying or selling, rather than simply holding, is the belief that the new situation is likely to mean greater

---

[1]The substantial evidence available that stock prices follow a random walk demonstrates that there are no systematic patterns of response to cyclical, periodic, or otherwise predictable events. This does not preclude the possibility of finding systematic responses to unpredictable events. See the collection of papers in Paul H. Cootner, ed., *The Random Character of Stock Market Prices* (Cambridge, Mass.: The M.I.T. Press, 1964).

or lesser profits for the corporation or corporations involved in the transaction. Expectations about a corporation's prospects are influenced by the view held concerning the effect of military involvement on the economy in general as well as on that corporation in particular.

This chapter considers four alternative perspectives for explaining and "predicting" the probable response of the market to the escalating Indochina war, based on different expectations about the way the financial community views the economic consequences of military intervention.

A *simple Marxist* perspective, as noted in Chapter 2, imputes to businessmen a belief that war is good and necessary for the capitalist American economy. Wartime mobilization provides "assured demand at assured profits for the specific interests in armaments research and production and a powerful stimulant to demand and production throughout the economy."[2] According to this perspective, war is bullish. Investors would be expected to respond positively to escalation and negatively to conciliatory moves throughout the war. This is essentially the perspective of hypothesis 1.7 in Chapter 2:

1.7 *Businessmen will be less likely to regard the American intervention in Vietnam as a mistake, less likely to think the war was bad for the economy in general, and less likely to think they personally are worse off as a result of the war, than will other elites.*

Of course, here we will be looking at evidence on the attitudes of investors only (whether they basically view the war as having overall negative or positive effects on the economy), and not comparing them with the beliefs of other elite groups.

An opposite perspective, which we can call *simple inverse Marxist,* but which might otherwise be labeled "liberal," "business pacifist," or even simply "realist," assumes that there are other effective ways of stimulating the economy without causing the negative side effects commonly resulting from war, such as inflation, increased budget deficit, adverse effect on balance of payments, and the possibility of wage and price controls. Throughout

---

[2]Ronald Aronson, "Socialism, the Sustaining Menace," in K. T. Fann and Donald C. Hodges, eds., *Readings in U.S. Imperialism* (Boston: Porter Sargent, 1971), p. 334. See also Ernest Mandel, *Marxist Economic Theory,* tr. Brian Pearce (New York: Monthly Review Press, 1970), Vol. 2, p. 524. Mandel does point out, however, that the arms economy implies a permanent tendency to inflation.

the war, this view recurred in the "Abreast of the Market" column of the *Wall Street Journal*, which reported on informal samplings of opinion about the current market scene. In a typical example the author of the column estimates that "most brokers asked for an opinion on the market's strength in the light of U.S. peace feelers expressed the view that a cessation of hostilities would be bullish." One particular broker is then quoted as saying, "Peace is never bearish. It could be disruptive in some stocks for a short period, but in the long run the investor always makes more money out of butter than he can out of guns."[3] According to this view, enough investors will recognize that in the long run peace is more beneficial to the economy than is war, and will expect the market to respond negatively to escalation and positively to conciliation from the very beginning of the war. This is essentially the perspective of hypothesis 1.10, the converse of 1.7 (again recognizing that we are looking at investors only):

1.10 *Businessmen will be more likely to regard the American intervention in Vietnam as a mistake, more likely to think the war was bad for the American economy in general, and more likely to think they personally are worse off as a result of the war, than will other elites.*

The third perspective, *modified Marxist/inverse Marxist*, is a combination of the first two. This view assumes that because it increases aggregate demand, a little war is good for the economy — as long as there is a prospect of victory, and there is little risk that the war will escalate into a major confrontation with another major power or that the negative side effects on the economy will become serious enough to outweigh the benefits. This belief in the positive effect of a limited military effort is demonstrated in two other quotations from the *Wall Street Journal* analysis columns. When the market rose slightly in the middle of the Tonkin Gulf crisis, one commentator was quoted as saying, "We are on a war footing in localized areas. If we can keep it that way, this good market performance probably will get better. If the war spreads, though, we could go a lot lower."[4] When the crisis appeared to be simmering down, the analyst estimated that "the consensus of the Street is that the primary threat of more than a brush war developing in Asia is past and stocks could be in for a sizable rally."[5] According to this perspective, the market would respond positively to escalation and negatively to conciliation in the early period, and in the

---

[3]*Wall Street Journal*, December 31, 1965, p. 13.
[4]Ibid., August 6, 1964, p. 27.
[5]Ibid., August 10, 1964, p. 23.

reverse manner in the later period, when the military stalemate as well as the negative effects of the war upon the economy had become apparent. This reflects both hypotheses 1.7 and 1.10, if we recognize that each may be accurate at different points in time. We found a fair amount of evidence to support precisely this view in Chapters 3 and 4.

According to a fourth perspective, the *neoimperialist*, businessmen regard war as necessary to protect vital economic interests abroad, both actual and potential. Communist revolutionary movements and other nationalist movements that might seize or limit American capitalist enterprise abroad must be resisted. Insofar as this belief gives rise to a certain predilection on the part of the entire business community for military intervention, the prediction would in part be the same as for the simple Marxist perspective: overall, the market should respond positively to the United States escalatory and unconciliatory moves during most of the war. In contrast to the simple Marxist perspective, however, a neoimperialist perspective would predict no strong opposition to communist conciliation, nor any approval of communist escalation. The stakes of investments and markets abroad, rather than the domestic level of economic activity, are of central importance here. This also brings to bear one of our hypotheses about differential motivations *within* the business community:

2.1 *Executives from corporations with substantial foreign sales or investments, or with expectations of substantially increasing foreign activities, or with expectations of increasing activities specifically in less developed countries, will look more favorably upon the effects of the war (as specified in 1.7) than will executives from other corporations.*

In the context of this chapter, this implies that stocks of firms with large holdings in LDCs would show a similar but even stronger response to events than that just specified for the overall stock market average. We also have proof of the converse:

2.4 *Executives from corporations with substantial foreign sales or investments, or with expectations of substantially increasing foreign activities, will look less favorably upon the effects of the Vietnam war (as specified in 1.10) than will executives from other corporations.*

Similarly, we can bring some evidence to bear on the hypothesis concerned specifically with executives from defense industry firms:

3.3 *Executives from such corporations [firms making substantial sales to the Department of Defense] will look more favorably upon the effects of* *the Vietnam war (as specified in hypothesis 1.7) than will executives from other corporations.*

Here we would expect the stocks of heavily defense-dependent firms to follow the pattern (but even more strongly) specified by the simple Marxist perspective. Hypothesis 3.3 is not, of course, necessarily a Marxist one but rather is also consistent with a variety of military-industrial complex views or other simple economic interest views.

Events and Stock Changes

All Vietnam events between August 1964 and December 1970 that were reported on page one of the *Wall Street Journal*, in the first paragraph of the "World-Wide" news summary column, were coded when they indicated a "positive event" with a relatively clear message for escalation or de-escalation of the war, and when they fit into certain categories specified on p. 151. A positive event is defined as a military action, a statement, decision, opinion, or judgment that actually occurred or was made. Statements including "reportedly" or "implies" were included on the communist side, in order to amplify the number of entries, but were not included when actions by the United States and South Vietnam were coded.

From this list, one day per month was selected as the one on which the most important event or events of the month occurred. Occasionally, more than one type of event occurred on the same day and both were reported in the top paragraph. We chose to use only the most prominent event or events of the month, rather than to look at the effect of *all* Vietnam-related events, on the assumption that the effect of less prominent events would likely be masked by the "noise" of other events. This allowed us to compare the relative effect of the various types of events we were concerned with; it was not our intention to compare the effect of these events with that of all other national and international events.

The *New York Times Index* was also coded according to similar procedures and a monthly event selection was made from this list. The concurrence of events on the two lists was a factor in the final selection. When a choice between two or three days was difficult, all were included. In some months no events were coded. The resulting list consisted of ninety-three event-days. In the analysis, each of these event-days was related to the net change in the stock market on the day the event was *reported* in the *Wall Street Journal*, except when the market analysis column or news report indicated that the news had reached the investing public before closing time the preceding day, and then that day's net change was used.

For the purposes of coding, the events have been divided into six mutually exclusive categories—two military and four political. *Military escalation*, which is divided into United States (including South Vietnam) and communist categories, is defined as an increase in weapons, troops, advisers, and/or ships, or the use of new tactics or techniques. "Record number" and "first time" are two key phrases indicating escalation. De-escalation is confined to the two political categories designated as United States (and South Vietnam) and communist *conciliatory* actions. In addition, there are two political escalatory categories, termed United States (and South Vietnamese) and communist *unconciliatory* actions.

Conciliatory actions are defined as those which indicate a peace initiative, that is, a proposal to reduce military operations or initiate talks leading to a settlement of the war; any other kind of effort to de-escalate the war or reduce military operations; a softening of previous terms for de-escalation or political settlement. Unconciliatory actions indicate a negative response to a peace initiative; a nonmilitary escalatory event; a hardening of peace terms; threats to expand or prolong the war or accusations that the opponent is doing so. Statements indicating determination to win or to continue until the opponent stops waging aggression are included on the ground that this necessitates continuation of hostilities. Statements that vital interests or ideological principles are involved in the war are also included in this category. Increases in economic aid and all aid offers are regarded as nonmilitary escalatory actions; only military aid actually granted or agreed upon is considered military escalatory. Thus, the six categories are: (1) United States (and South Vietnam) military escalation, (2) communist military escalation, (3) United States conciliation, (4) United States nonconciliation, (5) communist conciliation, (6) communist nonconciliation.

The sources of the actions, statements, decisions, and opinions coded for the United States were the President or White House; Vice President; Secretary of Defense, Department of Defense or Pentagon; Secretary of State or State Department; and Military Command, Saigon. The sources for South Vietnam were the President, Vice President, diplomatic representatives in Paris, and other government spokesmen. For the communist side the official statements of North Vietnam, the National Liberation Front (NLF), the People's Republic of China, and the Soviet Union, as well as reports from their official publications, were coded. The categories were separately coded by two independent coders with an inter-coder reliability of 0.95. All these independent variables are essentially uncorrelated with one another.

This investigation into the relationship between stock market fluctuations and Indochina war events consisted of three separate analyses. First, the response of the overall market was examined. A multiple regression analysis was performed with each class of events (i.e., the occurrence or nonoccurrence of each event on a particular day) as independent variables and the net change in the closing Dow Jones industrial average on each of the ninety-three selected days from that of the preceding day as the dependent variable. The years 1964–1970 were divided in several different ways and separate regressions were run against the events in different periods, in order to estimate the approximate timing of any shift that occurred.

Second, the response of ten selected LDC stocks to the war was analyzed. The corporations were selected using the following criteria (see Table 5.1): foreign content (i.e., percentage of sales, earnings, and assets abroad); LDC content (i.e., percentage of less developed countries out of the total number or countries in which a firm has operations); size; and representation according to type with emphasis on raw materials. All corporations that were selected made at least 20 percent of their sales abroad and held over 30 percent of their assets abroad. At least 45 percent of the total number of states in which each firm had operations were LDCs. All of the firms were ranked in the top quartile of the *Fortune* listing of the largest 500 United States corporations. We did not mechanically use any single criterion (e.g., size, or percentage of sales abroad) because we wanted to cover a fairly broad range of different products and industries. A multiple regression analysis, using each class of events as an independent variable, was run against the net changes in prices for each stock, as well as the standardized composite value for the group of stocks, for the overall period and for the pre-Tet and post-Tet periods separately.

Third, we analyzed the response of fifteen stocks of defense-dependent firms to war-related events. The results of the analysis are shown in Table 5.5 (p. 165). In choosing the list of firms, we began with the twenty-five largest (in dollar value) Department of Defense contractors in 1968, deleted fourteen that either were not listed on the New York or American Stock Exchanges (notably, Hughes Aircraft Corporation) or for whom the percentage of defense sales fell below 30 percent, and then added four more firms

Table 5.1 *Foreign Content of Selected United States International Corporations*

Corporation	*Fortune* Rank*	% Foreign Sales†	% Foreign Earnings	% Foreign Assets	States with Operation LDC/Total §
Boise Cascade (paper products)	100	20	25	33	4/5
Corn Products	66	43	47	43	13/29
Goodyear Tire & Rubber	20		36	38	16/34
IBM	9	29	29	34	55/81
ITT	30	60	54	56	12/25
Pfizer (chemicals, pharmaceuticals, cosmetics)	125	46	60	56	24/44
Reynolds Metals (aluminum products)	91	26	4	32	7/12
Singer	65	54		64‡	35/61
Socony Mobil	6	48	59	46	37/52
Standard Oil (N.J.)	3	33	60‡	52‡	25/54

Fortune 57, No. 8 (September 15, 1968): 105.

†Figures for foreign sales, assets, and earnings for 1964 operations from Nicholas K. Bruck and Francis A. Lees, "Foreign Content of U.S. Corporate Activities," *Financial Analysts' Journal* 22, No. 5 (September–October 1966): 127–131.

‡Nicholas K. Bruck and Francis A. Lees, *Foreign Investment, Capital Controls, and the Balance of Payments* (New York: New York University Press, 1968), pp. 83–85.

§Juvenal L. Angel, *Directory of American Firms Operating in Foreign Countries* (New York: World Trade Academy Press, 1966), 6th ed.

that met the last two criteria and were of special interest because of type of industry. Table 5.5 lists them in order with the percentages of their DOD contracts relative to total sales in 1968, and identifies each by type of principal product. Again we wanted a broad range of different types of principal DOD contractors so we did not apply mechanical criteria such as simply the largest contractors by dollar value. Had we used these criteria, our list would have included such giants as General Motors, which, though large by total dollar value of defense sales, is actually much less defense-dependent (at 2 percent) than are most firms in American industry. As before, we ran multiple regression analyses for each individual stock, and for the standardized composite value for the group, over the entire period and for the subperiods on either side of the February 1968 Tet offensive.

Finally, an attempt was made, using multiple regression analysis, to "predict" net changes in the Dow Jones industrial average on the days the weekly casualty lists were reported from July 1965 through the end of 1970, using the Defense Department's official report of the number of deaths.

The Stock Market as an Indicator:
Some Explanations and Some Caveats

A number of difficulties, of varying degrees of seriousness, accompanied our effort. We were trying to infer the "average" investors' attitudes from the behavior of those investors who chose to buy or sell stocks on a particular day, or specifically from the prices at which stocks were bought and sold. This is not a substitute for, but does importantly supplement, our survey and interview work, in which we probed directly the attitudes of corporation executives on war, peace, intervention, and the health of the economy in general. We could have done the same for investors. But the interviewing approach has its own limitations, and cannot be used exclusively. There are, for example, the obvious difficulties of obtaining accurate data on such sensitive subjects from highly sophisticated interviewees. Another limitation is even more compelling. The modified Marxist/inverse Marxist hypothesis predicts a shift, perhaps a reversal, in investors' attitudes during the course of some wars. We might even find a reversal in attitudes toward military intervention in general. In other words, in the 1950s or early 1960s, an investor may have felt that a little war, far away, was a good thing for the economy. But after observing the Indochina debacle he may have changed his mind, on the ground that such wars carry very great risks of a "quagmire effect," with economic and political upheaval at home. Thus, he may reason, even little wars should in the future be avoided. The preceding chapter presented much evidence of a *recent* rejection of wars and intervention, but nevertheless it is clearly difficult to ascertain how much of this attitude had been present for a long time, and how much was a result primarily of learning from the experience of a war that went sour. Asking people directly about such changes in perceptions is tricky; memories are untrustworthy. The stock market study, despite the limitations we are about to specify, at least does tap the actual *behavior* of investors at the time of the political and military events that concern us.[6]

---

[6]One stock market analyst, for example, described stock and bond prices as "the most accurate gauge of Wall Street's real views." John H. Allen, "McGovern Speech Affects Stock Prices Only Slightly," *New York Times*, August 30, 1972, p. 23.

One caveat nevertheless concerns the limited impact the war itself had on investors' behavior, especially in the early stages when it was not so salient, or in periods when other events—domestic and international, political and economic, general or concerning particular firms or industries—were occurring. Surely these considerations greatly affected the selling prices of stocks, and we did not introduce them directly into the analysis. However, we did assume that, to the extent they matter, they reduce any correlations we find with our war-related events, appearing as random error. The evidence, then, that a particular kind of war event is an important influence will be the correlations we do find. Since our concern is with war-related behavior rather than with explaining the course of the market generally, we can leave to others the addition of other variables to our equations.[7]

The selection of the war events themselves had its problems. Those events of the war that are seen in retrospect as critical turning points were not always viewed as such at the time; conversely, certain crises, fraught with dire consequences, passed without altering the course of the war. The main criterion must be salience at the time, and thus the events selected cannot comprise a list of the important events of the war from a historical point of view. But all the events included on the list were probably regarded as important at the time, by virtue of the location in which they were reported in the newspapers.

Another problem was possible ambiguity in the implications of the various events for the termination of the war. A highly escalatory event could be favored as the best means for bringing about an early ending to the war, and conversely, a de-escalatory event could be opposed on the ground that such an approach merely prolonged the war. Such interpretations are not merely theoretical possibilities, as shown by the view expressed by a member of a major securities firm about the implications of Nixon's May 8,

---

[7]If our aim had been to develop a model to predict the behavior of the stock market generally, we would of course have added a control group of other days without major war events, and we would have controlled for major economic events. The latter, however, is easier said than done, as most economic influences are better described as rates or processes, *not* discrete events— even more so than are influences relating to the war. In any case, since our aim was merely to discover the negative or positive impact of the war, it was perfectly satisfactory to leave economic and other events as variables accounting for part of the unexplained variance, in effect as part of the "error" term. So long as they are not importantly correlated with the war events (and that seems reasonable so long as we are speaking of *events*, though obviously in the long term, trends in the economy and the war were related), this raises no difficulties.

1972, decisions to resume the bombing of North Vietnam, to mine that nation's major ports, and to interdict rail transportation. Asserting that these moves could very well serve as "the final major battle of the war," the author expresses the belief that "if we are correct in assuming that this latest military venture is the key to an eventual termination of the conflict, it is possible to assume that in the next few months a settlement will be reached."[8] The political and economic significance of any news item is not clearly and immediately self-evident; consequently, "hardly any event can happen of sufficient importance to attract general attention which some process of reasoning cannot construe as bullish and some other process as bearish."[9] In spite of the variety of interpretations that could be given to the meaning of the various events, escalatory and de-escalatory events were coded literally to minimize the use of arbitrary judgments.

The problem of signal ambiguity is further compounded by the manner in which major escalatory and de-escalatory events in the Indochina war were announced. The former often were de-emphasized with the insistence that this event did not represent a departure from past policies. On the other hand, peace moves were generally accompanied by assurances that the war would continue until a just peace was achieved and aggression ended. But again, it is the literal meaning of the event that was used in the coding.

In addition to problems relating to the significance of events, there was the question of the point in time at which to measure the response of the market to any given event. The full effects of an event may not be felt until days, weeks, or even months later. An analysis with a lag was not made in this study because the main concern was the *immediate* response of the financial community.[10] Furthermore, the "noise" of extraneous events obviously increases with each day that passes after an event. A more serious problem was the impact that events often appear to have upon the market even *before* they occur (i.e., traders buy or sell in response to

---

[8]Harris, Upham & Co., *Market Interpretations* 10, No. 30 (August 7, 1972).

[9]G. C. Selden, *Psychology of the Stock Market* (New York: Ticker Publishing, 1912), p. 66. Quoted in Arnold M. Rose, "A Social Psychological Approach to the Study of the Stock Market," *Kyklos* 19, No. 2 (1966): 273.

[10]There is independent evidence that our procedure taps the strongest reaction. An earlier study of the market's reaction to a variety of world events found a plunge on the first day following bad news, with rises on subsequent days. See Victor Niederhoffer, "The Analysis of World Events and Stock Prices," *Journal of Business of the University of Chicago* 44, No. 2 (April 1971): 211.

advance information that a certain event is imminent). By the time
the event does occur, it may already have been discounted in the
market and may produce little or no further reaction—or even a
reversal of the initial response. Peace moves, such as the extension
of peace feelers and announcements of impending troop withdrawals, are particularly likely to generate rumors and premature
market responses with effects that are diluted or otherwise altered,
or even reversed by the actual occurrence of the events. For example,
although President Johnson's announcement of a partial bomb halt
in April 1968 sent the Dow Jones industrial average up 20 points,
and throughout the month of October rumors that a total bomb halt
was imminent gave rise to a so-called peace rally, the market in fact
dipped two points when the long-awaited complete bomb halt was
announced on November 1. Obviously, premature market responses
to rumors of an event obscure the meaning of the response to the
actual occurrence. This is particularly true with regard to the
wilder and more drastic rumors that circulate. In July of 1965 the
market declined on several occasions, according to analysts, because of rumors that the economy was about to be put on a war-type
footing with the imposition of wage and price controls and an
excess profits tax. However, when President Johnson finally made
his statement on forthcoming war measures, he called for *only*
doubling of the draft, and consequently the market was said to
rise because of investors' relief that nothing worse was contemplated.[11] Similarly, a six-month high in stock prices, which occurred
during the Korean war when President Truman declared a state of
emergency and announced forthcoming wage and price ceilings, was
attributed to the fact that the mobilization message was "milder
than expected" and "contained no surprises."[12]

The accuracy of advance information varies greatly, from
speculative rumor to the texts of statements released before their
delivery. Because the market immediately reflects any new information that appears to have economic consequences, it is quite
possible that the market's responses to rumors are stronger than
its responses to actual occurrences. Indeed the "Abreast of the
Market" column in the *Wall Street Journal* frequently refers to the
apparent effect of some rumor that in fact was originally given a
relatively insignificant position as a news item or was not reported
at all. At one point in 1969 the columnist estimated that the spring

---

[11]*Wall Street Journal*, July 29, 1965, p. 23; and July 30, 1965, p. 25.
[12]Ibid., December 18, 1950, p. 17.

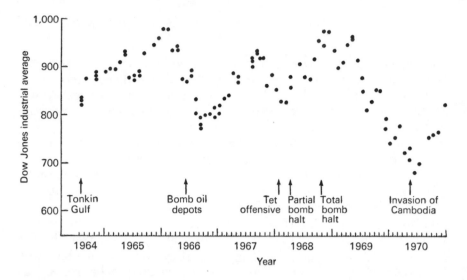

Figure 5.1. Dow Jones industrial average on days of important Vietnam events, 1964–1970.

rally from mid-April to mid-May was "based almost entirely on peace hopes," the hopes being inspired by a series of rumors.[13] But aside from the difficulties that would be encountered in systematically locating and coding rumors, there is their tendency to convey unclear messages and to evoke denials and additional conflicting rumors to cloud the message further. Therefore, in spite of the obvious responsiveness of the market to rumors, they are not included among the events. Official statements about intentions are included as a means of obtaining some of the early responses.

One final clarification should be made regarding the possibility of an upward bias or trend in the market as a methodological problem. An examination of the daily closing averages for the Dow Jones industrials indicates there was no major upward trend in the market during the period covered. The average for July 31, 1964, was 841; for December 31, 1970, it was 838. There were of course fluctuations, but these ranged between a low of 631 on May 26, 1970, and a high of 995 on February 9, 1966. All fluctuations were within a range of 25 percent of the mean—not enough to cause any methodological difficulties. (Figure 5.1 shows the range of averages for war event-days.)

These caveats make clear that we should not expect very high correlations between the market behavior of stocks and various

[13]Ibid., June 9, 1969, p. 33.

Table 5.2 *Predictions Attributed to Perspectives, and Summary of Empirical Results for Indochina War, 1964–1970*

	Events					
	United States			Communist		
Category	Con-cili-ation	Non-concili-ation	Esca-lation	Con-cili-ation	Non-concili-ation	Esca-lation
Predictions						
Simple Marxist	−	+	+	−	+	+
Inverse Marxist	+	−	−	+	−	−
Modified Marxist						
Early	−	+	+	−	+	+
Late	+	−	−	+	−	−
Neoimperialist	−	+	+	+	−	−
Results						
Dow Jones average						
Early	+	−	−	−†	−	+
Late	+*	+	+	+*	+	−
Total	+*	+	−	+*	−	−
LDC firm stocks						
Early	+	+	−	−†	−	+
Late	+*	+	+	+*	+	−
Total	+*	+	−	+*	+	−
Defense stocks						
Early	−	−	−	−†	−	−
Late	+	+	+	+*	+	−*
Total	−	−	−	+*	−	−*

*Indicates statistically significant finding (see Table 5.3).
†No entries coded for this variable during this period.

wartime events as reported in the newspapers. Other factors will introduce a good deal of additional variation that will seem, on the basis of our very imperfect knowledge, to be virtually random noise. But despite these other influences, we *shall* nevertheless show some important and statistically significant relationships.

Stocks and the Indochina War

Table 5.2 outlines the various predictions we have attributed to the four perspectives, and summarizes the results of our analysis for the Indochina war from 1964 to 1970. Tables 5.3–5.5 present the

Table 5.3 Stock Market Response to Indochina Events, 1964–1970: Regression Coefficients

Indicator	Number of Events	Multiple r^2	United States			Communist		
			Conciliation	Nonconciliation	Escalation	Conciliation	Nonconciliation	Escalation
Dow Jones average								
1964–1966 Early	38	.14	2.72	−0.59	−3.74	—†	2.15	0.64
1964–1967 Pre-Tet	54	.17	1.39	−0.38	−4.17	—†	−3.62	0.30
1967–1970 Post-disillusionment	55	.46	7.07 (7.13)	1.95	1.22	13.40 (18.15)	0.73	−2.90
1968–1970 Post-Tet	39	.50	7.23 (5.43)	0.18	1.72	12.85 (13.03)	4.15	−4.12
1964–1970 Total	93	.34	5.14 (5.62)	0.84	−1.19	11.64 (16.89)	−0.54	−2.47
LDC stocks (composite)								
1964–1967 Pre-Tet	54	.20	0.41	0.05	−0.25	—†	−0.13	0.02
1968–1970 Post-Tet	39	.48	0.63 (7.13)	0.26	0.22	1.07 (15.68)	0.51	−0.14
1964–1970 Total	93	.31	5.49 (9.12)	0.20	0.01	0.93 (15.37)	0.12	−0.09
Defense stocks (composite)								
1964–1967 Pre-Tet	54	.05	−0.31	−0.31	−0.38	—†	−0.47	−0.24
1967–1970 Post-Tet	39	.47	0.07	0.04	0.23	0.73 (4.68)	0.19	−0.58 (3.94)
1964–1970 Total	93	.15	−0.15	−0.14	−0.11	0.43 (2.95)	−0.19	−0.52 (4.58)

*F test given in parentheses where $p \leq .10$.
†No entries coded for this variable during this period.

Table 5.4 LDC Stock Response to Indochina Events, 1964–1970: Regression Coefficients

Corporation	Multiple r^2	Regression Coefficients*					
		United States			Communist		
		Concili- ation	Noncon- ciliation	Esca- lation	Concili- ation	Noncon- ciliation	Esca- lation
Boise Cascade (paper products)	.13	−0.03	−0.55	−0.45	0.95 (2.89)	0.41	0.04
Corn Products	.10	−0.34	−0.33	−0.64 (8.24)	0.30	−0.51 (4.04)	−0.19
Goodyear Tire & Rubber	.11	−0.04	−0.39	−0.40	−.01	−0.25	−0.66 (4.45)
IBM	.15	4.95 (4.75)	2.22	0.07	4.79	0.19	−2.39
ITT	.20	1.01 (6.97)	0.41	0.35	1.38 (7.18)	0.42	−0.52
Pfizer (chemicals, pharma- ceuticals, cosmetics)	.10	0.84 (3.65)	0.21	0.14	0.63	−0.26	0.12
Reynolds Metals (aluminum products)	.07	0.23	0.09	−0.07	0.71	−0.35	0.01
Singer	.14	0.57 (2.76)	0.50 (2.96)	0.05	0.81 (3.06)	0.24	−0.47
Socony Mobil	.08	0.12	−0.03	0.39	0.31	0.02	−0.12
Standard Oil (N.J.)	.17	0.72 (6.01)	0.50 (3.80)	0.17	0.92 (5.34)	0.01	−0.01

*F test given in parentheses where $p \leq .10$.

results in more detail, giving all the regression coefficients (b); when the results are statistically significant at the .10 level or above with this small "sample," the F test is shown in parentheses immediately below the coefficient. For the sake of simplicity, the standard errors have been omitted from this presentation.

Almost all of the statistically significant results concern *conciliatory* acts. Such acts in the later period of the war, whether by the United States-Saigon side or by the communist forces, are regularly associated with *rising* stock prices on that day. As might be expected, the apparent financial community approval of communist conciliation is greater than of American conciliation, but approval of both is evident. This basically applies to the set of LDC stocks and the set of defense industry stocks, as well as to the overall Dow Jones industrial average; it holds equally well for the period starting in January 1967 as for the period commencing in January 1968 with the Tet offensive. Thus the financial community did not wait for Tet or President Johnson's bombing halt to favor conciliation; rather the market shift barely preceded a discernible shift in the mass public's approval of the war, which occurred in 1967.[14] As early as February 1967 a *Business Week* editorial commented on a "peace offensive":

The bullish response of the business community to what would once have been called a "peace scare" shows that we have made an advance in our economic understanding which holds great potential for lasting good in the world. The securities markets in this and other countries now regard peace and prosperity as complimentary, not conflicting conditions.

If through intelligent management of fiscal and monetary policy nations can keep their economies fully employed in times of peace, then war simply diverts resources from uses that improve human welfare to those that reduce it.

Even earlier, after the resumption of bombing following a partial halt, the same journal remarked on the consolidation of a change in the business atmosphere, and of a fear among businessmen that the

---

[14]A Gallup survey conducted at brief but irregular intervals from August 1965, posed the question, "In view of the developments since we entered the fighting in Vietnam, do you think the U.S. made a mistake sending troops to fight in Vietnam?" In early February 1967, 52 percent of the national sample gave a negative response; this figure dropped to 50 percent in May, 48 percent in July, and 42 percent in October. It did not subsequently fall below 40 percent until August 1968. See *Gallup Opinion Index*, Report No. 39, September 1968, p. 3. The change is not well described as a steady erosion of support for the war. Rather it looks more like a set of epidemiological data, according to which contagion accelerates as the reservoir of "infected" grows, and then levels off as most of the susceptible population is affected.

government would impose economic controls that would adversely affect profit.[15]

If we ignore the defense industry stocks for the moment, no clear pattern of response appears either for *unconciliatory* acts or for *escalation*—whether early or late, for American or communist acts, for the overall market or for the LDC stocks. The only relationship that even approaches a level of statistical significance is that between the Dow Jones average and United States-Saigon escalation in the pre-Tet period (negative, at the .15 level). Essentially the same pattern appears from the simple correlation coefficients (also not shown), where only for conciliatory acts is the r^2 regularly above .10. Still excepting the defense industry stocks, no statistically significant relationships whatever appear in the *early* years of the war, regardless of precisely what time division is made.

Although it is not directly germane to our chief interests, the relatively high percentage of variance obtained for the entire equations (multiple r^2) for the late and total periods is worth noting. The fact that roughly *half* the variance in the Dow Jones average on these days during the post-Tet period was traceable to Vietnam events gives us some sense of the very great impact the war did make on investors' behavior.

No relationship during either the earlier or later periods was found between net changes in the averages and the number of *fatalities* reported by the Department of Defense. (This is not shown in the tables.) The squared correlation coefficient (r^2) for the Dow Jones industrial average and casualties was .00 for the pre-Tet period and .01 for the post-Tet period.

Table 5.4 reports the changes in the price of each of the ten LDC stocks during the entire period, 1964–1970. These stocks followed essentially the same pattern as did the market as a whole. Five of the ten stocks responded *positively* to United States *conciliatory* acts, and four of the ten responded positively to communist conciliation. There are only two significant correlations with escalatory acts, one each with United States and communist escalations. Both correlations are *negative*. There are two significant *negative* relationships with *unconciliatory* acts (one to United States nonconciliation and one to communist nonconciliation), substantially countered by two *positive* responses to United States *nonconciliation*. Lest much be made of the latter, however, stocks of these same two firms (Singer and Standard Oil) also went up when

[15]"A Look at What Peace Would Mean," *Business Week*, February 11, 1967, p. 140; and February 5, 1966, p. 21.

the American side took conciliatory actions. The multiple r^2 for each of the ten firms is much lower than that for the Dow Jones average or the LDC composite—although that for ITT is highest; for this corporation, the significant event classes have the effect that would be predicted by the *inverse-Marxist* perspective.

The situation for defense industry stocks is much the same. Apparent approval of communist conciliatory moves remains, and is reinforced by the statistically significant negative correlation of defense industry stock prices with communist escalation both over-all and in the later period: both findings are definitely *inconsistent* with the idea that investors in these firms expected a prolongation of the war to benefit them. The previous finding of a positive association of higher stock prices with United States conciliation in this later period, however, is absent for defense industry stocks. Replacement of the significant positive relation with American conciliation by a negative one with communist escalation does not change the picture notably. As with the other stock indices, we find no significant relations in the pre-Tet years. This last data set—defense industry stocks pre-Tet—is really a limiting case for many Marxist or military-industrial complex hypotheses. If the war was to be interpreted as favorable to certain business interests, the evidence ought to emerge here if anywhere. Thus we shall scrutinize these results in detail. Table 5.5 shows the behavior of stocks for fifteen defense-related firms during the pre-Tet period.

Looking down the columns of the table, we find that as many as seven of the fifteen firms show large *negative* responses to United States unconciliatory behavior, even though such a correlation does not appear for the defense industry stock index. This relationship is inconsistent with military-industrial complex theories. Looking at the individual firms across the rows, we see a variety of behavioral patterns. For some firms and for some kinds of events, expansion of the war must have seemed dangerous, and for other firms and events conciliation must have seemed detrimental. Even this is an oversimplification, since apparently contradictory results (e.g., disapproval of both United States conciliation *and* non-conciliation) sometimes appear for the same company (see Hazeltine, United Aircraft, and Norris).

Despite these within-firm contradictory findings, it still is worthwhile to look closely at what kinds of firms evidence what kinds of behavior. The figure representing percentage of sales to the Department of Defense covers many different kinds of activities. Some defense contractors benefited directly and substantially from

Table 5.5 Defense Industry Stock Response to Indochina Events, 1964–1967: Regression Coefficients

Corporation	% Sales to DOD, 1968	Multiple r^2	Regression Coefficients*					
			United States			Communist		
			Concili-ation	Noncon-ciliation	Esca-lation	Concili-ation	Noncon-ciliation	Esca-lation
Lockheed	84	.15	−1.01 (3.20)	−.07	−.61	—†	−.07	−.43
General Dynamics	84	.15	−.55	−1.35 (4.45)	−1.17 (3.17)	—†	−1.52 (3.50)	−.72
Hazeltine	74	.19	−.56 (8.41)	−.77 (4.45)	−.04	—†	−.05	−.31
Northrup	64	.12	−2.47	.81	.51	—†	2.23 (3.92)	1.61
National Presto	64	.26	−.29	−1.27 (7.64)	−.02		−.06	−.54
Martin Marietta	58	.11	−.16	−.21	−.11	—†	−.33	.15
United Aircraft	55	.25	−1.88 (4.45)	−1.66 (5.24)	−1.69 (5.15)	—†	−3.60 (7.35)	−2.45 (5.97)
Grumman	54	.14	.22	−.33	−.22	—†	−.41	.90
Thiokol	53	.10	−.55	−.66 (4.95)	−.61 (3.98)	—†	−.53	−.48
Norris	51	.22	−.46 (8.18)	−.65 (4.37)	.002	—†	−.07 (3.35)	.43
Avco	49	.03	−.34	−.35	−.45	—†	−.22	−.17
Raytheon	39	.13	−.16	−.92 (2.96)	−.69	—†	−.81	−.10
Olin	33	.09	−.19	−.59	−.46	—†	−.79	−.55
McDonnell Douglas	30	.11	−.32	.16	.13	—†	−.45	−1.12
Collins Radio	30	.04	.04	.45	.02	—†	1.01	.18

*F test given in parentheses where $p \leq .10$.
†No entries coded for this variable during this period.

the war. Others were engaged in other kinds of manufacturing—
for example, weapons appropriate to the European theater, or
strategic weapons, whose sales did not benefit, and even suffered,
from the diversion of resources to the Indochina conflict.[16] Several
of the companies listed in Table 5.5 can be identified as especially
dependent on the war effort. Hazeltine is a relatively small (smaller
than the *Fortune* 500 firms) electronics corporation that developed
and produced an electronic sensor for use in Vietnam. A high proportion even of its 74 percent sales to the DOD was surely war-
related. National Presto has been identified as the largest producer
of artillery ammunition outside of the Army ammunition plants.
The majority of its DOD sales stemmed from the war. Thiokol
produced Vietnam-related aircraft as well as ammunition. Norris
(also an ammunition producer) has been termed the largest corporate benefactor in percentage terms, and Olin has been referred to
as the largest in terms of total dollars (though its defense- and war-
related percentages are rather low).[17] Yet no particular pattern
emerges for them, except for the fact that Hazeltine and Norris are
two of the only four firms whose share prices showed big negative
responses (and the strongest responses at that) to United States
conciliatory acts. That is the sort of finding that military-industrial
complex theories (or more generally, self-interest theories) predict,
but by itself and given the same firms' negative association with
unconciliatory acts, it is not exactly overwhelming. Overall, we
really find no support for such theories. The relation of these
share prices to war-related events in the pre-Tet period is mixed,
perhaps almost random, and in the post-Tet period there is a fairly
consistent apparent approval of communist conciliatory moves and
disapproval of communist escalation of the war.

Why do the defense industry stocks show these unexpected
results? Certainly the variety of firms and products within the
defense industry forms part of the explanation. The total defense
budget increased only moderately during the Vietnam war, from
about 7.6 to 9.7 percent of GNP. (The rate of growth is less if
measured as a percentage of the federal budget.) What occurred was

---

[16]The Soviet journal *Literaturnaya Gazeta* (as cited in the *New York Times*,
July 15, 1971, p. 6) interpreted the Pentagon Papers affair as the outcome of
a struggle between one faction of the military-industrial complex concerned
with conventional weapons and Indochina, and another supplying strategic
weapons and seeking disengagement from Southeast Asia.

[17]This information comes from *Forbes* 101, No. 7 (April 1968): 66; and
Economic Priorities Report 2, No. 4 (January–February 1972): 37.

a substantial reallocation of funds from major weapons such as aerospace to ordnance and manpower; this was in some degree a shift from capital-intensive products to labor-intensive products for infantry, and could have depressed the overall share of profits in the defense industry. War production is a boom-and-bust operation—clearly good for some firms in the short run but having uncertain results in the long run and for the industry as a whole. By 1967 or 1968 it must have been apparent that the war was generating widespread hostility to military spending in general, threatening the prodefense, popular consensus that sustained the arms industry throughout the cold war. Some aspects of the war were clearly good for some companies, very good; but for defense-oriented corporations in general—those with long-term interests at stake—it must surely have been a mixed blessing.[18] Then too, only a few major companies were primarily dependent on Vietnam-related sales. Of the *Fortune* largest 100 industrial firms, only seven (General Dynamics, Lockheed, United Aircraft, Grumman, Avco, Raytheon, and McDonnell Douglas) sold as much as 30 percent of their total production to the Defense Department in 1968, and for most of these firms, as well as for the smaller companies listed in Table 5.5, Vietnam-related production accounted for well under half of their total sales. Thus the financial health of these firms depended primarily on the overall defense market, and more generally on the health of the entire American economy.

With respect to the hypotheses that we analyzed in Chapter 2, we find little evidence here in support of hypothesis 1.7; businessmen (here, investors) in general did not show any marked approval of the Vietnam war and did not see it as having positive economic effects for the economy or for themselves in particular. If anything, by 1967 they perceived it as a mistake (hypothesis 1.10), though we do not in this chapter, as we did in Chapter 3, compare their attitudes with those of other elites. Within the business and financial community, investors in corporations with substantial activity in LDCs looked neither more nor less favorably on the war than did investors in other firms (a rejection of hypotheses 2.1 and 2.4); nor did investors in defense-oriented firms look more favorably on the war than did investors in other firms (a rejection of hypothesis 3.3).

---

[18]See the editor's introduction to Steven Rosen, ed., *Testing the Theory of the Military-Industrial Complex* (Lexington, Mass.: D. C. Heath, 1973), pp. 17–18. Martin Marietta is among those corporations trying carefully to balance its business in what is known as a "war and peace" or "Tolstoy special" approach.

A comparison of these findings with the predicted results outlined in Table 5.2 clearly shows that none of the four perspectives
adequately predicted the findings:

The *simple Marxist* position incorrectly predicted the signs
of the coefficients appreciably more frequently than it predicted
them correctly; even when the sign was right, the results were
almost never statistically significant.

The *inverse Marxist* position was fairly accurate in its predictions for the later period, but not for the early period.

Thus, the *modified Marxist/inverse Marxist* position accurately
predicted the shift, in 1967, to a positive response to conciliation, a
response that was statistically significant. Furthermore, with the
nonsignificant coefficients, the sign predicted by the modified Marx-
ist/inverse Marxist position was correct in all but one instance
during the later period. (A very insignificant positive coefficient
appears for United States nonconciliation.) Nevertheless, the approval of escalation in the early period that was anticipated by this
perspective clearly was *not* forthcoming. If anything, there was a
moderate disapproval of American escalation in the early period of
the war.

The *neoimperialist* perspective seems to have had mixed results, being right slightly more often (especially in the later period)
than it was wrong. This conclusion is deceptive, however, since
most of the times when it was right, its detailed predictions were no
different from the predictions of the inverse Marxist position. In
the crucial prediction of market response to United States conciliatory actions, the sign of the coefficient was highly significant
in the direction *opposite* from that of the neoimperialist prediction.

The modified or inverse Marxist perspectives score partial
success for the *later* period in accounting for movements of *defense*
industry stocks.

Perhaps we have caricatured the four labeled perspectives,
though we have tried our best to extract fairly a set of empirically
testable predictions from each. Whether or not we succeeded, the
conclusion nonetheless emerges sharply from our results that *by
the beginning of 1967, the American financial community in general
clearly wanted to see the Indochina war de-escalated.* (We cannot make
any statement about the amount of de-escalation desired, or the
price these investors were willing to pay for it.) Moreover, the defense-dependent corporations and firms with substantial investment in less developed countries were no exception to this pattern.
In fact, the upward movement of LDC stocks in response to United

States conciliatory acts was slightly *stronger* than was the movement of the Dow Jones average, suggesting that investors in those firms were, if anything, still more anxious to end the war.[19] However, the fact that the stock movements of two firms were upward with United States nonconciliation, as well as with United States conciliatory acts, suggests that concern for the specific interests of these firms made their investors more particular about the terms of any settlement.

Although some slight disapproval of United States escalation in the early period is indicated, the absence, save for the defense industry stocks, of any strong relationship with either escalation or nonconciliation was unanticipated. Theoretically, we treated the last two types of acts as essentially the mirror image of conciliatory acts. In attempting to offer some post hoc explanation of the lack of relationship we can only tentatively suggest the following: (1) There may be some flaw in our data-making procedures, especially in the coding or selection of events, that is not apparent to us. (2) The response to escalation may have indicated mixed or unclear expectations about its military consequences. In other words, a positive response to escalation at that point might have stemmed as much from a hope that the extra effort would end the war quickly as from approval of the war; similarly, negative responses to escalation may have been rooted in quite different expectations. Much the same explanation may apply to the political category of nonconciliation, though there the explanation seems more tenuous. (3) Alternatively, the unpatterned response to escalation may have stemmed from a substantial degree of ambivalence within the financial community toward the military intervention in its earlier stages. The lure of a higher level of economic activity at home that would accompany a small limited war, plus the hope of containing communism and other nationalist movements in Asia, could have been motivations. But at the same time, those attractions could have been offset for many other investors by the expectation of inflation and other negative effects on an escalating war—not to mention the risk that the small conflict might become a superpower confrontation.

---

[19]For this comparison, the significance level for the Dow Jones average must be compared with that for the LDC stocks. Because of the way the averages were constructed, the regression coefficients of the two analyses are not comparable (though the regression coefficients of classes of events within either analysis are, of course, comparable).

Korean War Results

Because the Korean war probably antedates any widespread acceptance within the business community of Keynesian tenets that prosperity can be maintained by public spending for *civilian* needs, the Korean experience is presumably a good test of the proposition that businessmen used to (even if they do not now) think that a little war is a good thing. We investigated the relationship of stock market fluctuations to Korean war events according to procedures similar to those used for the Indochina war, but with two variations. First, the selection of important events was based on the location in the top paragraph of the *Wall Street Journal* news summary column, and on the length and location of headlines in the *New York Times* itself, rather than the *Index*. Second, we added two categories, United States victory and communist victory. (These initially had been used in the Indochina coding, but the final selection of events yielded such a small sample of these two types that they were excluded.) A victory was defined in terms of a defeat for the opponent, defeat being indicated by words clearly expressing military setback, such as "destroyed," "wiped out," "crushed," and "overrun." The period covered was June 1950 to July 1953; a total of seventy-six event-days resulted from the selection. Only the net changes in the overall market were examined.

The results of this analysis (see Table 5.6) showed a strong negative correlation between the Dow Jones industrial average and both communist escalation and communist victory. Hence there certainly was Wall Street displeasure at prospects that the communists might gain the upper hand. But there were *no* systematic patterns of response to United States escalation, victory, conciliation, or nonconciliation, nor to communist conciliation or nonconciliation. Thus, whereas the financial community had turned against the Indochina war by 1967, there was *no particular Wall Street enthusiasm either for the Korean war or for its end*. No division of Korean war events significantly affects this statement.[20]

The strong positive correlation between de-escalatory events and stock price increases during the Indochina war, and the ab-

---

[20]The only logical time division would be at the entry of China, which presaged a sharp decline in popular support for the war. The shift in support was the only significant one of the war. See John E. Mueller, "Trends in Popular Support for the Wars in Korea and Vietnam," *American Political Science Review* 65, No. 2 (June 1971): 358–375. The analysis of events from November 1950 through July 1953 yielded results similar to those for the entire period.

Table 5.6 *Stock Market Response to 76 Korean War Events: Regression Coefficients**

Regression Coefficient	June 1950– July 1953 (Overall)	October 1950– July 1953 (Post-China Entry)
(1) U.S. escalation	0.35	−0.23
(2) U.S. victory	−0.21	−0.51
(3) Communist escalation	−3.02 (9.80)	−2.29 (5.66)
(4) Communist victory	−1.80 (4.62)	−1.86 (4.71)
(5) U.S. conciliation	−0.90	−1.12
(6) U.S. nonconciliation	−0.12	−0.47
(7) Communist conciliation	−0.79	−1.13
(8) Communist nonconciliation	0.10	−0.09
Multiple r^2	.21	.20

*F test given in parentheses where $p \geq .10$.

sence of any such relationship for the Korean war, might be explained by two alternative propositions: (1) the economic effects of the Indochina war were perceived by investors as more serious than were those of the earlier war, or (2) a shift in investors' attitudes concerning the economic effects of military intervention occurred in the interim. Both propositions may hold some truth.

Domestic economic conditions in June 1950 were somewhat different from those in August 1964. The build-up during the Korean war was more rapid, was on a larger scale, and utilized a larger fraction of the nation's resources than the later war. However, inflationary pressures during the Korean war were most serious in the first year, after which they were checked in part by the correction of overstocked civilian inventories, and in part by the passage of three major pieces of tax legislation and the introduction of wage, price, and credit controls. Hence, the consumer price index rose by only 2 percent in 1951–1952 and less than 1 percent in 1952–1953.[21] By contrast, the military spurt of the Indochina war came at a time when the United States was rapidly approaching full utilization of its resources. The operating rate of

[21]Alvin Hansen, "Inflation: Korea vs. Vietnam," *Washington Post*, November 30, 1969, vi, p. 1.

industry was higher at that time than at the onset of the Korean war (90 percent versus 80 percent) and the unemployment rate was lower (4.5 percent versus 5.4 percent).[22] The stimulus of defense outlays creates problems of economic stabilization and allocation under any circumstances. If there is a high level of employment and little slack in the economy, aggregate demand becomes excessive, and inflation becomes serious, unless the government takes neutralizing actions. For a variety of political, economic, and other reasons, the right mix of appropriate monetary and fiscal policies and the reduction of nondefense government outlays needed to curb the inflationary pressures of the late 1960s were not achieved,[23] and in 1969 the consumer price index increased 6.1 percent.

It could be argued that the investor might welcome the inflationary tendencies created by war, and that because the value of common stocks is increased by inflation they are preferable to fixed-yield investments. There are indications of this view in the financial press at the time of the Korean war. On the other hand, a casual survey of the financial analyses in the *Wall Street Journal* during the Indochina war seems to indicate a much more negative attitude toward inflation as a market factor. Perhaps by the 1960s investors had begun to decide that inflation may temporarily boost stock prices, but that at the same time it may decrease corporate profits and dividend values. The increases and the introduction of controls to curb inflation tend to have—at least in the short run— a further negative impact on profits. According to the *Wall Street Journal* report of the semiannual meeting of the Business Council in May 1967, "The consensus of 100 leading industrialists was that business will be further strained by the Vietnam War, shrinking profits, higher taxes, a ballooning federal budget deficit, more militant labor, and more skittish shoppers."[24]

War and the Private Investor

Such a changed attitude toward inflation could be part of an increasing appreciation among investors of the destabilizing effects

---

[22]Figures supplied by Murray L. Wiedenbaum in Center for Strategic Studies, *Economic Impact of the Vietnam War* (Washington, D.C.: Georgetown University, 1967), p. 19.

[23]An extended explanation is contained in Arthur Okun, *The Political Economy of Prosperity* (Washington, D.C.: Brookings Institution, 1970), pp. 62–99.

[24]*Wall Street Journal*, May 16, 1967, p. 4.

of war on the economy and the difficulty of selecting, timing, and legislating the appropriate combination of measures that would make a war economy substantially more profitable than a peacetime one. Evidence of a shift in attitudes toward war among business leaders may be found in a 1969 series of *Fortune*-Yankelovich surveys of more than 300 top executives of companies listed in the annual *Fortune* 500 directory. When asked which national problems seemed "most pressing and critical," 49 percent cited the Indochina war and 43 percent cited inflation. In answer to another question, 56 percent cited the Indochina war as "one of the most serious threats to the economy at the present time."[25]

By March 1968 the financial community had become sufficiently outspoken that, according to David Halberstam, a "bluechip Establishment group" of senior political advisers reported to President Johnson that Wall Street had turned against the war. Their reasons are said to include: "It was hurting the economy, dividing the country, turning the youth against the country's best traditions."[26] This nevertheless reminds us of the evidence in the preceding two chapters that their reasons were varied and complex—certainly their economic objections were not limited to inflation, nor were all their objections by any means economic.

Lest we conclude that the business community will keep the United States out of war in the future, the following points should be made. First, both the stock market analysis and the survey data we have discussed reflect disillusionment in the later stages of a prolonged war that had particularly detrimental effects on the economy—a war initiated in a period of prosperity. Moreover, although there is no stock market or survey evidence of extraordinary business community support for the Korean war or the Indochina war in its early stages, there certainly is not any evidence of widespread active opposition under those circumstances. The stock market evidence suggests an attitude that was, on balance, basically neutral. Second, this last evidence, plus the absence at any point in either war of a negative pattern of response to escalation or American nonconciliation, leaves open the possibility that a future war initiated under different economic circumstances (e.g., a recession) might generate a different set of attitudes and responses, despite the "lessons" that appear to have been

[25]"What Business Thinks," *Fortune* 80, No. 4 (September 1969): 94, 208.
[26]David Halberstam, *The Best and The Brightest* (New York: Random House, 1972), p. 653.

learned in Indochina.[27] Third, this chapter has had little to say about business attitudes toward a much wider set of policy options; for example, attitudes toward defense spending, policy toward communist major powers, or "low-level" political and economic interventions in the third world. All these are subjects where mistaken policies could lead to major war, even though no such war was desired. The survey evidence of Chapter 3 indicated that on these questions business executives were usually—but not always— more dovish than senior military officers but were otherwise more hawkish than every other major civilian elite group except— sometimes—Republican politicians.

Insofar as negative attitudes were indicated in this chapter, they are in opposition to war, not necessarily to weapons or political intervention. Most businessmen may well perceive war as creating too many imponderables, carrying too many risks, and further complicating the adjustments necessary to maintain the balance between aggregate demand and productive capacity, as well as creating a host of dangers to the American domestic political and social system. The fact that investors showed no particular enthusiasm for the continuation or escalation of the Korean or Indochina wars does not eliminate the economic factor as *a* root of war, especially as a fundamental cause that must operate through more proximate political acts. But the results do suggest that economic influences may operate in more subtle ways than is always recognized. We must continue our exploration with other kinds of evidence, especially keeping alert for indications of an at least partially independent impact of ideology.

---

[27]It is nevertheless worth noting that after every one of the major wars of the past century in which the United States intervened (Spanish-American and the two World Wars, as well as the two examined here), the stock market experienced a steep rally that lasted for a year or more. On the first four wars, see Harris, Upham & Co., *Market Review*, July 1972, p. 3. (The post-Vietnam rally lasted less than a year, but almost certainly it was foreshortened by the oil crisis of October 1973.)

CHAPTER SIX

Intervention
in the
Third World

If the Army and the Navy ever look on
heaven's scenes
They will find the streets are guarded by
United States Marines.

Marines' Hymn

American Intervention and the Business Press

The attempt to explain American intervention in the developing nations is the heart and focus of most current economic theories of foreign policy. Therefore, the task of assessing the importance of economic influences on foreign policy choice—and more generally the economic sources of American foreign policy—requires that intervention receive particular attention.

In the preceding chapter attitudes concerning the economic consequences of intervention were investigated indirectly and inferences were made from stock market performance during the two most serious postwar American interventions. The survey analyses reported in Chapters 3 and 4 took a more direct approach, soliciting views from a sample of top executives on a broad range of foreign and domestic policy issues and attempting to find patterns and interrelationships among these views. Policy preferences were sought on American involvement in Vietnam, as well as future, hypothetical political and military interventions to assist certain specific nations or to protect American investments abroad.

The survey data represent views recorded at a single point in time—a particular point, in fact, that marked the final stages of a disastrous war. Furthermore, these views were given in response to specific, rather sensitive questions posed by academic interrogators. We cannot avoid the possibility that the respondents may have been eager to tell us what they believed we wanted to hear, rather than their true opinions; or to provide a pacific image of American business enterprises. Also, their recollections of earlier opinions could have been unconsciously modified in the light of their later perceptions.

In order to supplement, check, and enhance the validity of these results, we turn now to a different method, content analysis. This approach has two principal advantages. First, the data are provided by individuals in the business community spontaneously and without concern for the manner in which a researcher might interpret the views. Second, content analysis enables us to compile evidence for the period ranging from 1947 to the early stages of the Vietnam war, that is, the period before any widespread disillusionment with the domestic, economic, and social costs of Vietnam could have changed businessmen's attitudes. Hence the data derived in this manner constitute a nonreactive, contemporary measure and provide some historical perspective.

Ideal source materials for the content analysis would be board meeting transcripts of the *Fortune* 500 corporations over the past twenty-five years. Because these are not available, and because public statements on such sensitive political questions are seldom made by business executives, we shall analyze the views expressed in the business press. Obviously, the preferences will be those of journalists, but the *audience* is composed primarily of businessmen. We are assuming that, for pragmatic if not for other reasons, the business press reflects to a considerable extent the views of the community it serves.

In the next two chapters we seek to determine what kind of policy preferences and recommendations have been expressed by the business press on the question of American intervention in the less developed countries during the post-World War II period. What kinds of rationales—ideological, strategic, economic—have been given for these positions? Under what circumstances and for what reasons has the business press favored the use of force? What other kinds of intervention were advocated and for what reasons? Are economic motivations expressed, and if so, are they related to policy preferences? Or is policy preference related less to economic interest or motivation than to ideological or strategic concerns? Do the preferences change during the postwar period and in response to different kinds of crises? What kinds of comparisons can be made between the views of the business press and military press?

If economic influences are crucial determinants of American foreign policy, then they should prove more important than other influences in explaining businessmen's foreign policy preferences, and they should be more closely associated with policy preference in the business press than in the military journals. This is the perspective of hypotheses 4.1 and 4.2:

4.1 *Economic motivations will be more closely associated with the foreign policy preferences expressed by businessmen than with the preferences expressed by other elites* [here, the military].

4.2 *Economic motivations and interests will be more closely associated with the foreign policy preferences expressed by businessmen than will domestic ideology or strategic motivations.*

It was necessary to determine not only the importance of economic motivations as influences on policy preferences in the business press, but also the kinds of specific policy choices made on the basis of these influences. Most economic theories of foreign policy variously attribute an aggressive or interventionist foreign policy to the structural dependence of the total capitalist economy on foreign earnings; to the influence of certain groups that stand to profit directly from increased military expenditures, or groups that pressure the government to protect their actual and potential investments abroad; or to the prevalence in the federal government and the nation of "corporate values"—the belief in the interconnection between democracy and free enterprise and an obsession with preserving and extending these values throughout the world. All these variants share the perspectives of hypotheses 1.5 and 1.7:

1.5 *Businessmen will be more hawkish on a variety of foreign policy issues than will other elites.* [Specifically, they will favor intervention.]

1.7 *Businessmen will be less likely to regard the American intervention in Vietnam a mistake, less likely to think the war was bad for the American economy in general, and less likely to think they personally are worse off as a result of the war, than will other elites.*

A very different view emphasizes the pacific influences that business interests exercise on foreign policy and international relations in general. According to this view, capitalist enterprises prosper and profit best in an atmosphere of international peace and security. Wars, even victorious ones, consume resources and give rise to high taxes, government controls, and inflation—hence lower profits. War also disrupts trade patterns and routine business operations. As General Motors told the readers of a *New York Times* Op-Ed Page advertisement, "We can operate at a profit in a foreign country as long as there's peace. There is no greater danger to multinational corporations than war."[1] This is the perspective of hypotheses 1.4, 1.9, and 1.10. (The last two are the converse of 1.5 and 1.7.)

1.4 *Military men will be more "hawkish" on a variety of foreign policy issues than will civilian elites, including businessmen.*

1.9 *Businessmen will be less hawkish on a variety of foreign policy issues than will other elites.* [Specifically, they will be less likely to favor intervention.]

1.10 *Businessmen will be more likely to regard the American intervention in Vietnam as a mistake, more likely to think the war was bad for the American economy in general, and more likely to think they personally are worse off as a result of the war, than will other elites.*

These are the general questions that are investigated in this chapter and the next. This chapter focuses on the preferences expressed in the business press concerning nine cases of intervention: the extent to which various types of intervention were favored (or opposed) and the kinds of circumstances under which these policies were advocated. Chapter 7 examines the reasons given for these preferences and attempts to assess their relative importance. In both chapters the military press is used as a basis of comparison. The quantitative analysis of press content is supplemented by an in-depth discussion of the business press response based on a close reading of the materials. The discursive type of analysis in the later parts of both chapters is appropriate to communicate the varied tone and nuance of views that eluded our coding procedures, just as the interviews were a necessary supplement to the closed-ended questionnaires. A description of the methods used to analyze business press and military press opinion on the question of American intervention in developing nations is now in order.

The Content Analysis of the Business and Military Press

"Intervention" is a particularly ambiguous and controversial term to define. It is used here to mean organized and systematic efforts

---

[1]*New York Times*, October 19, 1973, p. 21.

to affect the political authority structure of the target nation.[2] The use of the term is limited, as in Rosenau's restricted definition, to actions that constitute a sharp break with the existing pattern of relations between two states. Military, economic, political, and "unspecified" are the four types of intervention that are examined here; these are operationally defined in the coding rules and discussed in the following paragraphs. The coding sheet for the content analysis is reproduced in the Appendix.

The military press was selected for comparison with the business press for both practical and theoretical reasons. The use of the same basis of comparison in both the survey and content analyses provided a certain consistency and permitted the results of each to supplement the other. We could think of no better alternative. Clearly, the *New York Times* cannot reflect the views of any single elite group. From their extensive survey, Bauer, Pool, and Dexter conclude that business executives are remarkably homogeneous in their reading habits. "It would be difficult," these authors assert, "to find another occupational group in the United States comparable in size to the business community—unless it be physicians—in which at least 40 percent read any one paper (*Wall Street Journal*) and 80 percent read a small group of general occupational magazines."[3] In the absence of any group comparably homogeneous in reading habits and sufficiently concerned with foreign policy issues to make an analysis possible, the military press was chosen.

In addition, good theoretical reasons impelled this choice. Because intuitively the military might be assumed to be one of the most hawkish elite groups, it provides a useful basis of comparison. Gabriel Kolko attempts to demonstrate that the United States has intervened in the third world in numerous instances for reasons that are "irrelevant to American security, save as they threaten U.S. economic interests." In a chapter entitled "American Military and Civil Authority," he attempts to show how businessmen and their "political cohorts" have "freely utilized the Military Establishment as a tool for advancing their own interests" over against

[2]See James Rosenau's description of the disagreement he encountered in his efforts to provide a restricted definition of the term in "The Concept of Intervention," *Journal of International Affairs* 22, No. 2 (1968): 165–176. Also see Oran Young, "Intervention and the International System," *Journal of International Affairs* 22, No. 2 (1968): 177–187.

[3]Raymond A. Bauer, Ithiel de Sola Pool, and Lewis Anthony Dexter, *American Business and Public Policy* (New York: Atherton, 1963), pp. 159, 162.

those of the "docile generals."[4] More common, perhaps, are the various military-industrial complex perspectives that might predict from the convergence of military and business interests that the results of the two samples would not vary significantly.

The cases.   The analysis focused on nine cases of United States intervention, either actual or contemplated, that were widely discussed in the press:

1. *Greece and Turkey.* September 1946 (large-scale conflict between Greek army and guerilla leadership breaks out) to October 1949 (guerilla leadership announces no further operations will be carried out).

2. *Early Indochina.* May 1950 (United States promises aid to Indochina) to July 1954 (Geneva settlement).

3. *Korea.* June 1950 (North Korean troops cross South Korean border) to December 1950 (six months after United States troop commitment).

4. *Guatemala.* May 1954 (Czechoslovakian government sends arms shipment to Arbenz government) to June 1954 (pro-Armas faction prevails).

5. *Lebanon.* May 1958 (civil strife intensifies) to October 1958 (United States troop withdrawal completed).

6. *Cuba.* January 1, 1959 (Castro assumes leadership of Cuban government) to November 1962 (post-missile crisis).

7. *Congo.* July 1960 (Congo gains independence, followed by civil strife) to December 1964 (Stanleyville forces subdued, strife subsides).

8. *Vietnam.* November 1961 (President Kennedy and National Security Council decide to strengthen South Vietnam, send specialists to train forces) to December 1965 (six months after United States troop commitment).

9. *Dominican Republic.* April 1965 (revolt begins) to September 1965 (provisional government established, followed by reduction of United States troops).

Crises in Iran, Iraq, the Formosa Straits, and Laos were also coded and included in the overall analyses but have not been analyzed as separate cases.

The most important consideration governing the selection of this list was the amount of attention a given case received in the

---

[4]Gabriel Kolko, *The Roots of American Foreign Policy: An Analysis of Power and Purpose* (Boston: Beacon, 1969), p. xiii and pp. 27–47.

business press. A number of interesting cases were eliminated when business press commentary was found to be too insignificant to be analyzed, either because the crisis simmered over a long period and lacked critical points, or alternatively because it covered too brief a span of time. An effort was also made to produce a representative selection of a variety of forms of intervention: military, economic, and diplomatic; overt and covert. Finally, because neo-imperialist explanations of American foreign policy are an important concern, the list concentrates on crises in the developing world.

The duration of each case and the events that were included therein were determined by the salience of the question of intervention as an issue in the business press and by a logical key-event demarcation. Some cases thus included several crises that occurred over an extended period. Cuba, for example, covers a span from Castro's assumption of power through the Bay of Pigs invasion and then the missile crisis. However, the two prolonged military interventions in Korea and Vietnam were arbitrarily cut at a point six months after official commitment of American combat troops.[5] This was done for two reasons. First, the central issue here was predisposition to intervene; hence it is the preferences expressed during the period leading up to and immediately following an act of intervention (or potential one), that are most relevant. Second, after troops have been committed, concern in the press shifts away from the question of the appropriateness of intervention to more tactical questions regarding pursuit of the war. Attitudes on escalation, de-escalation, and negotiation represent policy preferences on such issues as war termination and extrication from commitment rather than the resort to force; they have been considered at length in previous chapters. But basic attitudes on the appropriateness of the original commitment to intervention by force cannot be inferred from positions on tactics, as indicated by the advocacy of extreme hawkish means as the quickest, most cost-effective way to end the war. In short, the original commitment and the continuation of the war are two separate questions, but they are seldom treated as such in the press.

The sources.   As in most content analyses, the original coding scheme had to be modified in a number of ways to accommodate the particular type of material. The initial plan, which would have

---

[5]The small number of policy-oriented articles in the military press necessitated the inclusion of all relevant Korean war articles in the military sample.

simplified the coding and selection process, specified that all editorials and only editorials on the selected cases be coded for both the military press and the business press. However, the use of professional or interest group journals tends to limit the amount of editorial material that is codable for foreign policy preferences —at least this was true with the military press and the business press. The problem with the military journals is the not-surprising tendency to focus on strategy rather than policy. In fact, editorials do not even appear in a number of military journals. As might be expected, economic issues receive the bulk of attention in the business press, and much of the political discussion that does appear concerns national rather than international issues. On the international level, much of the writing is of a more technical nature, regarding investment climate and growth rates of various countries and regions abroad—topics that would be of interest to the American investor and businessman. General foreign policy analyses as well as articles on specific international developments do appear, but explicit opinions on specific crises appear less frequently. This is due in part to the infrequency of publication. Only the *Wall Street Journal* appears daily.

Of the business weeklies, treatment of international political events that occurred during the periods considered was negligible in *Forbes* and *American Business*. During the 1950s, *Barrons* instituted a policy of "responsible citizenship" and, for a subsequent period, devoted considerable editorial attention of a highly prescriptive nature to international crises. *Business Week* summarizes and analyzes international developments in articles and in its weekly "International News" section, but the aim is relatively objective information and preferences often are not clear, whereas the editorial page tends to focus on domestic economic issues. The *Kiplinger Washington Letter* appears weekly and is chatty on world crises but prefers to make forecasts and advise readers of the administration's thinking and probable courses of action rather than to express opinions on those matters. *Fortune* runs solid, substantial foreign policy articles, but this monthly publication tends to limit the number of articles that offer specific policy recommendations. When it became clear to us that confining the source base to editorials would result in an unacceptably small sample, policy-prescriptive articles were added. All articles in which a preference and rationale for intervention were explicit enough to be coded were included in this category.

The sample of periodicals from which the articles were selected also had to be modified. An earlier plan had relied exclusively on the listing of articles in the *Business Periodical Index*[6] and the *Air University Periodical Index*.[7] This method proved workable for the military periodicals, as checks indicated that most of the relevant articles were cited in the *Air University Periodical Index*. The survey of all articles that were listed in that index relating to the cases and the specified periods produced a total of 101 coded articles from 16 periodicals. (These are listed in the Appendix.)

Use of the *Business Periodical Index* survey did not prove workable for the business press; in fact, it was the editorials that most successfully eluded the index. In addition, the coverage of the *Business Periodical Index* did not begin until 1958 (the military index began in 1949), and the coverage of its predecessors, the *Industrial Arts Index* and the *Applied Science and Technology Index*, was even less adequate. Preliminary checks indicated that foreign policy discussion in the business press appeared primarily in the *Wall Street Journal, Business Week, Kiplinger Letter, Fortune* and *Barrons*. As this list with two exceptions coincides with the Bauer, Pool, and Dexter list of business press sources most widely read by high-level executives,[8] we decided to confine the analysis to an intensive search among these five sources. The business sample derived by this means from these five sources consisted of 250 editorials and policy-prescriptive articles.

Coding scheme.   The coding scheme was designed to identify the kinds of intervention favored (or opposed) and the rationales given. Types of intervention were categorized as military, economic, political, and unspecified. Rationales for favoring or opposing intervention were broadly categorized as ideological, strategic, economic, and "other." An additional category for opposing intervention was "disinterest"—a clear statement that there was *no reason* for intervening. More than one rationale could be coded, and the predominant rationale was noted.

Each article was also coded for the type of crisis (as perceived by the writer); that is, whether the issue was an external attack,

---

[6]*Business Periodical Index* (New York: H. W. Wilson, 1958).

[7]*Air University Periodical Index* (Maxwell Air Force Base, Alabama: Air University Library, 1949–1966).

[8]Bauer, Pool, and Dexter, op. cit., pp. 156–158. The *Harvard Business Review* was also on this list but was eliminated from ours, because discussion of foreign policy crises was minimal. *Barrons* was not on their list but was included in ours because of its editorial policy.

an internal revolt with substantial outside aid, or an internal revolt with little or no outside aid. Furthermore, the target or potential target of the intervention was coded to distinguish cases in which action would be taken against communists or communist "tools," on the one hand, from cases in which action was taken to assist neutralist or pro-West forces, on the other hand.

The coding unit was the individual article as a whole. Only the preferences and reasons of the writer were coded. Views merely mentioned or attributed to other individuals or groups (e.g., President, State Department, or even "some people") were considered those of the writer only when no contradictory argument was given and the sense of the article as a whole clearly indicated that the view was also held by the writer.

The first fact to be established was the presence or absence of a preference regarding one or more types of intervention. Each type was defined by a series of subcategories. Military intervention was coded on a scale of 0–3 denoting levels of commitment to the use of force. Level 1 was military assistance, including advisers, and covert operations. The second, intermediate level, which was termed passive troop deployment, included combat field support of advisers, as well as the following kinds of actions: deployment of troops to protect American personnel and installations, blockade, symbolic show of force. The third level designated active aerial or naval support or ground combat support or action. Only one military preference could be coded; in the event that more than one was present, the highest level favored was coded.

The category of economic intervention was limited to economic sanctions—that is, withdrawing economic aid, trade, or investment, or changing the terms of trade agreements to the disadvantage of the target nations for the purposes of affecting their internal and/or external politics. The *extension* of economic aid might have been included here, but such a definition of "intervention" becomes too readily extended to more subtle exercises of influence.[9]

A number of different kinds of actions were classified as diplomatic or political intervention: a change in official diplomatic

---

[9]For an effort to distinguish between influence and intervention in the extension of foreign aid by analyzing various political outcomes, see Howard Wriggins, "Political Outcomes of Foreign Assistance: Influence, Involvement or Intervention?," *Journal of International Affairs* 22, No. 2 (1968): 217-230. David Baldwin, on the other hand, equates intervention with influence in his analysis of links between particular types of aid and intervention. See "Foreign Aid, Intervention, and Influence," *World Politics* 21, No. 3 (April 1969): 425–447.

representation; a change in the level of support (of a country) in a regional or international organization; an alteration of a treaty commitment; Executive censure or support; any positive action by official United States representatives to alter the composition or performance of a local government; any positive effort to negotiate between contending sides; the use of a propaganda campaign to alter perceptions of the crisis; warnings; and the organization of collective action or policies.

Preliminary scanning of the editorials revealed frequent references to actions that would clearly constitute intervention, but the particular type of intervention was left unspecified. A typical example was the recommendation that "something must be done to bring the Castro government to an end." This type of action was coded as unspecified intervention.

The direction and intensity of preference were then coded on a five-point scale: strong pro (1), weak pro, pro-con (neutral or ambivalent), weak con, strong con (5). Categories were coded according to emphasis, substantiation, and explicitness of opinion.[10] Articles and editorials that gave only arguments pro or con but did not explicitly express a preference were coded in the direction of the argument as a 2 or 4 on the scale. Category 3 was comprised solely of editorials that gave equal emphasis to arguments for either side or that expressed no opinion. All policy-prescriptive articles, by definition, expressed a preference; otherwise they were not coded.

Although this investigation was systematic and quantitative, it did not employ the most sophisticated techniques that have been developed for the analysis of communications. The sample was acceptably large and complete, categories were precisely defined and applied consistently to the subject matter, and relative frequencies of certain preferences and motivations were tabulated and analyzed. Independent coders have checked the reliability of the categories.[11] But in two respects this approach departed from the standard operating procedure currently applied in most quantitative analyses of content. First, the meaning of the content

---

[10]See Appendix. Category classification suggested in *Illinois Associational Code for Content Analysis* (Urbana, Ill.: University of Illinois Press, 1953), pp. 20–23. A separate five-point qualification scale was also used throughout the business sample, but it was found in the analysis to be so highly correlated with the intensity scale that it was eliminated.

[11]Three independent coders were used in the initial formulation of the coding scheme. Categories on which agreement was difficult were eliminated or refined at this stage. The authors, after extensive discussions on the scheme, coded the same sample independently with a 95 percent intercoder reliability.

analyzed was sought in the article as a whole rather than in the "atomistic combination of measurable units,"[12] such as the sentence or word. Second, the computer was used only for the tabulations and the statistical analyses of the results—not for the coding process itself. These decisions were based on the character of the materials used and the type of information sought. The focus of this inquiry is on motivations, preferences, and rationales—the most difficult kinds of phenomena in verbal communication to ascertain and measure. Various kinds of contingency analysis, which require mechanical coding, might have been employed to establish consistent and repetitive patterns in which certain words were used in conjunction with other words. Such techniques *might* have afforded *some* insight into "latent content," that is, those preferences, rationales, and motivations not overtly expressed either because the writer was not aware of them or because he was reluctant to express them for some reason. However, machine coding methods require substantial outlays of time, money, and energy to develop dictionaries or to adapt existing ones for the retrieval and categorization of the information. After some preliminary experimentation it appeared doubtful that the amount of additional information that could be obtained by means of such methods would justify the costs. Furthermore, a more sophisticated and refined method than the one used would have given an aura of precision to results that, by virtue of the subject matter, must be limited in the degree of accuracy and precision that can be achieved.

Businessmen, Soldiers, and Intervention

In the next chapter we analyze the rationales given in the business press for the various policy preferences—that is, the question of motivations. In this chapter we look mainly at the overall distribution of preferences in the business press and military press, comparing the two samples and indicating variations across crises. Which kinds of intervention are most frequently the object of commentary and opinion in the military and the business press? Is military intervention, and specifically the use of force, favored more frequently in the military press or the business press?

Table 6.1 summarizes the preferences of the two samples with respect to the four kinds of intervention. Although there were 250

---

[12]Bernard Berelson's phrase used in his efforts to distinguish qualitative and quantitative content analysis, in *Content Analysis in Communication Research* (Glencoe, Ill.: Free Press, 1952), p. 126.

Table 6.1 Business Press and Military Press Discussions of Intervention, by Type of Intervention and Direction of Preference

Direction of Preference	Type of Intervention*											
	Military		Economic		Diplomatic		Unspecified		Total		% by Direction	
	Bus.	Mil.	Bus.	Mil.	Bus.	Mil.	Bus.	Mil.	Bus.	Mil.	Bus.	Mil.
Strong pro	55	64	11	1	47	15	12	3	125	83	41	72
Weak pro	52	7	4	1	4	2	4	0	64	10	21	9
Pro-con	18	3	0	0	1	0	2	1	21	4	7	3
Weak con	33	17	7	1	6	0	3	0	49	18	16	16
Strong con	21	0	2	0	21	0	1	0	45	0	15	0
Total	179	91	24	3	79	17	22	4	304	115	100	100
% by type	59	79	8	3	26	15	7	3	100	100		

*Absolute frequency.

articles for the business sample and 101 for the military sample, some articles expressed opinions on more than one form of intervention, so 304 total preferences were coded for the business sample and 115 were coded for the military sample.

Military intervention obviously was the primary focus of attention for both the business press and the military press, as can be seen by reading the column totals for the two categories. This is notable although perhaps not so surprising in view of the tendency of editorials to respond to the more critical and dramatic types of situations. Moreover, attitudes toward all forms of intervention were usually favorable, as can be seen in the last two columns: 62 percent of all discussions of some form of intervention were favorable, either strongly or at least weakly, in the business press, and 81 percent of the discussions in the military press were favorable. Perhaps this reflects our selection of cases; in every one at least some form of American military intervention did occur. Thus these elite groups basically supported what was already, or eventually became, government policy.

Nevertheless, the differences between these two groups are striking and bear directly on some of our hypotheses. Either way we look at the totals, the business press, although hawkish, is markedly *less so* than is the military press. Military intervention discussions constitute 59 percent of the business total but 79 percent—almost four-fifths—of the military total. To some extent this simply reflects a narrow, professional focus of concern for the military, but it may also indicate greater willingness on the part of businessmen to consider alternatives to force. And, as previously noted, the frequency of approval—strong or weak—of all kinds of intervention was 62 percent for the business press and 81 percent for the military press. Moreover, this same pattern applies when we compare various cells within the tables. For example, discussions specifically of military intervention are generally favorable (60 percent) in the business press, but overwhelmingly so (78 percent) in the military press. And although sizable minorities of the business references to other forms of intervention are unfavorable —9 (37 percent) of the discussions of economic intervention and 27 and 4 (34 percent and 18 percent), respectively, of the diplomatic and unspecified discussions—there is only one such opinion in the military press. All these differences are statistically significant at the .001 level, using a two-tailed test.

A similar pattern appears in Table 6.2, which focuses solely on preferences expressed about the use of American combat forces

Table 6.2 Business Press and Military Press Discussions of Intervention by United States Combat Troops, Other Military Intervention, and Nonmilitary Intervention, by Type of Intervention and Direction of Preference

Type of Intervention*

Direction of Preference	Combat Troops		Lesser Military		Nonmilitary		Total		% by Direction	
	Bus.	Mil.	Bus.	Mil.	Bus.	Mil.	Bus.	Mil.	Bus.	Mil.
Strong pro	37	42	18	22	70	19	125	83	41	72
Weak pro	46	4	6	3	12	3	64	10	21	9
Pro-con	17	3	1	0	3	1	21	4	7	3
Weak con	31	14	2	3	16	1	49	18	16	16
Strong con	17	0	4	0	24	0	45	0	15	0
Total	148	63	31	28	125	24	304	115	100	100
% by type	49	55	10	24	41	21	100	100		

*Absolute frequency.

—the "highest" form of military intervention. Only 83 out of 148 (56 percent) of the business press references to this highest level were favorable, in contrast to 46 out of 63 (73 percent) in the military press. This difference is significant at the .05 level. The discrepancy is even more striking if these favorable opinions are considered in relation to the total number of preferences expressed in favor of all forms of intervention in each sample. Only 83 out of 304 (27 percent) of all business preferences expressed favor for the use of combat troops, whereas 46 out of 115 (40 percent) of the military press preferences did so. This difference is significant at the .01 level. Moreover, a glance at the breakdowns in Table 6.1 shows that support for military intervention was much *less* likely to be strong in the business press than in the military press, and that the opposition of the military press to military intervention, when it occurred, was *always* weak.

Hawkishness in the business press becomes more significant when the preferences of the four other business press sources (*Business Week, Kiplinger Letter, Fortune*, and *Barrons*) are aggregated into one group separate from the *Wall Street Journal*. Table 6.3 compares the distribution of preferences of the *Wall Street Journal*, the four other business press sources, and the military press. The percentage breakdown by types of intervention discussed by each group is given, and within each type the percentage of preferences that were pro-intervention (strongly or at least weakly) is shown in parentheses. We find that the preferences expressed by the *Wall Street Journal* for nonmilitary and lesser military forms of intervention roughly approximate those of the four other business press sources, but they are strikingly different for the highest level of military intervention. Only 32 percent of all the *Wall Street Journal* opinions on troop intervention were favorable, in contrast to 85 percent of those for the four other business press sources, a considerably higher figure even than the 73 percent for the military press.

This significant intrabusiness difference leads us to consider whether the results indicated for the business press as a whole, in comparison with those indicated for the military press, have been distorted by the greater frequency of the *Wall Street Journal* editorials, which we found to be considerably more dovish than those of the rest of the business sample. This question in turn leads us to reconsider our sampling procedure as well as certain basic assumptions underlying it. Are we justified in weighting the sample according to the frequency of editorials, which is essentially the procedure

Table 6.3   *Percentage Distribution of Preferences for Intervention Expressed by* Wall Street Journal, *Four Other Business Press Sources, and Military Journals*

Type of Intervention	*Wall Street Journal*	Four Other Business Press Sources	Military Journals
Combat troops	52	45	55
(% pro)	(32)	(85)	(73)
Lesser military	10	10	24
(% pro)	(75)	(80)	(89)
Economic	6	10	3
(% pro)	(67)	(60)	(67)
Diplomatic	25	27	15
(% pro)	(61)	(67)	(100)
Unspecified	7	8	3
(% pro)	(73)	(73)	(75)
Total	100	100	100
(% pro)	(49)	(76)	(81)
N =	156	148	115

that has been followed, thus according very substantial significance to the views of the *Wall Street Journal*? Or should we assume each of the five sources to be equally representative of business views? We can explore the implications of this assumption procedurally by giving equal weight to each source, reducing the *Wall Street Journal* from 51 percent to 20 percent. We then find that 72 percent of this adjusted total of business press references to troop intervention was favorable, compared with the 56 percent obtained by the weighting-by-frequency procedure. According to this method, the business press is about as hawkish as the military press, the comparable figure for which is 73 percent. How do we reconcile the discrepant results of these two sampling procedures? Do the views of the *Wall Street Journal* or those of the other business press sources represent more accurately the views of the business community? More appropriately, what kind of mix of the two sets of views most nearly corresponds to the mix of attitudes among businessmen?

Although there is no definitive way to determine this correspondence, we can use certain crude indicators of relative degrees of influence among the five sources. Three separate studies of the reading preferences of business executives were conducted during the mid-1950s, an appropriate point in the period we are considering.[13] These three sets of results provide some indication of the relative importance of various business press sources of information on which executives based their foreign policy attitudes during this period. Bauer, Pool, and Dexter found that almost half of their sample of respondents, consisting primarily of "heads of firms," regularly read the *Wall Street Journal*, and the figure rose to 64 percent for heads of large firms. In his study, Edward Bursk found that 75 percent of his "top executives" regularly read that newspaper. By comparison, all three studies found the *New York Times* to be habitually read by only about one-third of their respondents. Lest it be concluded that the *Wall Street Journal* represents the views of the Eastern establishment press, we cite Bauer, Pool, and Dexter's findings that, at least in 1954, the farther their respondents lived from New York, the more they relied on the *Wall Street Journal*: 50 percent and 53 percent of the Southern and Western respondents, respectively, read the *Wall Street Journal*, in contrast to 43 percent of those living in New York, who relied relatively more on other New York newspapers.

Although there were some marked disparities in the three sets of results for general business magazines, the patterns of the relative importance of the magazines were similar for all studies: readership was consistently highest for *Business Week* and *Fortune*. Two of the studies found that *Business Week* was read regularly by about 45 percent of their samples, while the third found this to be true for only 30 percent. The figures of the three studies for *Fortune* were 38, 25, and 16 percent, respectively. The Bursk study, using an aided recall procedure, found that the *Kiplinger Letter* was read by 48 percent of the respondents, but only 10 percent or less of those analyzed by the other two studies did so. *Barrons* was read to an even lesser extent. These studies of the reading habits of business executives suggest that weighting the five sources equally may cause a more serious distortion of business press attitudes than does "overweighting" the *Wall Street Journal*.

---

[13]Edward Bursk reported the results of the mail survey he conducted in 1957 in "New Dimensions in Top Executive Reading," *Harvard Business Review* 35 ((September–October 1957): 93–112. The results of *Wall Street Journal* surveys conducted in 1952, 1954, and 1957 by Erdos and Morgan Research Service were reported in "The Reading Preferences of Corporate Officers and Executive Personnel," which was circulated privately but discussed in Bauer, Pool, and Dexter, who compared the results from their own interview data obtained in 1954 with the preceding two studies. See Bauer, Pool, and Dexter, op. cit., pp. 154–162.

A different kind of readership statistics may be found in a 1971 article on the *Wall Street Journal*, which indicates that 80 percent of that newspaper's circulation is composed of subscribers, who constitute a "city of businessmen" inhabited by 173,390 corporation presidents and 112,320 vice presidents.[14] Such a high proportion of subscription readers suggests regular rather than casual readership of the *Wall Street Journal* and provides additional support for assuming a considerable correspondence of views between that newspaper and its readers.

Another small but different piece of evidence to support the relative importance of the *Wall Street Journal* is the Pulitzer Prize editorial award for 1954, which was given to Vermont Royster of the *Wall Street Journal* for "distinguished writing and ability to influence public opinion."[15] William Grimes, who was head editor of that newspaper's editorial page until 1958, had earlier received a similar award.

All these pieces of evidence taken together would seem to provide some justification for heavily weighting the *Wall Street Journal*, although it is possible that we have overweighted this source and thus exaggerated the dovishness of the business press as a whole. Because only *Business Week* appears to have a readership comparable to that of the *Wall Street Journal*, and because it is the only other source that publishes a substantial number of editorials, the results for the business press undoubtedly would have been different had these two sources alone been considered representative. Discussions of troop intervention in *Business Week* were 79 percent favorable. (This is not shown in Table 6.3.) Thus the mean percentage of favorable opinions about this form of intervention for *Business Week* and the *Wall Street Journal* is 56 percent, which is exactly the same figure we got when we included the other four business press sources and weighted the *Wall Street Journal* by virtue of its greater frequency. This is, of course, only a statistical compromise. We simply cannot know the extent to which the *Wall Street Journal*, *Business Week*, or any one of the less widely read sources reflect the views of the business community. (Similar reservations might be expressed concerning the military press as a reflection of military opinion and the relative importance of the various military journals as expressions of this opinion. However, there was no selection of military journals, nor were the articles

---

[14]*Fortune*, August 1971, p. 140.
[15]*Wall Street Journal*, May 4, 1953, p. 1.

from any one journal disproportionately represented. Military press data represent the universe of military articles on the cases analyzed from the major military journals.)

Some clear findings do emerge from the data. The fact that the business press favored all forms of intervention—including the use of troops—more often than it opposed them indicates considerable hawkishness. Furthermore, a substantial part of the business press (excluding the *Wall Street Journal*) does appear to have been more pro-interventionist than the military press. However, hypothesis 1.5 (that businessmen will be more hawkish on a variety of foreign policy issues than will other elites) is supported only when the most widely read source is excluded. Because such a sample is highly unlikely to be representative of the business community's views, this conditional support is tantamount to rejection of the hypothesis, at least when military journals are the basis of comparison. Furthermore, the fact that the most widely read and influential source in the business press so frequently opposed overt military intervention is a significant finding, which in itself would seem to diminish considerably support for the hypothesis predicting greater hawkishness in the business sample. By the same token, hypothesis 1.4 (that military men will be more hawkish on a variety of foreign policy issues than will civilian elites, including businessmen) is supported. However, the degree of support that our data give to the opposite hypothesis, 1.9, which assumes that businessmen will be less hawkish on a variety of foreign policy issues than will other elite groups, is to some extent contingent on the relative weight accorded to the *Wall Street Journal*. If we consider the less widely read sources to be just as likely as the *Wall Street Journal* to reflect the views of businessmen, and if we give all sources equal weight, the business and military samples appear to be equally hawkish, thus supporting military-industrial complex theories that postulate a convergence of interest of the two elite groups. On the other hand, when the *Wall Street Journal* is given a weight proportionate to its greater frequency of editorials (i.e., when each article is counted as one unit of analysis regardless of source), the business sample is significantly less hawkish than the military. The business press sources were much more likely than the military periodicals to oppose military intervention—especially in its strongest form— and to favor forms of action other than military intervention. We have given reasons to justify our original weighting procedure, and on that basis we conclude that hypothesis 1.9 is supported.

Table 6.4 *Approval of Military Intervention by United States Troops, Expressed by Business Press and General Public*

Crisis	Approval Expressed by	
	% of Business Press Editorials	% of Public with Opinions
Greece, 1947	16	34
Korea, 1950	56	67
Indochina, 1953–1954	27	19
Lebanon, 1956	50	69
Cuba, 1962	12	13–29
Dominican Republic, 1965	88	70
Vietnam, 1964–1965	50	68

Perceptions of Business and the General Public

Some skepticism—that we partly share—may arise regarding the rationale of comparing the business press with no other press but the military. The finding that business is merely less hawkish, or no more hawkish, than the military, may not be considered very exciting or surprising. A more appropriate, or at least an additional, control group would seem to be in order. We have indicated why it is in fact difficult to identify any other appropriate control group of press sources, but it may be useful to compare the business press editorials with expressions of opinion among the populace. Table 6.4[16] makes this comparison concisely and very approximately. The first column gives the percentage of all business press editorials that expressed favorable comments about use of United States troops in the given crisis. The second column gives the percentage of a national sample of the members of the general public *with an opinion* who favored the use of troops. "Don't know" responses have been excluded in order to make the public opinion surveys comparable with the business press editorials and articles, which generally included only those with a definite policy recommendation either way.

---

[16]Sources and comments regarding public opinion data in Table 6.4: *Greece:* George H. Gallup, *The Gallup Poll: Public Opinion 1935–1971* (New York: Random House, 1972), Vol. 1, p. 675. Dates are August–September 1947. Response given was in favor of the option, "In cooperation with the United Nations organization, send United States troops to patrol the Greek border

These comparisons must be made with great caution. On the one hand, the expressions of business preference are subject to the kind of sampling error that is to be expected because of the nature of our sources and our treatment of them. On the other, the public opinion materials are subject to sampling error, to variation according to the time the survey was taken, and most important, to variation according to the wording of the question. Further severe difficulties arise when editorial statements are compared with survey responses. Given these cautions, some tentative conclusions nevertheless emerge. First, both the business press and the general public were very reluctant toward the use of American troops in Indochina and in Cuba (premissile crisis). Second, the business press was sometimes a bit more hawkish than the general

---

to stop armed men from coming into the country to make trouble." Perhaps this option, incorporating an assumption of United Nations approval, seems too mild. On the other hand, an even stronger option, "In cooperation with the United Nations, tell Russia that further moves into Greece will be considered a declaration of war against the rest of the world," gained the approval of 48 percent of the population. Thus the figure of 34 percent in the table probably understates popular hawkishness on this issue. In another version, the question was prefaced by the comment, "Some experts say that Russia will have atomic bombs in a year." When this version was asked, the responses changed from 34 to 30 percent and from 48 to 57 percent.

Korea: John Mueller, *War, Presidents, and Public Opinion* (New York: Wiley, 1973), p. 45. Average of six surveys taken July–December 1950; wording of question varied.
Indochina: Gallup, op. cit., Vol. 2, pp. 1146, 1170, 1236. Average of four surveys taken May 1953–May 1954 asking, "Would you approve or disapprove of sending United States soldiers to take part in the fighting there?"
Lebanon: Gallup, op. cit., Vol. 2, p. 1561. Question was, "Do you approve or disapprove of United States action in sending troops into Lebanon?" Sample was not national; only from New York-Chicago-San Francisco, July 1958.
Cuba: Gallup, op. cit., Vol. 3, pp. 1785–1786. Average of two surveys taken in September 1962. The first survey asked, "Taking everything into account, what action, if any, do you think the United States should take at this time in regard to Cuba?" The answer choices were "Bomb, invade, belligerent action." The second survey asked, "Some people say that the United States should send our armed forces into Cuba to help overthrow Castro. Do you agree or disagree?" The comparable figure for business editorials refers only to 1962, *before* the missile crisis emerged.
Dominican Republic: Gallup Opinion Index, December 1965, p. 7. Question was, "Do you think the U.S. did the right thing or the wrong thing in deciding to send troops into Santo Domingo?" Survey taken in December 1965.
Vietnam: Mueller, op. cit., p. 54. Average of five surveys taken November 1964–November 1965; wording of question varied.

All responses were calculated as a percentage of those giving a definite opinion; that is, excluding respondents who "don't know" or admit not having heard of the problem. No survey data for Guatemala and Congo.

public (for at least two crises), but often the general public was about as hawkish as the business press or more so. In general, we find no evidence here to support the proposition that businessmen are more likely to advocate military intervention than are members of the public at large. This interpretation is strengthened when a modification is made in the control group. Until the later Vietnam years, support for American military action abroad was generally higher among upper-income, educational, and professional groups. Although this was not true for each "crisis," we know it to be true at least for Korea, the Dominican Republic, and the early Vietnam period.[17] Thus the percentages in the second column may often be *understated* if the aim is to compare businessmen with those individuals in the general population of comparable income and social status. Beyond this fairly weak and cautious statement (that businessmen do not seem to have been more hawkish than were comparable members of the public at large) it does not seem safe to go.

How did the business press as a whole and the military press respond to specific cases of intervention? Table 6.5 allows us to compare the responses of the two groups of periodicals to ascertain whether there was any definite evolution of opinion over this rather long period. We can also pick out a few patterns. The table gives percentage breakdowns by type of intervention discussed in the business press and the military press at the time of each crisis; for each type the percentage of preferences that were pro-intervention (strongly or at least weakly) appears in parentheses. The number of discussions of each case is given at the top of each column. Finally, Table 6.5 indicates some of the characteristics of the crisis as perceived by the writers. Because the potential target of intervention in some cases changed considerably over time, either in its personnel (e.g., Congo) or in the way it was perceived by commentators (e.g., Cuba), it was important to include this kind of characterization. However, the information could not always be extracted from an article and occasionally the categories were inappropriate. These missing data are indicated by "percent not coded."

Let us look first at some of the differences in the ways the military press and the business press characterized each crisis.

---

[17]See among others, Mueller, op. cit., pp. 132–133; *Gallup Opinion Index*, loc. cit.; James D. Wright, "Life, Time, and the Fortunes of War," *Transaction*, January 1972, pp. 42–52; and Philip E. Converse and Howard Schuman, "'Silent Majorities' and the Vietnam War," *Scientific American*, June 1970, pp. 17–25.

Table 6.5 *Percentage Distribution of Preferences for Intervention in Nine Cases Expressed by Business Press and Military Press by Type of Intervention, Type of Crisis, and Type of Target*

	Greece		Korea		Indochina		Guatemala*	
	Bus.	Mil.	Bus.	Mil.	Bus.	Mil.	Bus.	Mil.
N =	14	3	34	23	49	11	16	—
Type of Intervention								
Combat troops	22	0	100	100	51	46	25	—
(% pro)	(67)		(56)	(85)	(44)	(40)	(25)	
Lesser military	64	67	0	0	8	27	6	—
(% pro)	(89)	(100)			(75)	(67)	(0)	
Economic	0	0	0	0	0	0	25	—
(% pro)							(25)	
Diplomatic	14	0	0	0	37	18	31	—
(% pro)	(50)				(100)	(100)	(40)	
Unspecified	0	33	0	0	4	9	13	—
(% pro)		(100)			(0)	(100)	(100)	
Type of Crisis (% of Articles)								
External attack	83	100	100	100	24	0	0	—
Aided revolt	17	0	0	0	69	80	0	—
Unaided revolt	0	0	0	0	2	10	22	—
% not coded	0	0	0	0	5	10	78	—
Type of Target								
Communist	100	0	100	100	93	60	45	—
Communist tool	0	67	0	0	0	30	33	—
Nationalist	0	33	0	0	7	0	0	—
Pro-West	0	0	0	0	0	0	11	—
% not coded	0	0	0	0	0	10	11	—

These differences are worth noting, although the small size of some of the military subsamples prevents us from concluding too much from them. It appears, for example, that the business press was more likely than the military press to express concern about threat of an external attack. This difference is particularly ap-

Lebanon		Cuba		Congo		Vietnam		Dominican Republic		Total	
Bus.	Mil.	Bus.	Mil.	Bus.	Mil.	Bus.	Mil.	Bus.	Mil.	Bus.	Mil.
20	8	82	14	33	11	27	34	10	11	285†	115
Type of Intervention											
85	100	31	21	12	18	75	35	70	91	49	54
(53)	(50)	(65)	(67)	(25)	(50)	(60)	(67)	(100)	(100)	(56)	(73)
5	0	13	37	3	27	2	44	0	0	10	25
(0)		(100)	(80)	(0)	(100)	(50)	(93)			(77)	(89)
0	0	22	14	0	0	4	3	0	0	8	3
		(67)	(50)			(100)	(100)			(62)	(67)
10	0	18	14	82	55	7	18	20	1	26	14
(100)		(93)	(100)	(15)	(100)	(100)	(100)	(100)	(100)	(64)	(100)
0	0	16	14	3	0	7	0	10	0	7	4
		(77)	(100)	(100)		(100)		(100)		(73)	(75)
Type of Crisis (% of Articles)											
22	0	0	0	0	0	21	3	0	0	27	21
72	50	0	0	13	67	79	97	100	100	30	48
0	25	7	0	87	22	0	0	0	0	17	14
6	25	93	100	0	11	0	0	0	0	26	17
Type of Target											
6	0	54	39	0	0	100	93	100	0	65	56
39	0	31	61	13	0	0	7	0	100	14	18
50	75	15	0	20	89	0	0	0	0	12	22
0	0	0	0	67	0	0	0	0	0	8	0
5	25	0	0	0	11	0	0	0	0	1	4

*Not coded for military—no data.
†This figure does not include miscellaneous cases.

parent with regard to Indochina and Lebanon, about which the business press expressed concern regarding attacks by China and the Soviet Union even though the root of each crisis was internal revolt. The business press also appears more likely to perceive the target of American intervention as communist. Nevertheless, the business press was, on the whole, less likely to recommend the use of force.

An analysis of the distribution of preferences by case reveals that there was virtually no opposition in either the business press or the military press to military assistance to Greece and Turkey or to the dispatch of troops to the Dominican Republic. Opposition to the two prolonged interventions in Vietnam and Korea was somewhat stronger in the business press. With regard to Vietnam, the two presses disagreed mainly on the lesser forms of military intervention. This reflects the general enthusiasm in the military press for the military advisory efforts of the United States—a topic rarely discussed in the business press. On the matter of troop intervention, the difference between the samples amounts to only 7 percent (at least up to six months beyond the actual commitment of American troops) and is not statistically significant. There had been considerably more opposition in both samples to intervention in Indochina fifteen years earlier. Opposition to military intervention in Lebanon was also substantial, and was roughly the same in both the military press and the business press. The ratio of favorable to unfavorable preferences for military measures against Cuba was three to one for both samples. Since these opinions concerned to a great extent the Cuban missile crisis, the strong favorable response is not surprising. The military press overwhelmingly favored American support of United Nations action in the Congo, whereas the majority of business press preferences was opposed to such action. This was the one case in which the military press generally saw the threat as a communist-aided revolt, while a majority of the business articles referred to it as basically an internal unaided revolt because the Katanga secession remained the focus of concern. Finally, there is no indication of a time trend.

In the following section we discuss the bases for these opinions in the business press. Here it is important to note that there is a marked divergence in the proportion of favorable opinions to unfavorable opinions in the two samples only for the two large-scale military interventions and the special situation in the Congo. With respect to Vietnam, the evidence fails to support hypothesis 1.7 (when the military is the basis of comparison), predicting that business will be less likely to view the Vietnam war as a mistake. Nor, however, is there very strong evidence, at least in the early stages of the war, in support of the contrary hypothesis 1.10, predicting that businessmen will be more likely to view the Vietnam war as a mistake.

At this point it is useful to supplement our findings on the distribution of preferences expressed by the business press and the military press with regard to specific cases of American intervention with a more detailed analysis of the business press response, based on close reading of the editorials. The business press was analyzed in this manner for the duration of the Vietnam and Korean wars, although only the initial period (first six months after official commitment of American combat troops) was coded. The following section presents an overview of the business press response to specific cases of intervention, indicating the general direction of preference, as well as significant variations among sources. The structural characteristics of each case are summarized, particularly the kinds of intervention considered and the perception of target or potential target of the action in question.

Crisis, Structure, and Intervention

In the Greece-Turkey and Dominican Republic cases we found the least resistance to intervention on the part of either sample. In both cases the target of intervention was perceived to be communist. Although the situation in the Dominican Republic could hardly have been regarded as anything more than an aided revolt, the perception of the Greek threat primarily as an external attack is notable, if not surprising. "Top Communists in the Balkans encouraged guerillas to enter Greece," explained a *Fortune* editor.[18] The internal struggle raging in Greece was generally portrayed as a mere pretext for Soviet expansion. The far-reaching implications of the Truman doctrine for a new policy of global responsibility were generally appreciated, and few qualms were expressed. Sending Marines to the Dominican Republic required a higher level of military commitment, but the rebellion was generally assumed to be communist-dominated, despite much evidence to the contrary. The *Wall Street Journal*'s editorial writers were apparently unconvinced even by that newspaper's own staff reporter, whose dispatches cast doubts on the American Embassy version of a "serious threat of communist takeover."[19] Once this assumption was made,

---

[18]*Fortune*, June 1947, p. 86.

[19]See Philip Geyelin's editorial page article in the *Wall Street Journal*, June 25, 1965, p. 7, in which he analyzes the official records and cables and describes the events of the Dominican crisis as he personally viewed them. The "Cuban reflex" theory is given as the explanation for the decision of the administration to intervene, even though there was little evidence at the time of intervention to indicate communist direction of the rebel movement. His views are also quoted in Theodore Draper, "The Dominican Crisis," *Commentary*, December 1965, p. 39.

there seems to have been no question about the necessity of preventing "another Cuba."

This enthusiastic, decisive approval of whatever steps were necessary to prevent the establishment of another communist beachhead in Latin America contrasts sharply with the hesitant response to the establishment of the first one. The differential response to the Dominican Republic and Cuban cases illustrates the way in which structural characteristics of a crisis circumscribe the response to it. In the case of Cuba, two such characteristics operated as restraints.[20] One was the absence of any organized, internal conflict threatening the existing Cuban government. Just as virtually every internal war creates a demand for foreign intervention,[21] so the absence of internal war appears to make such intervention exceedingly difficult. Although dissension existed, there was no focal point of opposition in Cuba sufficiently well organized and broadly based to make aid to insurgents a viable or justifiable alternative. Certainly there was no competing political authority with some degree of *de facto* control to request this aid.

The second structural characteristic that operated as a restraint on intervention in Cuba was the initial absence of any concrete manifestations of outside intervention. This uncertainty regarding the extent of the threat posed by Castro, combined with the problems of justifying the displacement of a *de facto* ruling group, appears to have minimized the pressures for intervention in the business press for slightly more than a year following Castro's takeover. As the perception of the potential target changed, willingness to intervene increased.

The yearly breakdown in Table 6.6 indicates that during the first year of Castro's rule, little prescriptive attention of any kind was given to Cuba, and only two recommendations were made for some unspecified kind of action. Indeed, Castro received a certain

---

[20]For a theoretical and empirical analysis of conditions that promote or restrain overt American military intervention, see Herbert T. Tillema, *Appeal to Force: American Military Intervention in the Era of Containment* (New York: Thomas Y. Crowell, 1973), especially ch. 1.

[21]For discussion of this phenomenon, see George Modelski, "The International Relations of Internal War," in James Rosenau, ed., *International Aspects of Civil Strife* (Princeton, N.J.: Princeton University Press, 1964), pp. 14–44. See also the study of Frederic S. Pearson, who tests empirically the proposition that "structural" conflict (i.e., widespread domestic conflict that could entail major changes in government policies and institutions) is more likely to result in foreign military intervention than are other kinds of conflict, in "Foreign Military Interventions and Domestic Disputes," *International Studies Quarterly* 18, No. 3 (September, 1974): 259–286.

Table 6.6 *Distribution of Business Press Preferences with Regard to Cuban Case, 1959–1962, by Year**

	Military Inter- vention	Economic Inter- vention	Diplomatic Inter- vention	Unspecified Inter- vention	Total
			1959		
Pro	0	0	0	2	2
Pro-con	0	0	0	0	0
Con	2	1	0	2	5
			1960		
Pro	6	12	7	4	29
Pro-con	1	0	0	0	1
Con	4	5	1	1	11
			1961		
Pro	10	0	4	0	14
Pro-con	0	0	0	0	0
Con	1	0	0	0	1
			1962		
Pro	11	0	3	4	18
Pro-con	0	0	0	0	0
Con	1	0	0	0	1

*Absolute frequency.

amount of support in some quarters as a "middle-class revolutionary" whose primary goals were land reform and diversification of the island's sugar-based economy.[22] This was the early line of *Business Week*, which tended to regard the Cuban problem as one of misguided tactics on the part of Castro. The Cuban leader was trying to do too much too fast, thus helping to create confusion that "opened the door to increasing communist activity." Thus communist influence was incidental; "what Castro's policy adds up to is a violent case of Latin American nationalism."[23]

[22]*Business Week*, January 10, 1959, p. 84; and August 1, 1959, p. 75
[23]*Business Week*, August 1, 1959, p. 75.

Other business press sources were less inclined to give Castro the benefit of the doubt and viewed communist influences as more serious; but no articles in 1959 described him as communist-dominated. Furthermore, even the more critical articles generally opposed not only overt military intervention but also economic and diplomatic sanctions, until March 1960. Military intervention was considered impossible unless Castro threatened Guantanamo base or permitted the establishment of a Soviet military base. It was thought that such measures as reducing the Cuban sugar quota and eliminating the preferential pricing would only drive Castro further to the left and alienate many Latin Americans at the same time. "Turning the other cheek" is not always a diplomatic virtue, asserted the *Wall Street Journal*, but Castro's insults were best met with quiet dignity.[24] Besides, Cuba was only inflicting pinpricks and did not endanger American security. The situation would be different should Cuba come under Soviet domination. This philosophical view was expressed editorially in the same issue with a front-page article bearing the headline, "Cuba and Communism: Leftist Power Grows; Businessmen Near Disaster."[25] Pervading all the sources, at least after the first year, was the expectation— or hope—that Castro would "hang himself by his own rope." Castro's political and economic policies could only lead to massive discontent. "A disaster has befallen Cuba and the United States should be concerned, but it should be the Cubans who find the remedy," insisted the *Wall Street Journal*.[26]

By the summer of 1960 Castro had signed an aid and trade pact with the Soviet Union and had taken over the operation of most American businesses in Cuba. Economic and diplomatic measures, previously considered ineffective, were generally recommended in business press sources, and there was increasing awareness of the security threat posed by a Soviet base in Cuba. From this point a variety of economic and diplomatic measures, such as reduction of the sugar quota, imposition of a trade embargo, and efforts to mobilize opinion and action through the OAS, were favored in the business press. *Business Week*, in an editorial entitled "Time to Blow the Whistle," approved reduction of Cuba's sugar quota and efforts to rally Latin American support for other "tougher measures."[27] The American business community, accord-

---

[24]*Wall Street Journal*, January 28, 1960, p. 8.
[25]*Wall Street Journal*, March 9, 1960, pp. 1 and 14.
[26]*Wall Street Journal*, December 23, 1959, p. 8.
[27]*Business Week*, July 9, 1960, p. 148.

ing to this editorial, had applauded when Castro overthrew Batista, because they believed Castro could give Cuba many things it needed—stable government, democratic institutions, land reform, and a more balanced economy. But Castro had imposed his own form of state-controlled economy, restricted imports, seized United States properties without compensation, and turned to communism.

Before the Bay of Pigs invasion in April 1961, there was some support in business press sources for American aid to insurrectionist forces; but a campaign proposal by John F. Kennedy suggesting such aid was criticized by the *Wall Street Journal* on the ground that "some things are better done surreptitiously—not publicized."[28] The Bay of Pigs invasion was unanimously deplored in the business press, but not so much for the failure of the United States government to support more openly and effectively the anti-Castro rebels as for what was regarded as an attempt to play dirty tricks without getting dirty hands. According to *Business Week*, "If you are going to play it heavy, play it heavy all the way. Otherwise play it clean."[29] The Bay of Pigs disaster removed for the time being the alternative of covert support of Castro opposition as an effective means of eliminating him.

Throughout the remainder of 1961 and 1962, increasing frustration with the obvious ineffectiveness of lesser measures, with the failure of the Castro government to collapse, and with the apparently increasing Soviet influence and arms build-up in Cuba, permeated the business press. Editorials began to refer more often to the possibility that force "might eventually" be necessary to rid the hemisphere of communism and to the necessity of showing greater firmness and determination vis-à-vis the Soviet aspirations in Latin America. But nothing specific was recommended, and the implied assumption underlying most of the commentary was that any overt military measures against Castro would require a more concrete manifestation of the threat he posed to American security.

The missile crisis of October 1962 at last provided the opportunity to display the firmness and resolution that the business press had so long recommended in vague terms. Business press sources not only acclaimed Kennedy's blockade against all shipments of offensive military equipment to Cuba, but reported from their own surveys the "virtually total support" in the business community for this action.[30] The *Wall Street Journal* found that the majority

---

[28]*Wall Street Journal*, September 24, 1960, p. 7.
[29]*Business Week*, April 29, 1961, p. 128.
[30]*Business Week*, September 27, 1962, p. 55.

of businessmen throughout the country "expressed relief that at last some kind of positive action against the communist threat in Cuba was being taken."[31]

The incentives for taking some kind of action in Cuba, at least after the middle of 1960, were stronger than in any other crisis. Yet at the same time, certain aspects of the situation militated against any action that could be conceived. A similar situation existed in Guatemala in 1954. Among the cases considered in this analysis, only in Cuba and Guatemala was there no internal conflict. The problem in both instances was to displace an incumbent government in the absence of any well-organized insurgents. In addition, the prior intervention of another country such as the Soviet Union was not clearly established.

Although the Guatemalan crisis yields a very small number of preferences to analyze because of its brief duration, it is noteworthy that the opinions of the business press about all forms of intervention (except the unspecified category) were predominantly negative. Searching for an appropriate "bad neighbor policy," Barrons suggested that "some inter-American substitute for the U.S. Marines" was needed.[32] But the other sources generally expressed disapproval of economic and diplomatic actions on the ground that "any deviation from non-intervention policy would unite Latin America against us, drive them into the arms of demagogues, and might even produce a chain of expropriations."[33] As in Cuba, strong incentives for intervention existed. A Business Week editorial posed the dilemma: "It [the United States government] cannot allow Moscow Communism or know-nothing fascism to inflict the Americas; but it can't set the hemisphere against it by open intervention."[34] This suggests support for the kind of policy actually adopted by the American government, namely, the use of covert means to bring down the Arbenz government. Views on the use of such techniques are difficult to tap, because they are seldom expressed, particularly when they are positive. One negative view was strongly stated by Business Week two weeks before the rebel forces that were covertly trained by the United States invaded from Honduras. Tinkering with internal revolutions was viewed as a dangerous position for the United States as it would encourage Latin American fears and sus-

---

[31]Wall Street Journal, September 23, 1962, p. 18.
[32]Barrons, May 31, 1954, p. 1.
[33]Business Week, April 18, 1953, p. 162.
[34]Ibid.

picions. "Winning Guatemala back to the free world would hardly be worth losing the support of half the hemisphere."[35]

The strongest opposition to American intervention to be found in the business press occurred in connection with the Congolese civil war. The type of intervention at issue here was the American diplomatic and political support of United Nations efforts to restore order and unity to the Congo. The multilateral nature of the intervention was one source of distress, particularly when it became apparent that American views would not always prevail.

Alone among the sources, *Business Week* initially saw the "Congo Test" as revealing a potentially important new role for the United Nations, that is, preventing newly independent nations from becoming pawns in the East-West struggle.[36] Hence, according to this view, American support of United Nations efforts to arrange a compromise solution and help to build a viable nation should be commended. Even the first Asian-African-sponsored resolution to strengthen United Nations efforts in the Congo and to authorize the use of force if necessary was favored by this journal. Recognizing the risks and problems inherent in this policy *Business Week* nevertheless saw it as an alternative preferable to direct American intervention.

The *Wall Street Journal* saw a third and better alternative, namely, complete noninvolvement. The United States could not guard the entire world against communism; priorities had to be set. Those who "do not understand or want freedom or order" should be off the priority list altogether.[37] In rather condescending rhetoric the Congo was pictured as "a darkling plain in which ignorant armies clash by night,"[38] and in which the central characters were all "a bunch of lunatics running around trying to get power."[39] Consolidation of a viable Congolese nation-state could not be an aim of United States policy, because "the man in the Congo bush does not have a national concept in his head."[40] In short, United States support of the United Nations efforts in the Congo was a "jungle bungle."[41]

Opposition mounted in all business press sources when it was perceived that the conduct of the United Nations operation was

---

[35]*Business Week*, June 5, 1954, p. 130.
[36]*Business Week*, August 6, 1960, p. 148.
[37]*Wall Street Journal*, September 15, 1960, p. 7.
[38]*Ibid.*
[39]*Wall Street Journal*, September 16, 1960, p. 8.
[40]*Wall Street Journal*, December 12, 1961, p. 9.
[41]*Wall Street Journal*, August 22, 1960, p. 8.

bringing about the very outcome that it was supposed to prevent, namely, a communist Congo. Objections were repeatedly raised to what were considered to be American-supported United Nations efforts to force a political settlement favorable to leftist factions, at the expense of Katanga, the "only viable pro-Western base in the whole area."[42]

The resort by the United Nations to military coercion against Katanga in the effort to unite the Congo was the subject of vehement criticism. The United States was supporting intervention against the wrong target; it was favoring a "war of aggression" by its enemies against its friends.[43] "How do we fight communism by fighting communism's foes?" queried the *Wall Street Journal*.[44] Thus the central issue for the business press in this case was the pro-Western, anticommunist character of the target of American intervention in the Congo; the overwhelming opposition to this action proceeded logically.

Different perceptions of the target of American military intervention in Lebanon appear to have affected the response of the business press to that action. Table 6.5 shows that 53 percent of the preferences were positive; half the articles viewed the target as essentially nationalist rather than communist. Opposition to intervention came primarily from the *Wall Street Journal*, which pushed the following line of argument. First, it was erroneous to assume that communist thrusts must be met wherever they occur. "Not every piece of ground is of equal importance" in justifying the risks and costs of intervention.[45] Second, in this case the problem was not even one of communist military aggression; this was primarily an internal revolt, abetted by the United Arab Republic. The United States could not in the long run gain by a policy of using force to hold back the tide of Pan Arabism; force would simply "translate Pan Arabism into anti-U.S. hatred."[46] United States military assistance to help Chamoun stabilize his pro-Western government might instead help his enemies. The other four business press sources held quite a different point of view. Two revolutionary forces were perceived to be behind the Middle East ferment: Arab nationalism and "the expansion of Soviet im-

---

[42]*Fortune*, October 1962, p. 84.
[43]*Barrons*, September 18, 1961, p. 1.
[44]*Wall Street Journal*, December 15, 1961, p. 11.
[45]For an interesting elaboration of these views, see the editorial entitled "Losing Our Way," in the *Wall Street Journal*, June 27, 1958, p. 8.
[46]*Wall Street Journal*, July 16, 1958, p. 7.

perialism." Essentially the upheaval in this area was a "world power struggle," in which the Soviet Union was trying to take over the Middle East. Although to some extent the pressures reflected legitimate needs and aspirations of the Arab peoples—and the United States, particularly businessmen, should be more sensitive to these—"Nasserism" was "backed by Soviet agents," and Arab leaders were simply Soviet stooges.[47] "Communist forces moved on Lebanon and played their own game regardless of Nasser's time-table." The rebellion against Chamoun was in fact "ordered" by Moscow, not Nasser.[48] Thus, these business press sources strongly recommended and supported the military action.

Korea, Indochina, and the High Cost of Intervention

The remaining three cases—Korea, the Indochinese crisis in the early 1950s, and the Vietnam war—are structurally similar in several respects. In each instance an incumbent government was threatened by insurgents who appeared to be receiving support and aid from at least one external communist power. Table 6.5 indicates both certainty and unanimity regarding the target or potential target of the American actions in these three cases, namely, communist or communist-dominated forces. Although the Indochinese and Vietnam crises were considered internal revolts that were receiving substantial outside aid, whereas Korea involved an external attack, the assumption of the communist monolith permeated the business press response to each of these three crises. "Moscow authorized an oriental satellite regime to march its Russian-trained and Russian-equipped army accoss the South Korean frontier," asserted the *Wall Street Journal* with great conviction.[49] A *Business Week* editor maintained that his only question at this point was whether the thrust the Kremlin had "ordered" against the "non-communist world" in Korea was a local action or the start of "the showdown."[50] According to *Barrons*, "Soviet tyranny and treachery" had forced the United States to intervene in Korea."[51] In the Korean war the Soviet Union, rather than the North Korean troops or even the Chinese "volunteers," was seen as the real enemy. During both of the wars in Indochina the Chinese were seen as the

---

[47]*Business Week*, July 19, 1958, p. 130.
[48]*Business Week*, May 24, 1958, p. 109; and June 21, 1958, p. 123.
[49]*Wall Street Journal*, July 7, 1950, p. 8.
[50]*Business Week*, July 1, 1950, p. 80.
[51]*Barrons*, June 3, 1950, p. 1.

source of aggressive designs in Southeast Asia, which United States intervention must counter. But the concurrence, if not actual encouragement and initiative, of Moscow appears to have been assumed until the late 1960s—well after the schism between China and the Soviet Union had become apparent.

The preferences expressed in the business press regarding these three cases also follow a rather consistent pattern. The necessity to halt further incursions by communist powers into the noncommunist world proceeded logically from the assumption of monolithic communism. Differences on tactics nevertheless reveal two different perspectives. One view, common to the four other business press sources, assumed that "U.S. security was diminished by any expansion of the Soviet bloc."[52] On the other hand, the consistent view of the *Wall Street Journal* during these crises (as well as the crisis in Lebanon) was that "not every foot of ground is worth defending" and "We cannot fight for every single piece of real estate in the conflict with communism."[53] American security could be just as seriously threatened by the attempt to defend indefensible places at unacceptable costs. This line of reasoning was not inspired by the economic consequences of the Vietnam war, but rather was first expressed at the very outset of the Korean war. The *Wall Street Journal* thought it crucially important to make carefully considered cost/benefit calculations before taking any stand against communism.

Along with the rest of the business press, the *Wall Street Journal* strongly supported both military aid to France to avoid a "Western" defeat and diplomatic steps to prevent Southeast Asia from being taken over by China.[54] A Southeast Asia pact that would formalize this determination was favored by all sources. As France's defeat became imminent, *Barrons*, which, as we shall see, was the most hawkish, favored the pact as an instrument for the joint deployment of military power, and as a means by which Western powers could "match words with deeds."[55] For *Business Week* the pact was the only way, since the signing of the Geneva Agreement, to "save Southeast Asia" both from the evils of colonialism and from Soviet imperialism.[56] But the *Wall Street Journal* saw the diplomatic efforts as a way of *avoiding* military involvement. A show

[52]*Business Week*, March 5, 1966, p. 25.
[53]*Wall Street Journal*, February 25, 1966, p. 7.
[54]*Wall Street Journal*, February 16, 1954, p. 10.
[55]*Barrons*, June 2, 1954, p. 1.
[56]*Business Week*, May 2, 1954, p. 192; and September 18, 1954, p. 200.

of strength and unity would encourage the Chinese to be more amenable to settlement and would thus promote a stalemate that would prevent the communists from taking over Indochina.[57] "If the pact is formed, it will make the contingency of sending troops to fight in Indochina that much more unlikely."[58] The deterrent value was in the commitment itself rather than its physical manifestations; after all, had not the Monroe Doctrine worked for well over a century without the expenditure of men or money?[59]

Joint declarations and a Southeast Asian defense pact were enthusiastically endorsed by the business press as the only hope of an alternative between sending in United States troops and watching Southeast Asia fall to the communists. For *Business Week* this loss was intolerable: "If France capitulates," an editorial warned shortly before the Geneva Conference, "we must face the prospect, however disagreeable, of military action in Southeast Asia."[60] For the *Wall Street Journal*, however, it was one thing to acknowledge the importance of Indochina in the struggle against communist expansion in Asia and quite another to insist that it must be held regardless of the cost. If true collective action were assured, the United States might consider greater efforts. But Indochina was "certainly not worth the price the U.S. would have to pay if it had to fight all alone."[61] The Indochinese, already exhausted from battle, simply wanted independence from France and did not make clear distinctions between communists and noncommunists. We would have less support than we had in Korea from allies as well as from the people on whose behalf we would be fighting, and the battlefield would be more remote. Furthermore, the theory on the basis of which we fought in Korea—that confronting the aggressor with military force will deter future larger aggressions—had been neatly disproved by the Indochinese crisis itself. Worst of all, we, the strength of the Western world, would once again be depleting our resources by fighting communism while the Soviet Union, strength of the communist world, would be risking nothing. "In frank cynicism, why should not the Russians fight to the last Chinaman?"[62] With prescience that is almost painful to read, the *Wall Street Journal* cautioned that "Americans should

---

[57]*Wall Street Journal*, May 19, 1954, p. 12.
[58]*Wall Street Journal*, April 21, 1954, p. 10.
[59]*Wall Street Journal*, April 15, 1954, p. 8.
[60]*Business Week*, May 22, 1954, p. 192.
[61]*Wall Street Journal*, April 28, 1954, p. 8.
[62]*Wall Street Journal*, April 19, 1954, p. 14.

know that in Indochina they are traveling an obscure road strewn with political uncertainties and combed with military pitfalls" and that "the road through Indochina will be a long one for the U.S. also."[63] Repeatedly the *Journal* warned against drifting into deeper commitments without first making sober calculations of costs and gains. "The descent into another frustrating and paralyzing fringe war could be all too easy if we do not watch our going. We should constantly bear in mind how difficult is the return."[64] Expressing some uncertainty about the advisability of the United States' filling the vacuum left by France in Indochina, an editorial warned that "a vacuum has tremendous power of suction. It could pull us further than we want to go."[65] To insist that Indochina be kept out of hostile hands regardless of the cost might well lead the United States "step by step into the Indochina jungle so deep that we would become prisoners of our past commitments and lose all our freedom of action."[66] Furthermore, "no one can truly say what it might cost to get out of Indochina once we got in."[67]

In Korea the discrepancy between the two perspectives is even more apparent in the attitude toward both the initial involvement in and the pursuit of the war. No article in any of the four other business press sources expressed opposition to American military intervention in the Korean war in the period before January 1951 (i.e., six months after the commitment of United States troops), whereas only 29 percent of the *Wall Street Journal*'s preferences were favorable to such intervention. The risks and costs were discussed in the four journals with varying degrees of specificity, but none expressed any doubt that the risks must be taken and the costs borne. *Fortune* acknowledged that America faced in Korea a real possibility of defeat, of being forced to pay costs disproportionate to any gain, of being weakened by the struggle and thus rendered more vulnerable in any military confrontation with the Soviet Union. Yet, *Fortune* insisted, the United States must take

---

[63]*Ibid.*; and *Wall Street Journal*, October 26, 1950, p. 8.
[64]*Wall Street Journal*, March 3, 1954, p. 10.
[65]*Wall Street Journal*, May 3, 1955, p. 12.
[66]*Wall Street Journal*, March 3, 1954, p. 10.
[67]*Wall Street Journal*, April 28, 1954, p. 10. In view of this strong negative position assumed by the major business press source on the question of American military intervention in Indochina, it is interesting to note the results of a study of the general press. Susan Welch found that the *New York Times*, the *Washington Post*, and the *San Francisco Chronicle* expressed no opposition to the proposed intervention in 1954. See "The American Press and Indochina, 1950–56," in Richard L. Merritt, ed., *Communication in International Politics* (Urbana, Ill.: University of Illinois Press, 1972), pp. 207–231.

these risks to avoid ultimately worse risks—"the defeat of our friends and the isolation of America, outmanned, outgunned." That a dangerous course, the course of risk, can be the safest course of all was a fact that should be particularly well understood by businessmen.[68] This was the implicit view of the four journals, which merely assumed the necessity of defending Korea.

A logical implication of this view was that "maximum counterforce" must be applied. The four journals strongly disapproved of the limited-war strategy pursued by the administration and the limited goals toward which they perceived the strategy to be directed. Conciliatory steps taken by the enemy were perceived as insincere propaganda moves, whereas those of the United States risked appeasement. The bombing of Manchuria and the reactivation of the Chinese civil war (or at least support of Chiang's raids on the mainland) were regarded as potentially necessary responses to communist truce-breaking and offensive build-up.[69] Barrons was most hawkish, advocating in addition the possible use of atomic weapons.

The skeptical, pessimistic editorials of the Wall Street Journal are in sharp contrast to those of the four journals. There was general agreement between the two perspectives that Soviet aspirations underlay the Korean conflict; all agreed that a firm stand must be taken against communist aggression. But the Wall Street Journal could not refrain from asking, "Must it be in Korea?" Considerable space was devoted to lamenting the haste with which the decision to intervene had been taken. The war was "an uncalculated risk, a war of inspiration."[70] "The shocking nature of Red aggression overrode all our reasoning."[71] More careful calculations should have been made to determine just "how much blood and tears is Korea worth? . . . Do we make a token effort or do we go all out for this remote peninsula?"[72] Furthermore, the war was portrayed throughout as an unwinnable one. We had taken a stand in the wrong place under circumstances that put us at a grave disadvantage, having forgotten the old adage, "Never wave your fists at a man when you are standing downhill with the sun in your eyes."[73]

[68]Fortune, August, 1950, pp. 53–57.
[69]Fortune, August 1951, p. 63; Barrons, November 11, 1950, p. 1; November 3, 1952; p. 1; February 9, 1953, p. 3; Business Week, April 14, 1951, p. 113.
[70]Wall Street Journal, November 19, 1950, p. 8.
[71]Wall Street Journal, December 8, 1950, p. 6.
[72]Wall Street Journal, June 30, 1950, p. 4.
[73]Wall Street Journal, December 4, 1950, p. 7.

The conviction pervading the editorial pages of the *Wall Street Journal* that the war was probably a mistake strongly affected the recommendations that newspaper made for the pursuit of the war. There was consistent opposition to steps that seriously risked extending the war in any way. One article opposed the idea of bombing Manchuria because "It is doubtful Korea is worth the lives we have already sacrificed on it. It is certainly not worth a world war if it can be avoided."[74] War aims that settled for nothing less than "total victory" were strongly rejected. Efforts to achieve total victory in World War II had led to the destruction of Japan as a power in Asia, thus creating the vacuum the communists were now seeking to fill.[75] The most to be hoped for was limited holding action until the Chinese showed a disposition to discuss a reasonable peace settlement.[76] Hence the urgency of a political settlement and the necessity for making concessions in order to achieve it. Once the North Koreans had been driven out of South Korea, the United States could evacuate without actually giving anything to the aggressor or sacrificing the victim.[77] In the days of allied retreat in the winter of 1950–1951, the *Journal* made frequent suggestions that to "cut our losses" by withdrawal might be the "least worst alternative."[78] But these were merely suggestions that evacuation was not an inconceivable alternative. With all the pessimism regarding the correctness of the involvement and its probable outcome, the *Journal* could not really advocate throwing in the towel. A pattern of ambivalence prevailed that would reappear in its editorial columns fifteen years later in response to another Asian war. This ambivalence was succinctly summarized in an editorial response to Truman's first steps at the outset of the war. "Are we willing to expend the wealth of lives and material that may be necessary to win a prize of uncertain value?" the editorial asked rhetorically. "But having committed ourselves this far, can we afford to quit?"[79]

[74]*Wall Street Journal*, September 12, 1951, p. 4.

[75]W. H. Chamberlain, well known for his revisionist views on World War II, was a regular contributor to the *Wall Street Journal*'s editorial page during this period. His views are typified by the title given to one of his articles explaining why we were fighting the communists in Korea: "They're There Because We Fought Japan," *Wall Street Journal*, November 17, 1950, p. 4.

[76]*Wall Street Journal*, April 13, 1951, p. 4.

[77]*Wall Street Journal*, December 1, 1950, p. 6; and August 21, 1951, p. 7.

[78]*Wall Street Journal*, December 1, 1950, p. 6; and December 12, 1950, p. 10.

[79]*Wall Street Journal*, June 3, 1950, p. 4.

This commitment imperative became the dominant concern of the *Wall Street Journal* during the Vietnam war. Again the crucial question was what to do about a commitment that may well have been a mistake in the first place. In Korea, the commitment had been made in too much haste; in Vietnam, it had been made incrementally, almost absent-mindedly. In neither case were the proper reasoned calculations made, defining objectives and assessing the costs necessary to achieve them. For ten years during the Vietnam war, the *Wall Street Journal* editorials emphasized the necessity for more thought and debate, more calculation of risks among the American public as well as in decision-making circles. Again it is this emphasis on the cost that distinguishes the *Wall Street Journal* response from that of the other four sources. The key may be found in a *Journal* editorial written in the earlier stages of American involvement: It would be worth the effort to deter further communist expansion in Asia "if it can be done quickly . . . if it is indeed feasible for the U.S. to win the Vietnam war reasonably soon without excessive loss of life and treasure."[80] From time to time the *Wall Street Journal* indicated that Vietnam might not be such a bad place to challenge the communists. In the autumn of 1961 it at least appeared to be a better place to make the stand than Laos. The South Vietnamese government seemed to have a strongly pro-American government interested in saving the nation from conquest, soldiers able and willing to fight, and a terrain that was a little kinder.[81] But this view was short-lived. The disadvantageous circumstances of an involvement in Indochina, which the *Wall Street Journal* had perceived in the early 1950s, became increasingly apparent again from the beginning of 1963. At this point the pattern of ambivalence that was evident in the *Journal*'s Korean editorials reasserted itself and persisted for the duration of the war. There was the fear that withdrawal would almost certainly mean a takeover by the communists.[82] Yet there was growing concern that certain facts of geography, as well as insufficient support from allies and the indigenous population, would make the cost of a full-scale commitment unacceptable. "The U.S. does have to stand firm against Red imperialism. But whether the stand is taken at Thailand, Malaysia or the Philippines or Australia should be determined by the cold considerations of a given nation's will to

[80]*Wall Street Journal*, October 21, 1961, p. 12.
[81]*Wall Street Journal*, October 12, 1961, p. 12.
[82]*Wall Street Journal*, June 2, 1964, p. 18.

fight, terrain, logistics, and all the normal military bases for judgment. We must not look to South Vietnam as the be all and end all of our Southeast Asian problems."[83] "In the long global conflict with communism we cannot expect to win every victory and never give up ground at all. Military strategy itself dictates withdrawal to a firmer position when a particular position becomes untenable."[84] Failure to understand this recommendation would involve us in so many enervating fringe wars that we would be ill prepared to fight the big confrontation with the real enemy, should the necessity arise.

But in the spring of 1965 the mood of the *Journal* changed. There was more sympathy and support for the "tougher line" and more emphasis on the necessity to curb the aggressor's appetite, as well as the recognition of the absence of an alternative to prosecution of the war.[85] When the issue of negotiations arose, a series of warnings was given against conceding too much and handing over Southeast Asia at the conference table.[86] The position of the *Wall Street Journal* may, ironically, have been hardened by the arguments and actions of the antiwar movement. The shift is first apparent in an article entitled "Hysteria over Vietnam," which deplored at great length those "ministers, professors, etc." who were demanding instant withdrawal and insisting that United States intervention was immoral.[87] The Dominican crisis served to strengthen this mood; it reminded and pointedly demonstrated to the *Wall Street Journal* that the Soviets were fomenting "wars of liberation" from Saigon to Santo Domingo—in Asia, Africa, and Latin America.[88] This was the only period during the entire war—approximately March 1965 to June 1966—in which a "larger war and greater sacrifice" were recommended. The response to American escalatory moves to bomb oil depots near Hanoi was positive. The editorial that appeared immediately after this action was devoted primarily to a vivid description of this "dubious enterprise," the Vietnam war. Stepping up the war seemed the only way to get out.[89]

There were no subsequent favorable responses to escalation, and by the middle of 1967 de-escalatory moves were strongly ad-

---

[83]*Wall Street Journal*, January 19, 1965, p. 16.
[84]*Wall Street Journal*, February 24, 1965, p. 18.
[85]*Wall Street Journal*, April 29, 1965, p. 11; June 17, 1965, p. 12; December 21, 1965, p. 12.
[86]*Wall Street Journal*, February 14, 1966, p. 12.
[87]*Wall Street Journal*, April 7, 1965, p. 18.
[88]*Wall Street Journal*, May 3, 1965, p. 14.
[89]*Wall Street Journal*, June 3, 1966, p. 10.

vocated. Even during the "hard-line" year the continued prosecution of the war, which was considered the only possible alternative,
was made conditional on the cost not becoming "exorbitant." Precisely because the communist threat to the United States was so
great was it important "not to get trapped in a side war in a distant
jungle" that would usurp all American strength. The problem was
one of proportion, the *Journal* repeatedly said. We should continue
to pursue the war unless "it constitutes an effort disproportionate
both to our military resources and to any conceivable gains from
the war."[90]

A *Journal* editorial of February 1966 set the tone for the duration of the war. It was entitled "The Question Remains," and the
question was none other than "Is Vietnam Worth It?" But, the
editorial concluded, the question was purely academic, "since we
are there and cannot now pull out without serious consequences."[91]
Thenceforth the editors vacillated between despair over the futility
of the war and outrage with those who were oblivious to the disastrous consequences that would proceed from a precipitate withdrawal. The despair was poignantly expressed in a May 2, 1967,
editorial calling for a bomb halt: "It is time to recognize that Vietnam has become a sickness without a cure." There were no solutions; the United States would have to search for the "least among
evils where every course inevitably means further anguish."[92]

By April 1968 the *Wall Street Journal* was inclined to believe
that the "risks of undermining our position in Asia may be out-
weighed by the risks of continuing the war—the blood, treasure,
and strain on our social fabric."[93] Furthermore, a major aim of the
war—to show the communists that aggression did not pay—had
already been lost.[94] Even so, the war must end in "a thoughtful
way." President Nixon's Vietnamization policy and the gradual
winding down of the war were enthusiastically endorsed. Every
possible effort must be made to enable South Vietnam to defend
itself before the American forces withdrew completely.[95]

The *Wall Street Journal*, as we have seen, believed from the
early 1950s that communism could not be challenged everywhere
at all times. The United States must reserve some freedom of

---

[90]*Wall Street Journal*, December 21, 1965, p. 12; and February 14, 1966,
p. 14.
   [91]*Wall Street Journal*, February 25, 1966, p. 16.
   [92]*Wall Street Journal*, May 2, 1967, p. 18.
   [93]*Wall Street Journal*, April 4, 1968, p. 12.
   [94]*Wall Street Journal*, February 15, 1968, p. 16.
   [95]*Wall Street Journal*, October 15, 1969, p. 22; and November 5, 1969, p. 22.

choice. If the cost of taking a stand in a given place were likely to be too high, American strength might be diminished, and that would constitute a greater threat to American security than the particular aggression that was challenged.

The other four sources, particularly *Business Week*, viewed the confrontation with communism in more absolute and rigid terms and showed less concern for the cost of the effort. Its view that "U.S. security is diminished by any expansion of the Soviet bloc"[96] is quite different from the overall view of the *Wall Street Journal*, which frequently maintained that the United States could tolerate some losses to communism. Before the Tonkin Gulf incident, *Business Week* declared that "there is no escape from this dirty war in Southeast Asia."[97] The domino imagery is far more prevalent in the journals than it is in the *Wall Street Journal*. If the United States did not challenge communist aggression in South Vietnam, "one shaky nation after another would tumble into the hands of the communists."[98] At least until 1967 *Business Week* did not consider that the war might be a mistake, and certainly evidenced little of the *Wall Street Journal*'s skepticism about the war's possible disastrous consequences.

There was not enough regular coverage in the four journals to permit comparison with the *Wall Street Journal*, but it is at least clear that a basic shift of thinking had taken place in *Business Week* before August of 1967, when an editorial with the headline "We Need a New Strategy in Vietnam" announced that "more blood and money will still probably not turn the tide of battle." A policy of limited military commitment, defending only those areas that were defendable, was recommended. This shift in strategy would cost less and would "bring into better balance the ends we wish to achieve and the cost of achieving them."[99] From this point on, the cost factor, so crucial to the *Wall Street Journal*'s approach to the question of intervention, became the central issue for *Business Week*. Toward the end of 1968 a *Business Week* editorial stated: "After the frustrations of Vietnam, future presidents will

---

[96]*Business Week*, March 5, 1966, p. 56.
[97]*Business Week*, May 23, 1964, p. 180; and August 15, 1964, p. 148.
[98]*Business Week*, August 2, 1964, p. 128.
[99]*Business Week*, August 12, 1967, p. 132. A member of *Fortune*'s board of editors also proposed a reassessment of Vietnam policy and "An Alternative Strategy" in an article by that title. This strategy, which emphasized the defensive and pacification aspects of the war, involved redeployment of American troops, clearly a retreat in some areas. The shift was a response to the Tet offensive. *Fortune*, April 1968, pp. 96–99, 196–204.

certainly weigh even more cautiously the time, place, and justification of any U.S. decision to intervene abroad."[100] There were no longer two different perspectives.

We have presented this overview to provide some indication of the kinds of situations in which the business press has been most likely to favor American intervention, as well as some conditions that seemed to limit this approval. Whether the contemplated action was intended to displace an unfriendly government or to stabilize a friendly incumbent certainly affected the direction of preference, as well as the types of intervention discussed by the business press. The business press also was unlikely to favor overt military intervention in the absence of an organized internal conflict in the target state or a perceived threat of outside intervention from a major power. Hence this kind of action was generally dismissed as an unfeasible method for removing Arbenz and, initially, Castro; relatively more attention was given to nonmilitary forms of intervention in the Cuban and Guatemalan cases than in most of the others. When the stabilization of a friendly government threatened by insurgents was the issue, and a clear threat of major power intervention was perceived, we found that the views of the *Wall Street Journal* diverged sharply from those of the other four sources. This cleavage appears to be based largely on the *Journal*'s more cautious, risk-avoiding, cost-conscious approach to foreign policy questions, as well as on the reservations the newspaper apparently held regarding the basic premises of containment. Although close reading of the business press in the later stages of the Vietnam war suggests that the rest of the business press may now view the prospects of future overt military intervention with more of the caution that was advocated for twenty-five years by the *Wall Street Journal*, it is nevertheless possible that the force of the reasons and pressures that underlay the earlier pro-interventionist views may be no less strong in the future than it was in the past. Hence we turn now to an examination of the reasons that were the basis for the preferences we have analyzed.

---

[100]*Business Week*, November 9, 1968.

CHAPTER SEVEN

Reasons
for
Intervening

When a man hath no freedom to fight for at home,
Let him combat for that of his neighbors;
Let him think of the glories of Greece and of Rome,
And get knock'd on the head for his labours.

Lord Byron, Don Juan

The Relative Salience of Different Reasons

The results of the content analysis thus far are consistent with the evidence obtained by the other two methods. Although evidence from Chapters 3 and 4 indicated that many businessmen held non-interventionist, if not isolationist, foreign policy views and suggested that a genuine shift in this direction may have occurred among businessmen in the late 1960s, it was clear that these changes were part of a more general shift in elite opinion away from a preoccupation with cold war concerns. Despite the dovishness of these views, businessmen nevertheless were found to be more hawkish than any other elite group except Republican party leaders and military officers. In Chapter 5, we concluded from our analysis of the stock market responses to escalation and de-escalation of the Vietnam war that after 1967, investors tended to anticipate that continuation of the war would have negative economic consequences. But the response of the market in the earlier stages of the war yielded no clear pattern. In our analysis of the business and military press we found a strong, persistent, isolationist strain in the editorials of the most widely read business press source throughout the post-World War II period. But in all five of our business press sources as a whole, intervention, especially in its military form, was favored more often than it was opposed in most of the nine crises we examined. Nevertheless, on the basis of the weight we accorded to the various business press sources, we found them to be *more* likely to oppose military intervention than were the military press sources.

The sharp divergence of views in the business press on the question of military intervention suggests that economic interests—to the extent that they do affect foreign policy choice—may exert contradictory influences. The absence of a systematic response of stock price changes to the escalation or de-escalation of the war before 1967 might also be attributable to just such a canceling-out effect. It is thus appropriate to focus again on the relative importance of different kinds of motivations, this time using non-reactive content analysis data to check the results of the survey. As in Chapter 4, we attempt here to assess the relative impact of each of the major types of motivation. On the basis of economic interest theories, we would expect to find economic motivations more closely associated with foreign policy preferences in the business press than are strategic or ideological rationales (hypothesis 4.2). We should also expect to find economic motivations to be more closely associated with policy preferences in the business press than in the military press (hypothesis 4.1). According to the view that economic interests promote expansion and conflict, we would of course expect to see economic motivations especially prominent in articles and editorials that advocate or support intervention; from perspectives that see economic motivations as basically a force for peace, we should expect those motivations to be especially salient in statements opposing intervention.

The determination of rationales is more complex than the identification of preference. The primary task was to assess the importance of economic considerations relative to other considerations. Although motivation is never easy to determine, the fact has been recognized throughout this study that economic motivations are even more elusive than most. Any content analysis coding procedure that relies on explicit statements of motivation will quite probably underestimate the importance of economic interest, which tends to be cloaked in broader, more altruistic terms. This concealment may be deliberate or unconscious, the effect of reticence to disclose economic interests or unawareness of their influence on policy choice. To attempt to meet these objections and to give every possible opportunity for economic interest to be illuminated, our coding scheme specified that *any mention* of economic interest in the entire article was sufficient to establish an economic motivation. (By contrast, the coding rules specified that the presence of other motivations could be established only if explicitly stated in the article as a rationale.) Economic rationale was defined as any reference to: American investments, trade, raw-material sources; the economy or economic interests of any ally; the defense of free enterprise or private property generally.

Strategic and ideological rationales, although broadly distinguishable from each other, become hard to distinguish in particular instances. Reasons stressing the national interest, power, security, commitments, and image of the United States, as well as international stability and peace, are clearly strategic; concern with the spread of communist ideology and threats to freedom and democracy are ideological. However, the strategic rationale that intervention is required to discourage the expansionist aspirations of an aggressive power assumes a more ideological cast when infused with anticommunist rhetoric. In view of this overlapping area, key words and phrases were identified to delineate strategic and ideological rationales.

Ideological symbols were selected to indicate the largely negative concern for *halting* the spread of ideology that threatened the values, beliefs, and ideals of the United States and/or Western civilization, as well as the more positive interest in *promoting* them. The following seemed an appropriate and reasonably defensible set of ideological key symbols: communism; Bolshevism; Marxism; communist movement, ideology, creed, or system of ideas; world revolution; wars of liberation; Red tide; Red banner; tyranny; barbarism; totalitarianism; democracy; freedom; free world; liberty; popular sovereignty; self-determination.

Words and phrases (and their variations) indicating a strategic concern included the following: power, balance of power (referring to United States hegemony), prestige, image, credibility, public opinion, commitment, responsibility, national interest, balance of power (meaning equilibrium, stability, order), peace, aggression, expansion, conquest, Russia, imperialism.

Note that although the noun "communism" is on the ideological list, the adjective "communist" is not, except in conjunction with words like "movement" and "ideology." The choice between "communist" and "Russian" would have been a convenient but not very reliable indicator of ideological and strategic categories, respectively. Because the pre-tests clearly confirmed a close association between the use of "Russian" and other strategic key words, it was added to that list. However, the use of "communist" was not so reliably associated with ideological symbols; the choice often appeared to be based on little more than the need to vary the language. Hence "communist" was specified not as a key word but as an indicator of general tone. Because of this ambiguity in the word "communist," a three-point scale was specified for the ideological categories to indicate the definite presence (2), possible presence (1), or absence (0) of ideological motivation.

A rationale was coded as either ideological or strategic if one or more key words in that category were identified in the article. If key words from both categories were found, both were coded. A predominant rationale was to be indicated wherever possible. Explicit statements about the nature of the main or real issue (e.g., "what is at stake is a battle against world communism, not a contest for world power") were taken literally. When such statements did not occur, the predominant rationale had to be ascertained by the general thrust and tone of the article and its emphasis on one set of key symbols or the other.

Using these categories and the 1–5 preference scales from the data sources described in Chapter 6, we obtained the following overall results. Table 7.1 shows the percentage distribution of various reasons for and against military intervention in both the business and military press during the entire period and distinguishes between those articles or editorials that basically favored military intervention and those that generally opposed it. Note that in this table, as well as in all subsequent tables giving frequency distributions, N refers to the number of different expressions of reasons, not the (somewhat smaller) number of articles or editorials; more than one reason was often discernible. The count of ideological reasons includes "possibles."

The results are clear-cut. Economic reasons are the *least*, not the most, commonly expressed reasons given in support of pro-interventionist policies. Strategic reasons are by far the most common. Ideological anticommunism is second in importance and economic reasons are a distant third. This pattern is virtually identical in the military and the business press. If both the business and military press supported intervention—as they usually did—the expressed reasons were rarely economic, and this was equally true for both.

Table 7.1 *Percentage of Reasons Given for and against Military Intervention in Business Press and Military Press*

	In Cases Where Military Intervention Was *Favored*			
	Reasons			
Press	Ideological	Strategic	Economic	N =
Business	31	61	8	194
Military	36	58	6	111

	In Cases Where Military Intervention Was *Opposed*					
	Reasons					
Press	Ideo-logical	Stra-tegic	Eco-nomic	Nation-alism	No Reason	N =
Business	2	66	13	11	6	102
Military	16	56	16	12	0	25

We notice nothing significantly different when we look at the reasons given for opposing military intervention. Strategic reasons (arguments urging caution, warning of the risks and relatively minor benefits to be gained) are more prominent than they were in the arguments for intervention. Ideological arguments were given only rarely in these editorials, perhaps because ideological anti-communism, the manifestation of ideology really tapped here, does not lend itself so readily to the cool calculation of costs and benefits. Economic arguments also appear rarely, about as often as those that argue against intervention because it violates the principles of national self-determination. Opposition to intervention on the ground that there was no reason to justify such action—that American security or national interest were not at stake—also occurs infrequently. This rationale was never mentioned in the military press. Otherwise, the number of military journals is too small for the slight differences between the business and military press to be in any way statistically significant. Thus in both parts of the table the economic interest hypotheses are rejected—from the point of view that sees economic interests as peace-promoting no less than from the perspective that sees them as a force leading to aggression and war.

The same basic results emerge from a different and more complex method of statistical analysis. Using a method analogous to that employed in Chapter 4, we ran stepwise multiple regression analyses using the frequency of each rationale (strategic, ideological, economic) as independent variables and the preference scale for military intervention as the dependent variable. Three control variables were added to the equation. The first designated the target of the possible or actual intervention as communist, communist "tool," nationalist, or pro-Western, measuring this crudely (but not, we think, with great distortion) as a simple interval scale. The second distinguished, on a simple three-point scale, among different interpretations of the "crisis" as an external attack, an internal revolt substantially aided from the outside, and an essentially internally generated revolt. We also controlled for the year in which the editorial or article appeared. The regressions were run separately on the business and military samples, and the results appear in Table 7.2. The presentation is basically the same as that used in Chapter 4 for regression equations; we shall look primarily at the relative strength of the F ratios, though the regression coefficients (b weights) and standard errors (S.E.) of each of the coefficients are given for readers who wish to examine them. The F ratios that suggest a contribution for the variable that is statistically significant at not less than the .01 level are indicated by an asterisk. As with all our other references to statistical significance in this book, by some criteria this test is not strictly applicable, given the nature of our "sample" of editorials and journals. It is merely a rough guide, for those who wish to use it, of the relative importance of certain variables.

The basic conclusions suggested by these analyses are not very different from those that emerged from the simpler use of frequency distributions. Again it is very clear that economic reasons are not notably associated—either positively or negatively—with military intervention preferences in the business press; their contributions to the equations are miniscule. The same is true of the military journals except that the economic arguments against intervention do carry some weight. The "sample" is so small, however, that the frequency distribution of Table 7.1 is a sounder guide than are the F ratios for this equation. Essentially the information in this table confirms the results shown in Table 7.1, with the qualification— suggested by our findings in Chapter 6—that perception of the target for intervention (communists, neutralists) does affect determination of whether military intervention is favored, and if so,

Table 7.2 *Contributions of Various Reasons to Military Intervention Preference: Business Press and Military Press*

	Business			Military		
	b	S.E.	F	b	S.E.	F
Arguments *Favoring* Intervention						
Reasons						
Ideological	.60	.10	33.86*	.45	.13	11.32*
Strategic	1.46	.17	76.89*	1.40	.27	27.41*
Economic	−.22	.28	.60	−.08	.41	.04
Controls						
Target	−.55	.12	20.02*	−.02	.15	.01
Crisis	.07	.09	.71	−.06	.15	.14
Year	.01	.01	.50	.02	.02	.62
		$r^2 = .50$			$r^2 = .34$	
Arguments *Opposing* Intervention						
Reasons						
Ideological	−.81	.38	4.45	.78	.26	9.05*
Strategic	2.06	.13	248.04*	2.49	.16	258.56
Economic	.05	.24	.05	2.51	.33	57.75*
National interest	.98	.26	14.28*	2.15	.31	49.05*
None	2.39	.39	38.22*	—	—	—
Controls						
Target	.44	.11	16.90*	.07	.08	.98
Crisis	−.14	.07	4.07	.03	.08	.16
Year	−.00	.01	.04	.01	.01	.30
		$r^2 = .70$			$r^2 = .83$	

*Significance levels at .01 or under.

how fervently. This certainly should not be surprising. The fact that preferences do not vary systematically over the years or according to the perceived type of crisis (external attack, internal revolt) is also in agreement with the detailed case-by-case analysis of the preceding chapter.

Since type of target did seem to be an important control variable, we ran separate regression equations for those cases in which the target was perceived as communist or a communist "tool" on the one hand, and neutralist or pro-Western on the other. These results appear in Table 7.3. Military arguments against intervention are too few to be analyzed with any degree of reliability, so

Table 7.3 Military Intervention Preference, Controlled by Perceived Target: Business Press and Military Press

Arguments Favoring Intervention

	Business			Military		
	b	S.E.	F	b	S.E.	F
Target Communist						
Reasons						
Ideological	.61	.11	31.66*	.46	.15	9.39*
Strategic	1.42	.19	58.38*	1.25	.30	16.90*
Economic	-.21	.31	.45	-.22	.45	.22
Controls						
Crisis	.12	.10	1.53	-.20	.17	1.39
Year	.01	.02	.54	.02	.02	.43
	$r^2 = .37$			$r^2 = .32$		
Target Noncommunist						
Reasons						
Ideological	—	—	—	.38	.44	.77
Strategic	2.00	.30	43.03*	1.91	.71	7.31*
Economic	-2.23	.65	11.70*	.78	1.25	.38
Controls						
Crisis	.37	.12	9.29*	.36	.74	.23
Year	.06	.04	2.31	.03	.08	.15
	$r^2 = .84$			$r^2 = .52$		

Arguments Opposing Intervention

	Business			Military		
	b	S.E.	F	b	S.E.	F
Target Communist						
Reasons						
Ideological	.89	.42	4.60	—	—	—
Strategic	2.07	.14	229.26*	—	—	—
Economic	.01	.25	.00	—	—	—
Nationalism	1.25	.31	16.19*	—	—	—
No reason	—	—	—	—	—	—
Controls						
Crisis	-.15	.08	4.03	—	—	—
Year	-.01	.01	.21	—	—	—
	$r^2 = .64$					
Target Noncommunist						
Reasons						
Ideological	-.33	1.67	.04	—	—	—
Strategic	1.42	.61	5.39	—	—	—
Economic	—	—	—	—	—	—
Nationalism	.42	.85	.25	—	—	—
No reason	1.60	.61	6.96	—	—	—
Controls						
Crisis	.02	.22	.01	—	—	—
Year	.10	.10	.85	—	—	—
	$r^2 = .57$					

*Significance levels at .01 or under.

Table 7.4 *Percentage of Reasons Given for and against Military Intervention, Controlled by Press Source*

	Arguments *Favoring* Military Intervention			
	Reasons			
Press Source	Ideological	Strategic	Economic	N =
Wall Street Journal	28	66	6	108
Other press sources	31	56	13	147

	Arguments *Opposing* Military Intervention					
	Reasons					
Press Source	Ideo-logical	Stra-tegic	Eco-nomic	Nation-alism	No Reason	N =
Wall Street Journal	3	70	8	12	7	97
Other press sources	5	61	18	14	2	44

the military columns in the second part of the table are blank. As can easily be seen, the findings shown in Tables 7.1 and 7.2 do not change in any notable way. Economic motivations remain of no importance except as they affect *opposition* to military intervention against regimes perceived as noncommunist. Hence, even though there were economic interests that might have been protected by military intervention, it is apparent, when the target was non-communist, that these interests alone were insufficient to warrant such action. This interpretation is tenuous, however, because the number of editorials analyzed is small (only 16); they concerned primarily Lebanon and secondarily Cuba and Indochina, in which the target was perceived as nationalist. We also find that ideological motivations fade to insignificance when the target is perceived as noncommunist.

In light of the results in Chapter 6 showing the policy orientation of the *Wall Street Journal* to be markedly different from that of the other business press sources, it is important also to establish a control for press source. Thus Table 7.4 lists simple frequency distributions, which are more directly interpretable than regression results. As can readily be seen, the patterns for the *Wall Street Journal* and the other press sources in this table are almost identi-

Table 7.5 *Percentage of Reasons Given for Military Intervention in Business Press, Controlled by Case*

Case	Reasons			N =
	Ideological	Strategic	Economic	
Korea	38	55	7	29
Indochina	15	78	7	41
Cuba	35	56	9	75
Vietnam	26	74	0	27

cal. Economic motivations are mentioned *slightly* less often in this Manhattan newspaper than in the other press sources, but in samples of this size the differences are insignificant. This means, then, that any reservations the reader might have had about the relative weighting of the *Wall Street Journal* and the other business press sources in Chapter 6 are not applicable here. The basic finding that articulated economic motivations are unimportant is entirely independent of the relative contribution of *Wall Street Journal* materials (i.e., editorials and articles) to the total set of materials analyzed. Table 7.5 shows the effect of introducing one other control variable; it also shows the separate frequencies for each of the four cases for which many comments were expressed. Once again the results are insensitive to the control; expressed economic interests are unimportant in all four cases; and reasons of strategic interest are by far the most prominent. No particular time trend or other pattern for distinguishing cases is apparent.

Summarizing our conclusions regarding military intervention as they relate to our basic hypotheses, we find *no* support for hypothesis 4.2, which predicted that articulated economic motivations and interests would be more closely associated with the foreign policy preferences expressed by businessmen than would ideological or strategic motivations. This is true despite the introduction of various controls, and irrespective of whether the preferences are for or against military intervention. All this holds despite our effort, when in doubt, to code economic motivations as being present in a text rather than absent from it. Nor is there any support for hypothesis 4.1, which predicted that economic motivations and interests would be more closely associated with the foreign policy preferences expressed by businessmen than with the preferences expressed by other elites, at least here when the business press is

Table 7.6 *Percentage of Reasons Given for and against Nonmilitary Intervention: Business Press and Military Press*

Type of Intervention	Reasons *Favoring* Intervention			
	Ideological	Strategic	Economic	N =
Economic				
Business	26	48	26	23
Military	33	66	0	3
Diplomatic				
Business	25	64	12	69
Military	32	60	8	25
Unspecified				
Business	25	55	20	20
Military	20	60	20	5

Type of Intervention	Reasons *Opposing* Intervention (Business Press Only)					
	Ideo-logical	Stra-tegic	Eco-nomic	Nation-alism	No Reason	N =
Economic	0	55	27	18	0	11
Diplomatic	3	66	9	17	6	35
Unspecified	0	50	0	50	0	8

compared with the military press. For both groups the strategic rationale was the most important basis for favoring intervention, ideological reasons were also significant, and economic motivations were expressed about equally rarely.

When we shift our focus to nonmilitary forms of intervention the picture looks only a little different. Table 7.6 shows the reasons given for and against economic, diplomatic, and unspecified forms of intervention. There are too few discussions in either sample to justify introduction of control variables. The military journals seldom discuss these forms of intervention, and expressions of opposition are too few to merit including them in the table.

Table 7.6 shows economic motivations as being expressed in the business press with slightly greater relative frequency than does Table 7.1, but not much importance can or should be attributed to this difference, given the small number of cases. For statements favoring diplomatic intervention the results shown in the two tables are in no way significantly different. Of the three favored types of intervention shown in Table 7.6, diplomatic is by far the most often discussed. Strategic motivations remain the most prominent, followed by ideological motivations; and then, last at some distance, come economic reasons. These statements are about equally true for both the business press and the military press. Economic motivations are tied with ideological motivations when economic and unspecified interventions are advocated, but given the small samples, this finding has no significance, and economic motivations still remain far behind strategic reasons in prominence. Strategic reasons also remain far ahead when reasons for opposing intervention are at issue in the business press. Again our data lead us to reject hypotheses 4.1 and 4.2, and give us no ground for thinking that articulated economic motivations systematically push businessmen toward either interventionist or noninterventionist foreign policies.

Summarizing the response of the business press to nine specific cases of postwar intervention, we note the following patterns. Economic concerns are rarely articulated. Ideological justifications are frequently given, but strategic considerations are overwhelmingly the most important basis for favoring or opposing all forms of intervention. In the remainder of this chapter, we offer a few speculative explanations for this particular configuration of preferences and provide some evidence to support our reasoning from the materials surveyed. Our discussion focuses on two central questions that emerge from these results: Why were economic reasons so seldom articulated in discussions of American military intervention in the business press? Why were strategic considerations so much more prominent than ideological concerns, particularly in the light of the survey responses discussed in Chapter 4, indicating that ideological influences were far more important than geopolitical perspectives in explaining foreign policy preferences?

Economic Interests

As indicated in the explanation of the coding procedure, we recognized at the outset of the analysis that economic motivations are elusive. Nevertheless, because the coding rules gave the benefit of the doubt to the existence of these motivations and particularly because the press discussions were addressed primarily to a *business* audience, we had expected this rationale to be more apparent than it proved to be. We suggest two explanations for these re-sults. It may be that economic motivations were indeed less im-portant than other considerations, and if they were, then the re-sults should simply be taken at face value. Alternatively, there is the possibility that economic interests, despite their inconspicu-ousness, were critically important, and predisposed the writers toward the strategic and ideological arguments they presented. According to this interpretation, businessmen may become aware of and attuned to strategic and ideological reasons for intervention merely because they have certain economic interests. In addition to pointing out the obvious difficulties in establishing such a linkage, we must reiterate that the primary purpose of the content analysis was to indicate articulated reasons rather than latent or sub-conscious motivations. A brief look at the materials from which the data emerged may shed some light on this issue. Because economic motivations were so rarely stated, it is possible to examine most of the specific situations in which economic interests were expressed and to see how these interests were related to preferences, and also to analyze the other considerations that appeared to be revelant.

Nowhere are economic interests revealed more explicitly or blatantly than in the discussions concerning American military assistance to Greece and Turkey, a program overwhelmingly favored in the business press. Making no secret of the enthusiasm with which some businessmen greeted the action, a large headline in *Business Week* proclaimed, "New Diplomacy, New Business," and in prose befitting the most radical of journals described the impli-cations for American capitalism of the Greek-Turkish loan and the "new world policy of checking Russian expansion."[1] The article speculated that "Private enterprise would hardly run the risk of setting up shop in Greece today. But as soon as the U.S. govern-ment assumes the responsibility for establishing and maintaining order in a region, private business will inevitably follow—first to serve the military and civilian personnel that will administer con-tinuing U.S. loans; later as order is restored to find new markets among the local population. . . . In every country in which American technicians are stationed, industrialization is likely to take an American pattern." Allusions were also made here and elsewhere to the necessity of preventing Soviet encroachment in the Middle East, the "gateway to the world's richest oil fields."[2] Other articles

---

[1]*Business Week*, March 22, 1947, pp. 15–17.
[2]*Ibid.;* and *Wall Street Journal*, March 17, 1947, p. 8.

simply noted that stabilization of the Mediterranean would improve the investment climate for American business.[3] These strongly articulated expressions of economic interest, in conjunction with the fact that the military aid program was overwhelmingly favored by the business press, certainly suggest a linkage between economic interest and preference in this case. On the other hand, we must point out that expressions of concern for the cost of such a program and recognition of the implications for the American economy occurred with the same frequency as the enthusiastic statements regarding investment opportunities.[4] Although the number of opinions expressed on this case in the business press was small (hence not separately noted in Table 7.5), economic reasons did not always point toward intervention.

Economic interests in Indochina—insofar as they were articulated—were of a different nature, involving the balancing of negative utilities only. They were also much more closely linked with strategic concerns. If the area that included "some of the richest natural resources in the world" and was "the great rice bowl of Asia" should fall into communist hands, "it would immeasurably strengthen the Red war potential" and it would be a "major disaster for American prestige and interests in [that] area."[5] But these concerns were expressed only by the *Wall Street Journal*, which, as we illustrated in the preceding chapter, opposed military intervention in Indochina, on the basis of cost-risk/gain calculations.

The economic stakes in the case of Lebanon may simply have been so obvious to all that there was no need to point them out. There was occasional mention of Arab nationalism and Soviet imperialism combining to "destroy strategic and economic interests that are vital to Western strength."[6] But the fact that the issues were articulated almost exclusively in terms of a power struggle against Soviet expansion is notable. One article even saw control over Middle Eastern oil as the means by which the Soviet Union might take over Europe: "What the Reds are really after is a death grip on Europe by gaining full control over oil going there."[7]

---

[3]*Business Week*, April 26, 1947, p. 117; and *Wall Street Journal*, March 13, 1947, p. 4.

[4]See *Barrons*, April 21, 1947, p. 1; *Wall Street Journal*, March 13, 1947, p. 4; and March 20, 1947, p. 4.

[5]*Wall Street Journal*, January 21, 1952, p. 6; and April 19, 1954, p. 14.

[6]*Business Week*, August 16, 1958, p. 120; and July 19, 1958, pp. 23–25.

[7]*Kiplinger Washington Letter*, July 26, 1958, p. 2.

In absolute numbers, there were more references to economic interests in the Cuban case than in any other. Only *Barrons* called on the government to "take whatever steps it can to protect the interests of its citizens," when Castro began to expropriate American firms.[8] Other expressions of economic reasons and interests were related to recommendations for economic sanctions—either elimination of the sugar quota and tariff privileges or imposition of an export embargo. The *Wall Street Journal*, for example, considered it not surprising that Latin American countries failed to see the "security threat" that Castro posed—"after all, it is the property of U.S. citizens, not of Brazilians, Argentinians or Venezuelans that Castro has taken." Hence it favored "positive action in defense of America's rights and interest"—namely, an export embargo.[9]

Similarly, in the Guatemalan case, *Barrons* was the only voice calling for military intervention to protect American investments. The other discussions of economic interest expressed concern regarding the potentially negative effects of American intervention on Latin American public opinion; one article anticipated that any deviation from a policy of strict nonintervention might "lead to a chain of expropriations."[10]

These examples can do no more than provide the context in which economic interests were expressed and illustrate some of the complexity of motivation. Of all the rationales coded in the business press, 6 percent were economic reasons *for* intervening and 4 percent were economic reasons *against* intervention. Thus, insofar as economic interests were articulated, they were almost as likely to point toward nonintervention as to indicate the necessity for some positive action. Although we cannot eliminate the possibility that latent or subconscious economic motivations predisposed writers in the business press to favor military intervention on strategic and/or ideological grounds, there is at least some basis for assuming that even these motivations did not always point in a single direction when intervention was at issue.

An independent survey of the business press, based on a broader range of sources but limited to the first three years of the Vietnam war, reached conclusions similar to our own. Thomas V. Dibacco searched thirty-three business periodicals representing a variety of business sectors, as well as some general business sources,

---

[8]*Barrons*, January 25, 1960, p. 1; and July 11, 1960, p. 1.
[9]*Wall Street Journal*, October 25, 1960, p. 18.
[10]*Business Week*, April 18, 1953, p. 162.

and found satisfaction or dissatisfaction with Vietnam policies rarely to be based on economic reasons. He concluded that the business press reactions to the war "mirrored those of the public," that is, they exhibited varying degrees of support, opposition, and/or indifference.[11]

Our basic finding that economic motivations were not associated in the business press with preference for military intervention is also consistent with a recent, different kind of analysis. John Odell found only a slight association between American *military intervention* and economic interests.[12] However, he also found the amount of United States *military assistance* given to a country to be positively related to the level of American economic interest in that country—specifically, to the value of the country as a source of raw-material imports, and the amount of trade with and investment in it.

One special caveat about interpretation is in order. Our focus has been on expressions of preference regarding relatively substantial acts of intervention in "crisis" periods during which political events in a less developed nation had become salient. It did not include acts contemplated or taken when the target nation was less prominently in the American public eye, nor the myriad exercises of influence that were considered to be at a lower level than required to meet our definition of intervention, but that clearly were intended to affect the policies if not the authority structure of foreign governments. No one could doubt that such actions have frequently been taken, from economic motivations, for the express purpose of modifying the target nation's economic policies. Import and export policies, the treatment of foreign investors, economic development plans—all have often come under pressure from the American government or from United States-dominated international organizations like the World Bank.[13] The

---

[11]Thomas V. Dibacco, "The Business Press and Vietnam: Ecstasy or Agony?," *Journalism Quarterly* 45 (August 1968): 427–435.

[12]"Correlates of U.S. Military Assistance and Military Intervention," in Steven J. Rosen and James R. Kurth, eds., *Testing Theories of Economic Imperialism* (Lexington, Mass.: D. C. Heath, 1974), pp. 143–161. In another study of circumstances underlying intervention, Frederic S. Pearson found foreign military interventions that were clearly associated with economic interest to be the rarest form, although he admits that this may be an artifact of dependence on public information sources. See "Geographic Proximity and Foreign Military Intervention," *Journal of Conflict Resolution* 18, No. 3 (September 1974): 432–459.

[13]For a recent, sharply critical attack on such practices, see Cheryl Payer, *The Debt Trap: The IMF and the Third World* (Harmondsworth: Penguin, 1974).

relative frequency of such attempts to influence, and the relative strength of the economic, ideological, and strategic motivations behind those attempts, are not investigated here. Very possibly economic motivations would be more manifest at such levels.[14]

Ideology in a Strategic Context

Let us turn now to those rationales which the writers articulated most commonly. We first consider the discrepancy in the relative importance of strategic and ideological bases of preferences indicated by the results of this analysis and the results described in Chapter 4. One explanation clearly lies in the different meanings attributed to ideological motivations in the two chapters. Ideology in Chapter 4 referred to a set of interrelated beliefs on domestic and foreign policy issues; it included anticommunism, but it basically applied to domestic policy views. In the foregoing analysis the ideological rationale was necessarily used in a much more restricted sense to mean a particular kind of foreign policy perspective; information on domestic policy views in the business press was rarely given in these articles, and hence was not coded. With this less comprehensive definition, it is not surprising that ideology appeared less often. But there may be another, perhaps more fundamental, explanation. The mere existence of an ideology or set of beliefs is not sufficient in itself to provide justification for intervention. Ideology must be linked with power to constitute a serious threat. Because communism, the official creed of a powerful political adversary, was perceived as a militantly expansionist ideology, it was also viewed as a threat to American interests and security. "International communism as a system of ideas could be defeated by superior ideas," explained one article. "But it is the combination of irrational dogma and national power that is the really mortal enemy," and as more specifically expressed in the *Wall Street Journal*, the combination of a "significant nuclear arsenal with an undampened, world-conquering ideology."[15] Hence most ideological justifications for intervention were also strategic ones

---

[14]In addition to the Odell study, the link between the extension of economic aid and economic interest has also been explored by Steven Rosen, whose comparative analysis of five major recipients revealed that American foreign assistance (military and economic) is correlated with the openness of a country to American trade and investment. See "The Open Door Imperative and U.S. Foreign Policy," in Rosen and Kurth, eds., op. cit., pp. 117–142.

[15]*Fortune*, February 1951, p. 121; and *Wall Street Journal*, October 6, 1967.

(i.e., they concerned American security and interests), whereas strategic reasons were not always perceived in ideological terms.

Although the interpretation and emphasis varies among cases and press sources, a set of common assumptions does emerge from the examination of these materials. Taken together they present a theme, which exemplifies the interrelationship between the two rationales. This theme may be summarized as follows:

Historically, militant, aggressive, and often tyrannical powers have threatened international order and certain libertarian values of Western civilization. Only when the aggressive actions were challenged by powers representing order and liberty were the hegemonial aspirations abandoned and international peace secured. The Soviet Union, which seeks to disrupt the status quo and extend its political system by force, is such a power—with a difference. Communist ideology imparts a particular militance and ruthlessness to Soviet foreign policy and impels that state toward world domination. Communist doctrine also provides the basis for use of certain methods (subversion, wars of liberation) that make the danger all the more insidious and difficult to confront.

Hence the spread of communist ideas and the expansion of communist political systems were portrayed as unprecedented threats to American security that were indistinguishable from each other. "It is the creed and power drive of the communists that makes them belligerent . . . and the chief external threat to the United States."[16] This is because "our own security is ultimately threatened whenever a powerful nation proclaims and follows a course of totalitarian world domination—a professed communist goal. Militant communist ideology creates a China exceptional for its belligerence and therefore a threat not only to Vietnam but eventually to the United States."[17] The call to "check militantly expansive communism before it threatens us directly"[18] sometimes assumed a sense of great urgency, as in this exclamation during the Korean war: "We are at war with communism—nothing less than the fate of our country is at stake."[19]

---

[16]*Wall Street Journal*, May 12, 1965, p. 16.

[17]*Wall Street Journal*, April 29, 1965, p. 16.

[18]*Wall Street Journal*, May 14, 1965, p. 10.

[19]*Business Week*, December 9, 1950. The role of the Korean war in spurring a general rearmament program is evident in such quotations as the following: "When North Korea smashed into South Korea, they smashed into our national consciousness this fact: if we want a fair chance to save our national freedom from destruction by communist aggression, we must race to restore some of the military power we had so speedily written off after World War II" (p. 108).

The sense of urgency was often dramatized by historical reference. During the crises in Cuba, the Dominican Republic, and Guatemala, the contemporary relevance of the Monroe Doctrine was frequently mentioned. Originally enunciated "to protect the system of freedom from older forms of tyranny," it was held to apply "with greater force and renewed vigor now that we are faced with an infinitely more powerful tyranny, communist imperialism."[20] The Truman Doctrine and the military assistance commitment to Greece and Turkey were "democracy's Monroe Doctrine," symbolizing the determination of the United States to fight "attempts to change governments by coercion and political subterfuge." Although the new policy would place a "block in Russia's road of expansion," the Greek question was essentially a conflict of ideas, a question of "whether the totalitarian ideas of Russia or the democratic ideas of the United States and Britain are to dominate the whole area from Gibraltar to the Suez."[21] "There is loose in the world a force which means to upset the social organization on which civilization is built," and "that force is reaching toward Greece,"[22] warned one editorial. Aggressors' appetites must be curbed—to "dull their lust for world enslavement." The age-old lust for power, invigorated by a "world-conquering ideology,"[23] was given particular immediacy by the prevailing images of Munich and falling dominoes.

The apocalyptic emphasis is most notable in the *Wall Street Journal* and *Barrons*, which reached quite different conclusions regarding intervention in specific situations, despite their shared imagery and historical perspective. This contrast was most pointedly revealed during the Korean war. Regarding the United States as the "standard-bearer of Western Christian civilization," *Barrons* clearly envisaged a Pax Americana—whatever world stability had existed had been brought about by "continuous application of power on the side of justice."[24] "Citizens of Athens, Rome, and Britain would know what we are about." American troops were fighting in Korea "in an ancient and honorable task—to stop the barbarian at the gate."[25] Hence the United States not only must

[20]*Business Week*, July 3, 1954, p. 112. Similar views may be found in the *Wall Street Journal*, September 5, 1962, p. 18; and May 8, 1965, p. 110.
[21]*Wall Street Journal*, March 13, 1947, p. 4.
[22]*Wall Street Journal*, March 28, 1947, p. 4.
[23]*Wall Street Journal*, August 9, 1965, p. 8.
[24]*Barrons*, June 3, 1950, p. 1.
[25]Ibid. A repetition of this theme appears in the issue of August 28, 1950, p. 1.

"contain communism wherever it breaks out," but also must attempt the "active redress of the balance of power against Russia." Such an activist policy was in the interest of the United States and in the "ultimate interest of preserving liberty under the law."[26] The *Wall Street Journal* also saw America as the embodiment of freedom in human history, but for that very reason opposed policies that risked the preservation and strength of the United States. "There is in the world today only one power that stands in the way of barbarism. So long as the United States stands, the way is barred. So soon as it falls the whole world will be engulfed." The United States should do its utmost to preserve the peace of the world but should clearly recognize the limits of its powers and scale the commitments accordingly. No policy should be pursued that would "debilitate American strength and thus jeopardize the overriding goal, which is to defend ourselves and so in the end defeat the forces of barbarism."[27]

These dramatic excerpts are presented not merely for their entertainment value, but to illustrate the particular manner in which national security requirements were linked with ideological justifications in discussions of intervention in the business press. The figures in the tables in this chapter indicate that the imperatives of maintaining national security, power, interests, and credibility, as well as regional and international power balances, were the predominant concerns. However, ideological reasons were expressed with such intensity that they must be assumed to have had greater influence than is evident solely from the tables.

Reluctance and Restraint

Let us now consider in greater detail the bases for opposition to intervention. Only by analyzing the reasons for both negative and positive preferences can we speculate about future predispositions. As previously noted and as might be expected, strategic reasons were most frequently mentioned. In general, these reasons were that intervention would be inimical to the national interest in some way, that it would be unlikely to accomplish the desired goal, or that the risks or costs were too high relative to the probable gains.

---

[26]*Barrons*, December 25, 1950, p. 1.
[27]*Wall Street Journal*, December 26, 1950, p. 6; and December 27, 1950, p. 7.

Prominent among the more specific reasons was the position that the situations that appeared to require American intervention would in fact be worsened by such action. Initially, the belief that intervention in Cuba might consolidate Castro's popular support and push him further to the left or produce someone even worse encouraged opposition to any form of action.[28] Similarly, *Business Week* feared that direct intervention in Guatemala would give a "tremendous boost to communism or fanatic nationalism, twin enemies of U.S. influence in Latin America.[29] The same kind of cautionary reasoning was particularly apparent in the *Wall Street Journal* editorials with respect to American intervention in Lebanon to help stabilize the pro-West Chamoun government. This kind of "meddling" was perceived as likely to increase Chamoun's opposition and the extremist elements within it.[30] In like manner, by "trying to do too much for the Southeast Asians" (i.e., restructuring their social and economic institutions), "we appear to smother them."[31]

The ineffectiveness of intervention in confronting the fundamental problems generating a crisis situation—particularly nationalism and poverty—was frequently mentioned. Seeing no means by which the United States might stem communist influence in Guatemala, *Business Week* admitted that the noncommunist world was "faced basically with a political aggression that is difficult to parry with blunt military and economic weapons."[32] By this reasoning, it was difficult to see how the United States could hope to solve the problems of Southeast Asia—"they are just too complex." About all we could do to try to contain communist expansion was to offer some financial and technical assistance and "hope the Asians will work out solutions that are not hostile to the West."[33] (Note that this statement was made one week before American military involvement in Korea.) The basis for much of the *Wall Street Journal*'s opposition to military intervention in Indochina was that the problem was primarily a political one—"We could win military victories and the political problem of allegiance and trust of the Asian peoples would still be there." Most Indochinese,

---

[28]*Business Week*, December 5, 1959, p. 118; and *Wall Street Journal*, July 20, 1959, p. 7.
[29]*Business Week*, July 3, 1954, p. 76.
[30]*Wall Street Journal*, May 26, 1958, p. 7; and May 29, 1958, p. 8.
[31]*Wall Street Journal*, April 21, 1959, p. 18.
[32]*Business Week*, June 5, 1954, p. 128.
[33]*Business Week*, June 24, 1950, p. 111.

the newspaper held, viewed communists as their liberators from colonialism and did not want to be defended against them. There was, therefore, great doubt that intervention would do any good. "A people can be saved only if they want to be. If the United States thinks otherwise, it courts disaster."[34] Similarly, the problem underlying the crisis in Lebanon was Pan-Arabism, and the United States would "have exactly the same problems after the Marines as before them."[35]

But the most forceful and consistent opposition to intervention in the business press was the *Wall Street Journal*'s challenge to containment and global commitment. Chapter 6 provided an overall view of the newspaper's positions during the various crises. The particular arguments given provide a theme that is both coherent and relevant to any projections concerning businessmen's foreign policy preferences in the future.

This particular perspective was a blend of pragmatism, nationalism, and conservatism. The fundamental premise was, as indicated earlier, that the preservation of American strength and security must be the paramount concern of foreign policy. Communism should be resisted only insofar as security was threatened —and even in those cases only when "the ground and the people were firm enough." The United States could not "police the world" or "guard the world against communism" or "save the world." A policy of "automatic intervention" against every communist aggression was based on questionable assumptions; it was expensive and risky. We had fought in Korea to prevent future aggression by China, but the intensification of the threat in Indochina at the end of the war had cast doubt upon that assumption. We had persisted in Vietnam in order to prove that aggression did not pay; yet the exorbitant costs of our efforts had proved the contrary. Because we are tied down in one place, can we assume the enemy will not strike elsewhere? The assumption that no communist gain can be tolerated was also fallacious; what the communists have gained has "often been more trouble than benefit to them." Containment required the commitment of tremendous resources to assure readiness to meet any threat at any time in any place of the enemy's own choosing. This put the United States at a logistical disadvantage on the battlefield with any immediate adversary. But worst of all, the

---

[34]*Wall Street Journal*, May 21, 1954, p. 4; June 4, 1954, p. 6; July 2, 1954, p. 4.
[35]*Wall Street Journal*, July 17, 1958, p. 8.

inevitable peripheral battles and the extended commitments drained the United States of the strength necessary to confront the real enemy if the contingency should arise in the future. Our trying to keep commitments around the world simply gave the enemy the opportunity "gradually to bleed us to death by the infliction of minor wounds." Meanwhile, the "real enemy," a nonparticipating observer, was shoring up its strength. Thus containment was antithetical to the national interest. And it ignored the fact that there were some things the United States could not do. When we try to "fix up all the bits and pieces in the world we cease to be masters of our own destiny," and some day the "price of the gamble lost may be a conflagration which will leave nothing of the world—and ourselves—save bits and pieces."[36]

We have demonstrated some of the more compelling reasons given in the business press for and against intervention. The survey data and the results of the stock market analysis indicated increasing dissatisfaction in the business community with the Vietnam war from early 1967. Considerable reluctance to become involved in similar military efforts in the future was expressed in the questionnaire responses. What does the content analysis suggest regarding the future predispositions of businessmen with respect to American intervention in the third world? The strength of anti-interventionist views in one segment of the business press during the peak of the cold war, taken in conjunction with the survey responses indicating that this perspective may well have gained ground, suggests greater reluctance within the business community to approve future direct military intervention. The basis for such a view is likely to be the supposition that intervention is simply not a very good risk. It is expensive, the duration of the conflict is uncertain, and the chances of general war are omnipresent. And with all that is risked, the gains are often ephemeral; many objectives cannot be achieved, even minimally, by this means.

Despite these misgivings, the American business executive of the future will be investing more extensively in the third world than ever before. Greater tolerance for nationalist regimes may have developed within the business community, as was indicated in the survey. Certainly American business enterprise has been adept at devising flexible arrangements for dealing with demands for local participation and ownership arrangements in developing nations. Continued domestic pressures in the United States may

---

[36]*Wall Street Journal*, November 7, 1950, p. 6.

give further impetus to investments abroad. Yet, the third-world nations are bound to experience increasing instability—at least in the near future. The need for a stable investment environment will surely remain a compelling force. The conditions may be stricter and the range of situations narrower, but quick, cheap, successful military intervention may again be contemplated—especially after the memory of Vietnam begins to fade. A minority that passionately desires a particular intervention can sometimes prevail over a majority that tepidly opposes it. Economic interests are far more likely, however, to involve the American government in influence attempts and in the support of governments that, though they may promote American interests, may have a shaky basis of support in their own countries. This kind of activity could, as in Vietnam, lead incrementally to commitments that might seem irrevocable. At some point in the process, strategic and ideological arguments would be marshalled to mobilize wider popular acceptance of the policy. Economic interests that require a stable and hospitable environment in the third world are nevertheless more likely to involve the United States in covert operations and other indirect means of influencing local government policies than in overt military acts. Indeed, resort to these cheaper, less dramatic, less risky forms of pressure might even increase if overt military intervention becomes a less feasible option.

CHAPTER EIGHT

Interdependence
and
Insularity

*O God, give us serenity to accept what can-
not be changed, courage to change what
should be changed, and wisdom to distinguish the one from the other.*

Reinhold Niebuhr

Summarizing the Evidence

We shall begin the process of summarizing by restating each of the
hypotheses offered in Chapter 2 and matching it with the evidence
accumulated to test it. First we compare business executives as a
whole with other elite groups.

1.1 *Businessmen will be more favorable toward military preparedness
than will other elites.*

In Chapter 3 we found businessmen to be less favorable toward
military expenditures than are members of most civilian elites, but
not military men or Republican party officials—a moderate confirmation of hypothesis 1.1.

1.2 *Businessmen will be more favorable than other elites toward
United States government activities to protect American business interests
abroad, and toward the promotion of governments in less developed countries
that are well disposed to the activities of foreign investors and maintenance
of the free enterprise system; similarly, they will be more hostile toward
socialist and communist governments in less developed countries.*

In the detailed examination of the parts of this hypothesis by a comparison of business and military elites in Chapter 3, we found some moderate support for it, and not significant evidence for its converse. And where we had information, we also found that it was confirmed with regard to other civilian elites, with the exception of Republican party officials and possibly labor union leaders.

1.3 *Military men will be more favorable toward military preparedness than will civilian elites, including businessmen.*

This hypothesis was strongly confirmed in Chapter 3.

1.4 *Military men will be more "hawkish" on a variety of foreign policy issues than will civilian elites, including businessmen.*

This hypothesis was generally confirmed in Chapter 3. It was also confirmed in the content analysis in Chapter 6, if we assume the correctness of our decision to weight the various business press sources.

1.5 *Businessmen will be more hawkish on a variety of foreign policy issues than will other elites.*

This hypothesis was generally disconfirmed in Chapter 3 when businessmen were compared with military officers or Republican party officials, but it was generally supported in the important comparison between businessmen and all other civilian elites. In Chapter 6 we found businessmen to be less hawkish than the military, given the way we weighted the press sources, or at most, about the same when a different weighting system was used. We rejected the hypothesis after our rough comparison (using the survey materials) of the business press with the general public.

1.6 *Businessmen will be more opposed to income redistribution (in an egalitarian direction) than will other elites.*

In the survey analysis in Chapter 3, this hypothesis was supported when the Columbia business sample was compared with all other elites including the military, but when the Yale business sample was used, the hypothesis was supported only when the businessmen were compared with most other *civilian* elites, and not when Republican politicians were the point of reference.

1.7 *Businessmen will be less likely to regard the American intervention in Vietnam as a mistake, less likely to think the war was bad for the American economy in general, and less likely to think they personally are worse off as a result of the war, than will other elites.*

The survey data in Chapter 3 clearly refuted this hypothesis when tested against attitudes among military officers—the only test available for such a comparison. Similarly, the stock market data in Chapter 5 indicated that, by 1967 at least, businessmen were generally opposed to the war. The situation in earlier years is more ambiguous. In Chapter 6 we at least did not find businessmen to be more in favor of intervention in Vietnam than were the military.

1.8 *Businessmen will be less favorable toward military preparedness than will other elites.*

The converse of hypothesis 1.1, this hypothesis was confirmed in Chapter 3 with regard to military officers but was generally refuted when businessmen were compared with most other civilian elites (but not Republican politicians).

1.9 *Businessmen will be less hawkish on a variety of foreign policy issues than will other elites.*

This hypothesis, the converse of hypothesis 1.5, was confirmed with regard to military officers but was generally refuted in Chapter 3 when businessmen were compared with most other civilian elites (but not Republican politicians). The content analysis in Chapter 6 also confirmed the hypothesis vis-à-vis the military, again assuming the correctness of our decisions on how to weight the journals.

1.10 *Businessmen will be more likely to regard the American intervention in Vietnam as a mistake, more likely to think the war was bad for the economy in general, and more likely to think they personally are worse off as a result of the war, than will other elites.*

This hypothesis, which is the converse of 1.7, was confirmed in the survey data in Chapter 3, in which military officers were the reference point. The evidence in Chapter 5 showed that businessmen were opposed to the war from 1967 onward, and, together with the survey data, provides modest support for the hypothesis. Chapter 6, however, showed that business and military sentiments were about equal in the early years of the war.

Of the five preceding hypotheses that were derived from economic theories attributing war and aggressive foreign policies to business interests generally, there was thus mild support for 1.1, 1.2, and 1.6; ambiguous results for 1.5; and disconfirmation of 1.7.

For the hypotheses tested in Chapter 4, comparing the attitudes of different groups within the business community, we have the following results.

2.1 *Executives from corporations with substantial foreign sales or investments, or with expectations of substantially increasing foreign activities, or with expectations of increasing activities specifically in less developed countries, will look more favorably upon the effects of the war (as specified in 1.7) than will executives from other corporations.*

This hypothesis was rejected in our analysis in Chapter 4. It was also disconfirmed in the stock market analysis in Chapter 5, which revealed no difference whatever between the behavior of the stocks of firms with large LDC interests and the behavior of other stocks in response to the war.

2.2 *Executives from the corporations specified in 2.1 will be more hawkish on a variety of foreign policy issues than will executives from other corporations.*

In Chapter 4 we found some support (although not strong) for this hypothesis.

2.3 *Executives from such corporations will be more favorable toward United States government activities to protect American business interests abroad, and toward the promotion of governments in less developed countries that are well disposed to the activities of foreign investors and maintenance of the free enterprise system; similarly, they will be more hostile toward socialist and communist governments in less developed countries than will executives from other corporations.*

The first clause of hypothesis 2.3, dealing with the protection of American business abroad, was rather strongly confirmed in Chapter 3, but there was no support for the remaining clauses.

2.4 *Executives from corporations with substantial foreign sales or investments, or with expectations of substantially increasing foreign activities, will look less favorably upon the effects of the Vietnam war (as specified in 1.10) than will executives from other corporations.*

2.5 *Executives from such corporations (as specified in 2.4) will be less hawkish on a variety of foreign policy issues than executives from other corporations.*

Hypothesis 2.4 was rejected in Chapter 4. Since we found 2.2 moderately supported in Chapter 4, we must treat its converse (2.5) as rejected also.

2.6 *Executives from corporations with expectations of substantially increasing sales or investments in the Soviet Union and/or China will be* *less hawkish on a variety of foreign policy issues than will executives from other corporations.*

We found no evidence to support this hypothesis, and thus must reject it.

3.1 *Executives from corporations making substantial sales to the Department of Defense will be more favorable toward military preparedness than will executives from other corporations.*

Hypothesis 3.1 was clearly confirmed in Chapter 4, at least for a fairly narrow range of military preparedness questions.

3.2 *Executives from such corporations [as specified in 3.1] will be more hawkish on a variety of foreign policy issues than will executives from other corporations.*

3.3 *Executives from such corporations will look more favorably upon the effects of the Vietnam war (as specified in hypothesis 1.7) than will executives from other corporations.*

These two hypotheses were clearly rejected in the material in Chapter 4. In addition, the stock market analysis in Chapter 5 found defense stocks, like the stocks of firms in other industries, basically rising in response to conciliatory acts by the communist side in Vietnam from 1967 onward, thus supplying additional evidence that it was correct to reject hypothesis 3.3.

Finally, there are the three hypotheses about the relative importance of economic motivations as compared with other kinds of motivations in determining businessmen's foreign policy preferences.

4.1 *Economic motivations will be more closely associated with the particular foreign policy preferences expressed by businessmen than with the preferences expressed by other elites.*

When businessmen were compared with military officers in Chapter 4, this hypothesis was clearly rejected—no difference was found between the two groups. Similarly, the content analysis in Chapter 7 supplied absolutely no evidence in support of this hypothesis.

4.2 *Economic motivations and interests will be more closely associated with the foreign policy preferences expressed by businessmen than will domestic ideology or strategic motivations.*

This hypothesis also was clearly rejected in Chapter 4. In fact, economic motivations and interests ran a weak third, well behind both domestic ideology and strategic motivations. In only a very few instances did economic interests and motivations account for even as much as 2 percent of the variance in foreign policy preference, whereas domestic ideology was consistently a very much stronger influence. The articulation of economic motivations was also found to be consistently weak in the content analysis in Chapter 7, despite a conscious effort to code the data so as to record economic motivations in every ambiguous case and thus to give the benefit of the doubt to economic interest theories.

4.3 *Among businessmen, foreign policy hawkishness will be more closely associated with a conservative position on income redistribution than with conservative attitudes on civil rights or civil liberties.*

This hypothesis also was clearly rejected in Chapter 4, and its rejection seems more important than the modest confirmation of hypothesis 1.6 about income redistribution—a hypothesis not directly related to foreign policy.

Nine of these last hypotheses tested propositions that asserted a role for economic interest in promoting war and aggressive foreign policy; three were in one degree or another supported by the evidence: 2.2, 2.3, and 3.1. But the other six were rejected moderately (3.2), strongly though with results that were not significantly different from those of the control group (2.1 and 3.3), or with results that actually ran in the opposite direction from those hypothesized (4.1, 4.2, and 4.3). Including hypotheses 1.1, 1.2, and 1.5–1.7, we thus have strong support for one and moderate support for five hypotheses of this sort and ambiguous results on a seventh, but moderate disconfirmation of two and strong disconfirmation of five others.

When all this evidence is brought together and combined with other information discussed in the appropriate chapters that was not directly relevant to the numbered hypotheses, we have, in general, only *weak and rather fragmentary evidence in favor of theories attributing war to economic interests.*

This result emerges not from the application of a single method to a single body of information, but from a multimethod approach of surveys and interviews, event analysis, and content analysis of a wide variety of materials. Although each of the separate applications is not without its serious methodological and conceptual problems, the consistency of the evidence throughout all applications is impressive and, we think, lends considerable weight to the overall conclusion. It is not a matter of finding that economic interest theories are wrong or mistaken; on the contrary, they are to some degree supported. But their relative explanatory power, when compared with that of strategic and ideological theories, is not impressive.[1] In terms of the problem as formulated in Chapter 1, such economic theories seem to make only a small contribution to our understanding of elite perspectives on American foreign policy. At the least, future research on the role of economic interest must invoke a much more complex theory—for example, one that considers the interaction of such interests with personality, life experience, and communication patterns.

Yet in light of the varying records of success of the different economic interest hypotheses when confronted with evidence, it is not very helpful merely to lump them all together and to evaluate them solely as a group. After all, different hypotheses had their origins in different theoretical perspectives, and should be distinguished. Table 8.1 lists a condensed statement of each hypothesis with our best judgment of its degree of support or disconfirmation on the basis of our data. Such a summary conclusion about some complex hypotheses causes a loss of subtlety in interpretation that we regret, and readers may disagree with a few of our evaluations. Nevertheless, we feel we owe readers an attempt at a summary even at the cost of some unintended distortion of detail. Degrees of support or disconfirmation are indicated by a scale from $++$ to $--$; the key at the bottom of the table explains the codings.

Some of the hypotheses were derived generally from a perspective we described as tracing aggressive foreign policies to *imperatives of the capitalist system* in general. Hypotheses 1.1, 1.2, and 1.5–1.7 are of this sort; they attributed to businessmen a

---

[1]This view, that ideology is a far more powerful influence on foreign policy behavior than is economic interest, is apparently shared by most members of the American intellectual "elite." See Charles Kadushin, *The American Intellectual Elite* (Boston: Little, Brown, 1974), pp. 156 ff. See also Allen Barton, "Consensus and Conflict among American Leaders," *Public Opinion Quarterly* 38, No. 4 (Winter 1974–1975): 523. Barton holds that the cold war was maintained not by a "military-industrial complex," but by "a political-government group; it consisted of politicians and officials with a thirty-year investment in anti-communism as a political issue and a government policy."

On the importance of a multimethod empirical study when single measures are necessarily unreliable, see Eugene J. Webb et al., *Unobtrusive Measures: Nonreactive Research in the Social Sciences* (Chicago: Rand McNally, 1966); and Paul Lazarsfeld and Morris Rosenberg, eds., *The Language of Social Research* (New York: Free Press, 1955). This is especially important in instances like this where, for example, businessmen's responses to survey questions may reflect their private opinions but not necessarily how they might act on behalf of their firm.

Table 8.1 *Summary of Hypothesis Testing*

	Capitalism Leads to "Aggressive" Foreign Policy	
1.1	Businessmen more favorable toward military preparedness	+
1.2	Businessmen more favorable toward protecting economic interests abroad	+
1.5	Businessmen more hawkish than other elites	0
1.6	Businessmen more opposed to income redistribution	+
1.7	Businessmen more favorable toward Vietnam war	−
2.1	Executives from foreign-oriented firms more favorable toward Vietnam war	− −
2.2	Executives from foreign-oriented firms more hawkish	+
2.3	Executives from foreign-oriented firms more favorable toward protecting economic interest abroad	+

	Defense-Oriented Firms Cause "Aggressive" Foreign Policy	
3.1	Executives from DOD-oriented firms more favorable toward military preparedness	+ +
3.2	Executives from DOD-oriented firms more hawkish	−
3.3	Executives from DOD-oriented firms more favorable toward Vietnam war	− −

	Ideology Merely as Superstructure	
4.1	Economic motives more closely associated with preference for businessmen	− −
4.2	Economic interests more closely associated than are ideology or strategic motives	− −
4.3	Income redistribution attitudes more closely associated than civil rights or civil liberties attitudes with foreign policy preference	− −

	Capitalism Leads to Peace	
1.8	Businessmen less favorable toward military preparedness	0
1.9	Businessmen less hawkish	0
1.10	Businessmen less favorable toward Vietnam war	+
2.4	Executives from foreign-oriented firms less favorable toward Vietnam	−
2.5	Executives from foreign-oriented firms less hawkish	−
2.6	Executives from China- and Soviet Union-oriented firms less hawkish	−

	Military Interests Lead to "Aggressive" Foreign Policy	
1.3	Military men more favorable toward preparedness	+ +
1.4	Military men more hawkish	+ +

Key:
+ + Hypothesis strongly supported; supported in two different analyses.
+ Hypothesis moderately supported; supported in one analysis and merely not disconfirmed in another; supported in comparison with most but not all groups.
0 Hypothesis neither supported nor clearly disconfirmed; two different analyses inconsistent.
− Hypothesis moderately disconfirmed; disconfirmed in comparison with most but not all groups.
− − Hypothesis strongly disconfirmed; disconfirmed in two different analyses; converse strongly confirmed.

capitalist class interest that would lead them to espouse an expansionist, aggressive foreign policy. Hypotheses 2.1–2.3 also are derivable from this point of view. They predicted we would find particularly hawkish policy preferences on the part of businessmen who were engaged in economic activities abroad, especially in less developed countries; according to Marxist and some other theories, the drive for foreign markets and investment outlets is a basic imperative of the capitalist system. The collective record of these hypotheses is better than that for most of the others. Of the eight, only two (1.7 about a favorable attitude toward American intervention in Vietnam among businessmen, and 2.1 about a favorable attitude toward the effects of the Vietnam war among businessmen with special interests in LDCs) were rejected, and the results for a third (1.5) were ambiguous. Support for the other five ranged from slight to moderate.

This record should not be dismissed. We feel that the modest degree of support evidenced for most of these hypotheses indicates that the needs of a capitalist system probably do make *some* contribution to producing an activist, globalist, interventionist United States foreign policy. Perhaps this is especially true when less developed countries are the targets, though the evidence is too weak to distinguish between a need for foreign markets for goods and capital, and a need for heavy military spending to maintain aggregate demand. In any event, we do not feel that the evidence indicates that the contribution of either of these theories is substantial. It is possible that economic interest theories once were more nearly correct, that our survey results from the post-Vietnam era primarily reflect businessmen's painful recognition that that particular war, fought in that particular way, did not advance their interests. We have, however, considered this possibility at various points in the analysis. The content analysis looked at data from periods well before Vietnam—as far back as the early 1950s—and found little evidence that business advocacy of a hawkish or globalist policy was stronger than that of the general public or the military. The stock market study found no consistent business approval of war.

The evidence in support of "merchants of death" theories is markedly weaker. Of three hypotheses attributing hawkish foreign policies specifically to the interests of defense-oriented industries, two were rejected (3.2 and 3.3) and only one was supported (3.1). The only one that was supported hypothesized that executives from defense-oriented firms would be particularly favorable toward military preparedness. Support for it was hardly a surprise; more unexpected was the absence among such executives of especially hawkish views on broader foreign policy issues.

Three hypotheses (4.1–4.3) were devised specifically to test the view that *ideology is merely a superstructure* erected (consciously or otherwise) to promote the economic interests of the capitalist class. Each of these hypotheses was unambiguously rejected. Surely broader ideological arguments are sometimes used to support economic interests; no one could seriously argue otherwise. But our evidence indicates that ideology—whether of the anticommunist variety, or a more comprehensive kind of conservatism embracing restrictive views on civil rights and civil liberties as well as capitalist values—has a strong and, in important ways, independent influence on foreign policy preference.

Note, however, that the opposite kind of economic interest hypotheses—that businessmen's economic interests will lead them to be markedly less hawkish than other elite groups—is also rejected. Despite the arguments of enthusiasts for the multinational corporation, theories that *economic interest is a significant force for a pacific foreign policy* and the avoidance of war find no important support in our data. This is certainly true regarding the hypotheses about the pacific influence of particular kinds of business activities abroad (hypotheses 2.4–2.6). It is also generally true for hypotheses 1.8–1.10, attributing less hawkish views to businessmen in general, except when the comparison is with military elites. This leads to one final summary conclusion here: hypotheses attributing particularly *hawkish views to military officers* (1.3 and 1.4) are regularly supported. The degree to which these views are effectively translated into the nation's foreign policy is, of course, another question, and deserves attention.

Although the results of these analyses provide only very modest support for specifically economic interest theories, they are nevertheless consistent with—if hardly a sufficient test of—some theories that fear the power of a military-industrial complex. We should not gloss over the fact that many of our empirical findings simply establish that businessmen are not more hawkish, or are on occasion somewhat less hawkish, than military officers. The survey results in Chapter 3 clearly show that military officers and businessmen—along with substantial segments of the Republican party leadership—constitute the most hawkish of the American elite groups. They are more likely than members of other groups, such as labor leaders, Democratic party officials, voluntary association leaders, senior civil servants, or major media figures, to support a basically cold-war-oriented foreign policy; they are also more likely to occupy conservative positions on the domestic political spectrum. Thus on both the foreign and the domestic scene, they are more likely to defend the policy outcomes and distribution of rewards characteristic of the American political system in recent decades. Their reasons for supporting these policies may not be identical, but whatever those reasons are they do seem to converge. Many businessmen may see their economic interests as being served by these policies; many military officers must see their bureaucratic and career interests as being served by them.

This view does *not* imply that the members of each group therefore necessarily conspire with one another in support of those policies; nor does it imply that they support those policies solely, primarily, or consciously in order to protect their own narrow interests. This view does not imply that they deliberately subordinate the welfare of their own society or that of the world at large to those interests. They may hold a set of hawkish-conservative beliefs for reasons quite independent of those interests, and we cannot lightly dismiss the possibility that their beliefs about the general welfare may be correct. We have found that some beliefs are, to an important degree, independent of interests. Yet interests do help to underpin a broader ideology. At the least, interests provide a reason for failing to challenge ideological beliefs under circumstances when some of the basic intellectual underpinnings might seem questionable to an "objective" outside observer. Interests may not, therefore, be the cause of an ideology, but they may, in ways that are not necessarily traceable to conscious reasoning processes, prevent, delay, or diminish the abandonment of that ideology. Here we are certainly in the realm of speculation, and, save for finding some important congruences between typical business and military beliefs, we are beyond the point where our quantitative data are of much help.

Although we have engaged in hypothesis testing only in a sharply circumscribed context—the United States in the third quarter of the twentieth century—we believe that is a crucial context for evaluating many theories that are intended also to apply to other contexts. In the interests of parsimonious scientific explanation, further theorizing about the role of economic interests will require careful choice among the diverse hypotheses considered. Moreover, if proponents of economic interest theories contend that the hypotheses we have tested do not adequately express the meaning of their theories, then perhaps the proponents will do better than we did in stating the hypotheses in a form that will both satisfy the theorists' intent and be, in principle, capable of refutation by empirical evidence. New hypotheses also must not predict results that could readily be "explained" by other than economic interest hypotheses. For example, some hypotheses that postulate that economic interest is the source of conservative ideology do not clearly tell us why we should prefer them to other hypotheses that predict widespread adherence to conservative ideology for very different reasons. Further rigorous theorizing about the sources of ideology and the prospects for its change is mandatory. From a policy-oriented perspective, such theorizing could lead to a consideration of the forces in American society that might, perhaps with deliberate assistance from those who do not adhere to conservative ideologies, produce a major shift in the way Americans view their political role in the world.

Ideology and Intervention

It is difficult entirely to sort out the relative contributions of strategic theories and of ideological ones, partly because of the difficulties, in evaluating a given statement of support for a policy, of deciding where "strategic" reasoning ends and "ideological" thinking begins, or vice versa. In the preceding chapter we suggested that they often work together in a reinforcing manner. Also, in our content analysis, we were unable to relate foreign policy views directly to the range of the writer's views on domestic policy, and we thus had to content ourselves with relating them to ideology in the more narrow sense of anticommunist ideology expressed in conjunction with specific foreign policy recommendations. In Chapter 4, however, we did have a good measure of domestic policy attitudes that we could relate to foreign policy preference. There we found quite strong correlations between the two—convincing evidence of an ideological explanation in the sense that

ideology is a *system* of beliefs. That is, its symbols have a certain integrated, unified quality. They "hang together" with a consistency which, while it may be artificial or illogical, is at least recognized as a general standard for imposing constraints on belief-elements. . . . the belief constraints allow us to predict . . . attitudes across a wide range of issues.[2]

---

[2]Douglas Rosenberg, "Arms and the American Way," in Bruce M. Russett and Alfred Stepan, eds., *Military Force and American Society* (New York: Harper & Row, 1973), p. 151. For a good review of meanings of the term "ideology" as employed in political science, see Robert D. Putnam, "Studying Elite Political Culture: The Case of Ideology," *American Political Science Review* 65, No. 3 (September 1971): 651–681. In no sense do we use the term as pejorative.

According to this definition, the political ideologies of many businessmen extend well beyond the mere protection or advancement of their commercial interests. One such specific ideology, anticommunism, appears frequently in our materials as well as in other available information on the political activities of businessmen; the behavior of ITT officials is a good example.

For those who hope for a long-lasting change in the purpose and methods of American foreign policy, it is perhaps very encouraging to find that ideology seems to be a more powerful explanation of preferences than does economic interest or motivation. Economic interest represents an extremely stable element of social systems. On the most basic level, the economic interests, whatever they are, of capitalists as a class are unlikely to change radically so long as private enterprise remains the dominant form of economic organization in the United States. Businessmen will retain an interest in holding and expanding their markets, and in maintaining a high level of employment and economic productivity. Businessmen whose firms have large overseas operations will retain an interest in protecting and enlarging those operations; businessmen whose firms prosper from making substantial sales to the Defense Department are unlikely to welcome a major retrenchment in military spending by the federal government. We have a good idea of how stable these latter interests are. Foreign trade, foreign investment, and defense spending all have remained within a range of 6–13 percent of the American gross national product in every year since 1950, and show little likelihood of dropping below this range in the foreseeable future. If these interests were very closely associated with foreign and defense policy preferences across a wide spectrum of issues, and seemed to be a major contributor to American foreign and defense policies, then the prospects for dramatic change in those policies would appear to be dismal. Means or methods might vary, but so long as the interests retained their entrenched share of the economy, their most basic goal—to keep and expand that share—would be expected to be constant.

Bureaucratic interests, vested economic interests, and many kinds of institutions share this characteristic ability to resist any reduction in their power and influence. These economic interests would therefore constitute a weighty inertial force in the way of new policies. If the direction and character of American foreign policy were attributable primarily to its capitalist economy *in toto*, then the prospects for a change in policy would be only as bright as the prospects for a drastic change in the basic economic organization of the country. Even a change in economic organization might well not suffice—remember, for example, the inertial power of those institutions in the Soviet Union that support heavy military spending and resist détente.

Ideology, on the other hand, may be somewhat more subject to change, especially over a period of a few years, than economic interest. In the previous chapters we discussed at some length evidence that the foreign policy beliefs of many people in the United States—mass public as well as elites—have already changed in major ways during recent years. Important material to support this interpretation was supplied by our survey results, the changing behavior of stock prices, and the content analysis, as well as some other bits of evidence that we referred to more briefly. The sense of external threat has generally attenuated, enthusiasm for an "internationalist," "activist," or "interventionist" foreign policy has waned, and support for high levels of defense spending has dropped drastically. On the subject of defense spending, every public opinion survey from 1937 to 1964 that asked whether it should increase, decrease, or remain the same found that less than 35 percent, and usually less than 20 percent, wanted to see it cut. From 1968 to the present, however, ten surveys asking the same question found the percentage favoring a reduction in defense spending to be at or near the 50 percent mark. As with many similar issues, the opposition to high levels of military expenditures is concentrated among younger voters.[3] Studies of the composition of Congress have shown that representatives born after 1920 (a relatively young age for congressmen in 1970) or elected for the first time after the Joseph McCarthy era are, on the average, significantly more dovish than are older representatives.[4] There are, of course, notable exceptions: not all old men are hawks (e.g., former Senator Fulbright), nor are all young ones doves, but this is the general pattern.

Partly it is a matter of younger men and women being more ready to shift to dovish positions from previously rather hawkish ones, but partly it is a matter more of changing bodies than of changing minds. Older congressmen retire, die, or are defeated for reelection, and their successors possess a different set of experiences and attitudes. Furthermore, there is an intriguing set of data from

---

[3]Bruce M. Russett, "The Americans' Retreat from World Power," *Political Science Quarterly* 90, No. 1 (Spring 1975): 1–21.

[4]Wayne Moyer, "House Voting on Defense: An Ideological Explanation," in Russett and Stepan, eds., op. cit.

Presidential speeches, compiled over a period of almost 200 years from the birth of the Republic, that imply a roughly 40-year cycle of interest—from relative "internationalism" to "isolationism" and back. Although we certainly should not give too much credence to this evidence, a generational interpretation would nevertheless make sense of it.[5] It will not be long before a generation with new experiences and outlooks moves into elite positions in America. Already those who knew Vietnam but not World War II are 40 years old.

It is important, therefore, in evaluating the importance of various influences on foreign policy, to consider not just which ones account for a high percentage of the variance, but also which ones are *subject to change*. In policy research, it is common practice to look for the "manipulables," those variables over which the would-be policy maker may have a relatively high degree of control.[6] Thus both bad driving and poor automobile design may be major causes of road accidents, but if, at the margin, automobile design is more subject to effective control, then the wise policy maker who wants to reduce accidents will concentrate on it.

Ideology may score fairly high on both the criteria of variance accounted for and susceptibility to change. Whereas ideological perspectives will not change dramatically in the short run, we have good reason to think they are subject to change over longer periods,

---

[5] See Russett, op. cit., for an extension and further interpretation of material originally compiled from Frank Klingberg, "The Historical Alternation of Moods in American Foreign Policy," *World Politics* 4, No. 2 (January 1952): 252–253. The generational interpretation was discussed in a bit more detail at the end of Chapter 4 of this book. At the risk of overusing a statement that has become almost a cliché, this reminds us of the remark by Max Planck that a new scientific point of view "does not triumph by convincing its opponents and making them see the light, but rather because its opponents eventually die, and a new generation grows up." Quoted in Thomas S. Kuhn, *The Structure of Scientific Revolutions* (Chicago: University of Chicago Press, 1970), 2d ed., p. 151. See also Michael Roskin, "From Pearl Harbor to Vietnam: Shifting Generational Paradigms," *Political Science Quarterly* 89, No. 3 (Fall 1974): 563–588.

[6] See, for example, the statement by Arnold Kanter and Stuart J. Thorson, "The Weapons Procurement Process: Choosing Among Theories," in Steven Rosen, ed., *Testing the Theory of the Military-Industrial Complex* (Lexington, Mass.: D. C. Heath, 1973). This practice is generally accepted in the peace research movement, and among many more traditional scholars as well. Note Hans Morgenthau's statement that theory must be "a map of the political scene not only in order to understand what the scene is like, but also in order to show the shortest and safest route to a given objective," in his "The Nature and Limits of a Theory of International Relations," in W. T. R. Fox, ed., *Theoretical Aspects of International Relations* (Notre Dame, Indiana: University of Notre Dame Press, 1959), p. 18.

especially as a result of the generational phenomenon. "Manipulability" is probably too strong a term, although deliberate efforts of political leaders, prominent people in the mass media, and even academic writers can have an effect; indeed perhaps the most important contribution that people not in immediate policy-making positions can make to a new foreign policy is to help change public perceptions of our world and the nation's role in it. Certainly, independent of the contribution that any single individual can make is the impact of major international events on domestic politics, and their consequent "linkage" with or feedback to future foreign policy.[7] The war in Southeast Asia is a vivid example. If, according to the Ellsberg or "democratic" interpretation cited in Chapter 1, previous decision makers had feared an anticommunist popular backlash for "losing" Indochina, then a point surely came when the greater danger of popular reaction stemmed from a continued refusal to pull out. (In game-theoretical terms, the time arrived when decision makers had to re-evaluate the payoff matrix.)

In an analysis of three strands of American thinking that have led to America's "activist" role in the world, historian Arthur Schlesinger, Jr., identified two that clearly come under our heading of ideological.[8] The first he traced to the impact of Stalinism: "For many people in the 1940's this necessary and correct anticommunism hardened into a series of conditioned reflexes which continued to guide their thoughts after communism itself was beginning to be transformed under the stress of nationalism." A virtually complete consensus, the boundaries of which were narrowed by the hysteria of the McCarthy period, held for at least a decade and weakened only slowly for some years thereafter. This consensus indicated much more than a mere suspicion of or even hostility to communism, which was certainly not without good cause and which remains today. But the sense of extreme external threat does seem to have eased greatly among most elites; the content

---

[7]See James N. Rosenau, "Theorizing Across Systems: Linkage Politics Revisited," in Jonathan Wilkenfeld, ed., *Conflict Behavior and Linkage Politics* (New York: McKay, 1973). Even Bernard Cohen, at the end of a book highly critical (and appropriately so) of many assertions about the importance of public opinion as an actual constraint on decision makers, concludes with "the paradox that a policy making system which has mastered all the modes of resistance to outside opinion nevertheless seems, from a long run perspective, to accommodate to it." *The Public's Impact on Foreign Policy* (Boston: Little, Brown, 1973), p. 205.

[8]See Schlesinger's comments in Richard M. Pfeffer, ed., *No More Vietnams* (New York: Harper & Row, 1968), pp. 7–9.

analyses and especially the survey material of this book testify to that.[9]

The second major ideological strain Schlesinger identified is "liberal evangelism"—"the concept that the United States has a saving mission to the world." In Woodrow Wilson's words, "It will be our fortunate duty to establish a just democracy throughout the world."[10] We have not discussed this concept at great length in this book, largely because it is now rather uncommon. At no point in our survey or interview work did we encounter much of this sentiment. On the contrary, liberal evangelism has to a great extent receded. The best evidence for this is the much-strengthened alignment of foreign and domestic policy positions. Whereas many liberals on domestic matters once advocated an activist or interventionist foreign policy, the hawk group is now composed overwhelmingly of domestic conservatives. We documented at length in Chapter 4 the fact that it is primarily conservatives who now favor high defense spending, still approve of the Vietnam venture, and favor military action on behalf of other states threatened by communist revolts or attacks.

A third strand of thought noted by Schlesinger is certainly not devoid of ideological connotations, but fits more readily into the general category of strategic theories that we have discussed. This is "Stimsonianism," the idea that "if aggression were permitted to go unpunished in one place, this by infection would lead to a general destruction of the system of world order." Such thinking is of course part of the general adherence to the idea of collective security typical also of Woodrow Wilson and a variety of academic theorists.[11] Undoubtedly this idea has exerted a major influence on

---

[9]As one example not discussed previously, note that on page 273 of the original edition of his *The Professional Soldier* (New York: Free Press, 1958), Morris Janowitz distinguished the two principal schools of thought among the military, the "absolutists" and the "pragmatists," by whether the considered foreign policy aims of the Soviet Union were world conquest or merely "expansionist." In our survey of military officers, 36 percent stated that they considered communist nations to be generally *defensive* rather than expansionist.

[10]Note also the rhetoric of the early Marshall Plan days, describing it as "infinitely more than a policy of containment of Soviet-Communist expansion," also "a constructive policy of building throughout the free world the conditions not only of peace but of a good life." From Joseph Marion Jones, *The Fifteen Weeks: February 21–June 5, 1947* (New York: Harcourt Brace & World, 1955), pp. 265–266, cited in Robert A. Packenham, *Liberal America and the Third World: Political Development Ideas in Foreign Aid and Social Science* (Princeton, N.J.: Princeton University Press, 1973), pp. 317–318.

[11]See, for example, Arend Lijphart, "The Structure of the Theoretical Revolution in International Relations," *International Studies Quarterly* 18, No. 1 (March 1974): 41–74.

American thinking, as evidenced in our content analysis. But now, we suspect, among American elites like our businessmen, this idea too is at ebb tide. Recall, for example, the answers to our questions about readiness to assist various countries if they were attacked by communist forces.

Some Roots of Anti-interventionism

We believe, therefore, that this change in attitudes is likely to last for some time, that it represents not a point in the yearly up-or-down fluctuation that may occur in economic activities, but something more akin to one extreme, peak or trough, in a long-term business cycle. Moreover, this skepticism about intervention, collective security, and the need for heavy military expenditures has deep roots in the conservative tradition of American business. It may well be that the majority opinion in business circles during the early cold war years was strongly in favor of defense preparedness and the acceptance of overseas military and political commitments; there really is no satisfactory way, at this time, to measure very precisely the degree of adherence to these principles at that time, more than twenty years ago. Nevertheless, influential voices were raised against them in the business and financial community, using terminology that seems applicable today; indeed, these views do not differ substantially from some of the ones we uncovered in our 1973 survey and interviews. For example, great concern was expressed in conservative circles during the 1950s that excessive military spending might bankrupt the economy, and there was widespread enthusiasm for the efforts of George Humphrey, Dwight Eisenhower's Secretary of the Treasury, to get "more bang for a buck" with the nuclear "new look." The following three comments convey these sentiments:

The idea of boosting defense spending to make more prosperity represents a rather crude approach to economics. Military spending is a necessary evil; it produces little of value to the economy. To use it in this way is just wasteful pump priming, and the reward of pump priming is pretty poor anyway. They [Kennedy Democrats] act like we are just emerging out of the depression.[12]

America could be defeated without firing a shot if economic solvency were allowed to go down the drain of ruinous inflation or if the glory and strength of our economy, its free, individualistic character, should be lost in a jungle of state controls.[13]

---

[12]*Wall Street Journal*, editorial, July 12, 1960, p. 12.
[13]*Wall Street Journal*, editorial by W. H. Chamberlain, May 29, 1953, p. 6.

Spending for military purposes means inflationary pressures on your own economy . . . those pressures may be as dangerous as the direct military threat of Russia. At some level extra amounts may weaken you more economically than it strengthens you militarily.[14]

Another editorial comment feared the consequences of American military commitments to allies. It warned of the "commitments unlimited" in the United States-Philippines mutual defense treaty and declared that "drawing lines" was no solution to the American security problem, for the Soviet Union might involve the United States in other wars. It cautioned that the American people must be advised of the total implications of their commitments: "They are entitled to know the cost of totality—in manpower, money, and freedom of action."[15] Another editorial counseled that "You cannot always contain communism because you do not have the manpower to do it or refuse to pour what manpower you have into an impracticable venture."[16] Most poignantly, at a time of fear of an American military intervention on behalf of the French in Indochina, readers were warned that a ground war would be long and difficult, and would have an uncertain outcome: "Are we to set ourselves up alone to save Asia from the Asians?"[17] Surely other comments appeared in the business press approving the military commitments or urging intervention; we have seen many of them and could have quoted them also. We are not here totaling up the ayes and the nays. What is relevant is the fact that there is an authentic, "respectable" strand of business conservatism—represented here especially in the East Coast *Wall Street Journal*—to which current anti-intervention sentiment in the business and financial community is the heir. With such ideological roots, current sentiment is not likely to be ephemeral.

We want to return to the argument of many liberals as well as Marxists, which is outlined in Chapter 2, that a conservative ideology is consistent with a preference for high military spending.

---

[14]*Business Week*, December 15, 1951, p. 24.

[15]*Wall Street Journal*, September 5, 1951, p. 8.

[16]*Wall Street Journal*, September 13, 1950, p. 8. Many of these comments, incidentally, sound like the "pragmatic" mainstream that Kadushin, op. cit., pp. 168 ff., identifies with the American intellectual elite's thinking about foreign affairs.

[17]*Wall Street Journal*, April 19, 1954, p. 14. For recent discussions of the tradition of "conservative isolationism," see Ronald Radosh, *Prophets on the Right: Conservative Critics of American Globalism* (New York: Simon and Schuster, 1975); and Thomas G. Paterson, ed., *Cold War Critics* (Chicago: Quadrangle, 1971), especially Henry W. Berger, "Senator Taft Dissents from Military Escalation."

At first blush we might expect conservatives to oppose all forms of big government, and surely some do. But, it is alleged, the reasons why many do not are that (1) defense preparedness accords with their general anticommunist ideology; (2) defense preparedness bolsters them against Soviet or other communist threats to their specific economic interests at home and especially abroad; (3) defense is an "acceptable" form of state spending because it maintains a high level of aggregate demand without competing with free enterprise or weakening work incentives. Military spending thus would fill a variety of requirements for its proponents.

Some of the editorial comments just quoted, however, certainly do not accept the proposition that defense spending is good for the economy. Nor in either our survey or in the stock market analysis did we find reason to think that such beliefs were held by the majority in the business community. For example, only 33 percent of our business sample replied that even as much as a 25 percent reduction in defense spending would have an adverse effect on the American *economy*—far fewer businessmen than military officers (62 percent), and far fewer than the number of businessmen who thought that such a reduction would have an adverse effect on American *security* vis-à-vis other nations. Similarly, only 38 percent of the business sample declared that a retrenchment of United States foreign policy commitments would have a negative effect on United States economic expansion abroad—again far fewer than the number of military officers (62 percent) holding this view. We suspect, therefore, that, at least in the current climate, the third reason listed in the preceding paragraph, although still advanced by some, makes the least contribution to the success of the argument. The major contribution probably comes from the first reason, ideological anticommunism—surely including a general feeling that communism represents a threat to capitalism but not otherwise or directly linked to any economic interests. And as the sense of threat from communism and the Soviet Union seems to have declined, much of the enthusiasm for a large defense establishment has waned.

This then brings us back to the question whether businessmen largely turned against an activist foreign policy, and especially against the Vietnam war, *merely* because Vietnam did not pay. Certainly they turned against it in large part because of its appalling costs relative to any prospective benefits—costs that were economic as well as political and social. Certainly future military actions, if they promised a much more favorable cost/benefit ratio, would not be greeted with the same hostility that developed to this war during its course. How widespread or deep would be the opposition to future military interventions is simply not something we can measure with any precision. However, we do know two things. First, in *none* of our major analyses—the survey, the stock market study, or the content analysis of the business press—did we find substantial *economically based enthusiasm* for Vietnam or other military interventions at any point during the cold war. With a few exceptions, most of the evidence suggests that economic interests were basically neutral or contradictory; at worst, they provided only mildly favorable support for intervention. Support was usually given or withheld on other grounds—ideological and strategic. The vivid image of at least one instance in which intervention most certainly did not pay is now superimposed on that base of previous economic near-neutrality. Second, we have repeatedly suggested more varied additional reasons why businessmen turned against the Vietnam war. We also explained that this reversal had to be intellectualized so that it would be consistent with other attitudes, and that consequently other attitudes on foreign policy frequently were also changed.

Generational and cyclical interpretations are part of the picture. As we explained in our brief historical sketch at the end of Chapter 4, with the establishment of an anticommunist consensus in the early cold war years, the historic far left in America was shattered. Radicals strained, or were forced, to prove their loyalty. In doing so they not only accepted this foreign policy consensus, but they abandoned or muted criticism of domestic American institutions—particularly criticisms of the working of the capitalist economy. To continue that kind of criticism would give the McCarthyites ample opportunity to question their loyalty. With most of the critics silenced, the traditional leftist concerns with poverty and injustice were neglected—so much so that by the late 1950s Michael Harrington could create a sensation by "discovering" that poverty existed in America. (The preceding discussion implies that domestic criticism was suppressed to produce the foreign policy consensus. Many radical critics would argue that the confrontation on foreign policy was created to suppress domestic critics. The effect was the same either way.) With the advent of the 1960s, radical demands were again heard in a strength unknown since the depression of the 1930s. Focused particularly on race relations in the cities, the new radicalism made economic demands, for resource allocations, that could have been met quickly only in one way—by diverting resources away from military expenditures and other cold war preoccupations. By this reasoning the drain of Vietnam exacerbated the domestic crisis, but certainly was not its sole cause. By this reasoning many former supporters of the foreign policy consensus would have broken with it even had the Vietnam crisis never occurred. The re-emergence of "expensive" liberalism required the abandonment of cold war policies not only by people on the left, but by "Tory Radicals" as well. Many of the businessmen we questioned must be part of the latter group.[18]

We emerge from all this with a sense that an activist or interventionist foreign policy will *not* in the near future be especially *urged* upon their government by the majority of top-level American business executives. The overt use of military force is especially unlikely (except *possibly* in the Middle East), as is almost any policy that demands sustained support from the elites or the general public. Quick military operations not requiring congressional approval or the voting of new appropriations will be the least constrained.

Substantial inferential jumps remain to be made from opinion as elicited in the course of the various studies described in this volume to predictions about elites' actions or advice in crisis situations or under circumstances in which specific interests are actually at stake. It may well be that under such circumstances a small minority with strong economic interests might carry the day against a much larger group of less active, less vocal, or less concerned individuals with different policy preferences. We noted this problem at the beginning of the book, and it cannot be resolved without utilizing a different mode of research that would, at best, encounter enormous difficulties. However, we can say with some certainty that individuals seeking so to defend their economic interests would require at least the passive support and acquiescence of many others whose interests were much less immediate. On the basis of our findings, we believe that the bulk of such support, if it emerged, would come not so much from those with some vaguely similar economic interests (either holdings elsewhere in the world, or merely the economic interests generally attributable to

---

[18]We owe the formulation of many points in this paragraph to a cogent statement by our colleague H. Bradford Westerfield. Barrington Moore has suggested that "especially in the most powerful business circles . . . those in the seats of economic power [are] actively looking for just what concessions to make." *Reflections on the Causes of Human Misery and upon Some Proposals to Eliminate Them* (Boston: Beacon, 1972), p. 160.

businessmen, by definition), as from the ideological brotherhood of those who, whatever their occupation or material interest, shared a similar world view.

More pointedly, our material, especially that obtained in the survey and interviews, indicates that foreign policy is generally not terribly important to most businessmen, whether they be hawks or doves. In this they probably are like most other Americans of this era. The author of a recent article in *Fortune* stated this view of the prospects for American foreign policy:

We are not going to tear up all those defense treaties, dismantle all those bases, bring home all those ships from the Western Pacific and those troops from Germany—thereby inviting the revival of Soviet (and other) aggressions. Nor are we going to turn our backs on $80 billion of direct U.S. investment abroad and on $90 billion of annual foreign trade. . . .

At the same time, the United States'

. . . shrinking of military presence is a sign not of our weakness but of increasing Asian strength—continuance at the old level might have stimulated Chinese paranoia and stunted the movement of other Asian countries toward accepting fuller responsibility.[19]

This same article nevertheless expressed a very real fear of isolationism among the general public. To apply the term "isolationist" to the businessmen we have studied here would be an overstatement and a distortion. They retain great interest in overseas economic opportunities, and many of them have a wide range of personal and cultural contacts throughout the world. Although they are not particularly hawkish or likely to press for hawkish policies, neither are they especially dovish or likely to fight hard for dovish policies. A certain "insularity" is perceptible. The business of American businessmen is business, and perhaps domestic politics.

By this interpretation they are likely, in company with other Americans, to be reluctant to approve the kind of military expenditures typical of previous decades, or to provide ready and sustained support to the Executive branch for vigorous foreign policy initiatives—the ready rallying around the flag that past crises produced.[20] Such lack of enthusiasm cannot, however, be equated with a more positive or direct constraint on some aspects of foreign policy, or

---

[19]Max Ways, "The 'National Interest' in a Multipolar World," *Fortune* 85, No. 6 (June 1972): 74.

[20]For further evidence of a decline, among the populace in general, of a sense of foreign threat (e.g., danger of war, threats posed by communism, the Soviet Union, or China), see William Watts and Lloyd A. Free, eds., *State of the Nation* (New York: Universe, 1973), p. 39.

a constraint that is peculiarly more characteristic of businessmen than of other American elites. There is little or no evidence in this study that businessmen will be a particular restraining force. We can nevertheless refer to our discussion, in the opening chapter, of why the new attitudes emerging among all elites will have some important effects on foreign policy formulation and execution. At the least, and especially if "democratic" theories are given credence, these attitudes greatly reduce the previous impetus, with its roots both in ideology and in strategic concepts, to an activist foreign policy.

Many radical critics do not draw much distinction between liberals and conservatives in America because they consider that range of views to be too narrow to encompass the kind of alternative policies that ought to be envisaged. Marxists insist that both liberal and conservative "ideologies" are derived from capitalist interests. Thus they might not anticipate the great importance (we found) of domestic ideology in determining different foreign policy preferences. Or if they did anticipate it, they might say that it did not lead to a sufficiently wide spectrum of foreign policy options—that the result was merely different styles of imperialism with the same basic goals.

We agree that in many respects the range of domestic and foreign policy options considered by most Americans is far too narrow. And we do not doubt that economic interests contribute importantly to narrowing that range; large-scale nationalization of industry, for example, is rarely contemplated. We are sure too that the long-run survival of mankind requires the most serious consideration of an extraordinarily wide spectrum of options, and an abandonment of the traditional view of world politics as being the interaction of always-sovereign nation-states. Certainly the current hawk–dove range is desperately lacking in the rigor and imagination of thinking that will be demanded. Very likely, all our existing political and economic institutions will have to change almost beyond what we could recognize if we could see them centuries hence. Yet we cannot agree that the contemporary distinctions are irrelevant to our near-term survival prospects. For those who think they are, we can allow Professor Georgi Arbatov, Director of the Institute for the Study of the U.S.A. of the Soviet Academy of Sciences, to reply:

It is important to distinguish, above all, between the "non"-communism intrinsic to the bourgeoisie and the petty bourgeoisie and the bellicose "anti"-communism of the most reactionary and aggressive circles of imperialism. . . . For the working class they may signify a distinction between a terrorist dictatorship of the fascist type and a bourgeois democracy (even a curtailed one under monopoly rule), while for the socialist countries and all the peoples of the world they spell the difference between a thermonuclear war and a policy envisaging methods of struggle in the world that would not undermine the principles of peaceful coexistence of states with different systems. Thus, although it is a question of a distinction of a tactical nature, these distinctions may be and are (particularly in the present epoch) of very great significance.[21]

"Real" Interests of America and the World

At this point it seems appropriate to conclude with some brief personal comments about the implications of our findings for the pursuit of a foreign policy compatible with "real" American or global "interests." Obviously there are myriad "national interests," with as many assessments as assessors. Any such evaluation as this is bound to be subjective, reflecting the writers' own prejudices.

If we were to limit the discussion to East-West superpower relations, we would not find ourselves very disturbed, and would even be heartened by the new attitudes. It seems to us that cold war anticommunism has long outlived whatever usefulness it had. Renewed efforts for détente are essential and are to be welcomed; and the relatively recent shift in mood makes them easier if not imperative for American leaders. This does indeed imply some fairly relaxed assessments about the degree to which the communist powers will be able, or rather unable, to pose really serious threats to really serious American interests in the next decade or two. It is one thing to be alert to external threats, as a country must always be in a world of nation-states, and to recognize the dangerous elements of hostile ideologies and nuclear power centers. It would be another to behave like the ram one of us recently witnessed. It saw a reflection of itself on the shiny surface of an automobile. When it glowered, the "other ram" of course glowered back. When it butted the glowering image the "other ram" butted back at the same time. The "fight" continued until the "aggressor-defender" finally departed with a sore head.

If American society is to be reformed in the direction of greater egalitarianism, as we hope it will be, such reform almost surely can be accomplished only by a reduction in the perception of external dangers to the nation's security. We doubt that the civil liberties of an open society can long endure the extreme perception

---

[21]*The War of Ideas in Contemporary International Relations* (Moscow: Progress, 1973), pp. 225–226.

of danger that characterized the worst of the cold war era. Moreover, one of us has previously documented the degree to which military spending in the United States has come largely at the expense of alternative expenditures for capital investment and for raising the level of national education and health.[22]

But a focus merely on domestic politics and on great power relations is myopic. It seems to us that the truly grave problems of international politics concern not relations among the "haves"— America, the Soviet Union, Europe, Japan, and even in some respects China—but rather relations between the rich and the poor. We live in a world of rising frustration as development efforts falter while images of rich people living well in their Northern Hemisphere citadels are diffused ever more widely across the globe. Modern communications have come to the slums, barrios, and bustees of the third world not in sufficient force to bring substantial economic development, but sufficiently to bring information about how well a rich minority is managing. The crumbling of traditional religious beliefs and respect for authority has meant that these rising frustrations are accompanied by a falling threshold of tolerance for frustration. The weapons of destruction come increasingly into the hands of those who are ready to use them. Sometimes those hands control governments, but more often now they control nongovernmental or transnational organizations quite prepared to take actions for which they cannot effectively be held responsible. The IRA, the Palestinian guerillas, and the Tupamaros are portents of things to come—movements whose grievances are deeply felt and often widely acknowledged as just. Cheap and abundant nuclear weapons lie in our future. Some transnational actors, and even some governments of poor states, may be quite prepared to go out with a

---

[22]Bruce M. Russett, *What Price Vigilance? The Burdens of National Defense* (New Haven, Conn.: Yale University Press, 1970), ch. 5; also Jong Ryool Lee, "Changing National Priorities of the United States," in Russett and Stepan, eds., op. cit. The process of arriving at a condition of reduced threat-perception is not, however, riskless—particularly in a period when economic pressures are imposing severe tensions on the political system. Note the remarks of Harold Lasswell in an essay that ought still to be read today: "If in the older industrial nations 'peace at any price' movements begin to win significant support, it is safe to predict that police measures will be strengthened against 'subversion.' The 'political vacuum' created by withdrawals of identification may be occupied, therefore, not by anticoercive elements, but rather by persons and programs having a militantly nationalistic coloration." "The Garrison-State Hypothesis Today," in Samuel P. Huntington, ed., *Changing Patterns of Military Politics* (New York: Free Press, 1962), p. 57.

nuclear bang if their frustrations cannot be assuaged. At the moment, the world system of political organization is not even remotely prepared to cope either with the violent symptoms of frustration or with the basic human needs that underlie them. The standard military procedures are unlikely to be effective here.[23] Nor is the world ready to deal with the enormous problems of global pollution, resource depletion, and population growth. These problems are not apparent in the structure of power relations as, for example, presented in Chapter 1, but they are real.

An America that turns away from the world, in a political if not an economic sense, will hardly make a sufficient contribution. The current disillusionment with foreign aid is illustrative. There is general agreement that the United States foreign economic assistance program has failed either to achieve the goals it has set for itself or the goals that it should have set for itself. As a result, its political backing—always tenuous at best—has evaporated, and economic aid as a proportion of gross national product has fallen from a peak of 1.6 in the Marshall Plan years, or even .8 percent in 1962, to .3 percent at present.[24] Perhaps that in itself is just as well; perhaps the program was a misguided effort that could not treat the true causes of international poverty and inequality. But the tragedy is that nothing very much is coming up to replace it.

In some respects it may be better that the United States do nothing rather than continue some of the wrong actions it has been performing; better, for example, that it cease certain kinds of intervention. But that cessation alone would constitute a rather minimal achievement. It is doubtful that the world's peoples will wait patiently for Americans to come naturally to their next period of great outward looking. We can already see clearly the silhouette of the world to come.

---

[23]For some comments on this, see Bruce M. Russett, *Power and Community in World Politics* (San Francisco: W. H. Freeman, 1974), ch. 9; and Karl W. Deutsch, "Between Sovereignty and Integration: Conclusions," *Government and Opposition* 9, No. 1 (Winter 1974): 113–119.

[24]U.S. Bureau of the Census, *Statistical Abstract of the United States, 1974* (Washington, D.C.: Government Printing Office, 1974), p. 787. According to a survey in 1973, only 13 percent of American adults thought the United States government was doing "more than it should . . . to fight domestic poverty," but 44 percent thought it was doing "more than it should . . . to fight poverty in other parts of the world." See Paul A. Laudicina, *World Poverty and Development: A Survey of American Opinion* (Washington, D.C.: Overseas Development Council, 1973), p. 97.

Appendix

This Appendix includes the business and military questionnaires, showing the percentages of responses or, where appropriate, the means. ("No answer" responses were eliminated from percentaging. Except for item 37 asked of the businessmen, such responses always amounted to well under 5 percent.) Asterisks denote business-military differences that are statistically significant at the .01 level.

The Appendix also includes a copy of the coding sheet used in the content analysis, and a list of the military journals that were analyzed.

Business and Military Survey Responses

	Business	*Military*
1. Which *one* of the following do you consider the most important approach to world peace?		
a. Trade, technical cooperation, economic inter-dependence	61.5	*44.1**
b. Narrowing the gap between rich and poor nations	7.8	*4.1*
c. Strengthening of international institutions	6.2	*5.9*
d. Military superiority of the U.S.	10.9	*15.8**
e. Collective security through alliance	1.8	*6.3**
f. Efforts to achieve a balance (equilibrium) of power	8.6	*22.1**
g. Arms control	3.2	*1.8*

2. Which *one* of the following major forces do you consider most important as a cause of war?

		Business	Military
a.	Human nature (aggressive, irrational, selfish, etc.)	23.2	21.9
b.	Nationalism (in developed and less developed countries)	20.8	18.4
c.	Ideology	14.9	16.0
d.	Economics (scarcity, drive for profits, technical dynamism)	19.4	25.0*
e.	Power politics	21.7	18.8

3. How would you estimate the probability of U.S. involvement in war during the next decade?

			*
a.	Highly probable	5.0	4.2
b.	Probable	13.8	25.3
c.	50–50	33.1	28.7
d.	Improbable	40.7	38.4
e.	Highly improbable	7.4	3.4

4. Where do you think international conflict in the decade is *most* likely to occur?

a.	Between nuclear superpowers (U.S., U.S.S.R., China)	2.3	1.5
b.	Between a superpower and one or more less developed countries	13.9	16.3
c.	Between less developed countries	83.8	82.3

5. What type of war is *most* likely to be fought by the U.S. in the next decade?

a.	Strategic nuclear exchange	0.4	0.5
b.	War with tactical nuclear but no strategic nuclear strikes	8.9	3.3*
c.	Major non-nuclear war	17.8	20.3
d.	Counter-insurgency	58.8	68.3*
e.	Major domestic civil disturbance in the United States that would involve the Armed Forces	14.1	7.6*

6. Below is a list of some of the major problems facing the United States today. Place a *1* by the one you consider the most serious. Mark the second most serious with a *2* and so on, *ranking all five:*

		Means	
a.	Military and technological advances of China and Russia	3.7	2.7*
b.	National and socialist movements in less developed countries	3.2	3.3
c.	World ecological problems: pollution and population pressures	3.1	3.3
d.	Domestic order and stability	2.3	2.6*
e.	Social and racial disparities within the U.S.	2.7	3.1*

7. Do you think the external and internal threats of communism to U.S. security have increased, decreased, or remained the same over the last decade?

	Increased		Remained the same		Decreased	
	Business	Military	Business	Military	Business	Military
a. External threat of communism	15.0	20.7	27.2	39.7	57.8	39.6*
b. Internal threat of communism	22.7	16.7	27.3	51.3	50.0	32.0

Do you agree or disagree with the following statements:

	Business	Military
8. Ground combat is no longer an effective means of settling disputes.		*
a. Agree strongly	15.1	2.4
b. Agree with qualifications	43.8	17.7
c. Disagree with qualifications	33.5	48.1
d. Disagree strongly	7.7	31.8
9. The United States should seek agreement to mutually dismantle alliances such as NATO and the Warsaw Pact.		*
a. Agree strongly	6.1	2.1
b. Agree with qualifications	28.1	20.2
c. Disagree with qualifications	39.8	35.1
d. Disagree strongly	26.0	42.6
10. The United States must always keep ahead of the Russians in strategic nuclear weapons.		*
a. Agree strongly	31.5	23.0
b. Agree with qualifications	46.3	51.2
c. Disagree with qualifications	20.3	24.1
d. Disagree strongly	2.0	1.6
11. The United States has sometimes contributed to the escalation of the cold war by overreacting to Soviet moves or military developments.		
a. Agree strongly	14.1	11.1
b. Agree with qualifications	37.8	46.5
c. Disagree with qualifications	29.6	27.7
d. Disagree strongly	18.5	14.7
12. The revolutionary forces in the "third world" are now basically nationalistic rather than controlled by the U.S.S.R. or China.		*
a. Agree strongly	23.8	22.0
b. Agree with qualifications	50.2	61.5

	Business	Military
c. Disagree with qualifications	19.7	14.9
d. Disagree strongly	6.3	1.6

13. The U.S. should be prepared to accept socialist governments in Latin America even if the communists play an important role in them.

a. Agree strongly	16.3	11.8
b. Agree with qualifications	61.9	66.3
c. Disagree with qualifications	15.9	17.7
d. Disagree strongly	5.9	4.2

14. At present, communist nations are generally expansionist rather than defensive in their foreign policy aims.

a. Agree strongly	21.6	12.8
b. Agree with qualifications	43.4	51.1
c. Disagree with qualifications	31.4	32.5
d. Disagree strongly	3.6	3.6

15. Poverty in the United States is now mainly due to cultural and psychological problems of the poor.

a. Agree strongly	16.2	10.7
b. Agree with qualifications	41.2	42.6
c. Disagree with qualifications	29.6	35.9
d. Disagree strongly	12.9	10.8

16. Differences in income between people in this country should be reduced.

a. Agree strongly	6.9	6.5
b. Agree with qualifications	29.0	31.8
c. Disagree with qualifications	37.5	42.7
d. Disagree strongly	26.5	19.0

17. Marijuana should be legalized.

a. Agree strongly	6.1	3.7
b. Agree with qualifications	24.8	25.0
c. Disagree with qualifications	20.5	21.4
d. Disagree strongly	48.6	49.9

18. Supreme Court decisions of the 1960's have imposed excessive restrictions on the police.

a. Agree strongly	49.6	39.8
b. Agree with qualifications	35.8	44.0
c. Disagree with qualifications	11.4	13.2
d. Disagree strongly	3.2	2.9

19. Practices of the FBI and military intelligence in recent years pose a threat to civil liberties.

	Business	Military *
a. Agree strongly	9.3	2.3
b. Agree with qualifications	21.2	15.3
c. Disagree with qualifications	40.4	44.5
d. Disagree strongly	29.1	37.9

20. The main cause of Negro riots in the cities is white racism.

	Business	Military
a. Agree strongly	1.8	2.3
b. Agree with qualifications	15.7	14.7
c. Disagree with qualifications	47.2	44.2
d. Disagree strongly	35.4	38.9

21. Racial integration in the schools is proceeding too rapidly.

	Business	Military *
a. Agree strongly	10.1	7.1
b. Agree with qualifications	34.0	27.8
c. Disagree with qualifications	46.3	50.3
d. Disagree strongly	9.6	14.7

22. In the event that one of the following nations is attacked by foreign communist forces *or* is faced with a serious insurgency problem led by an indigenous communist movement, *and* requests U.S. help, there are 3 courses of action the U.S. might take:
1. Use military force to extend all needed help
2. Provide help, but short of U.S. military involvement
3. Stay out

Please *indicate the number of the course of action 1, 2, or 3,* you think the U.S. should take for each nation.

Means

	a. Foreign communist invasion		b. Communist insurgency	
	Business	Military	Business	Military
Brazil	1.7	1.3*	2.3	1.9*
India	2.5	2.4*	2.7	2.6*
Japan	1.8	1.2*	2.3	1.9*
Mexico	1.3	1.1*	1.9	1.5*
Thailand	2.4	1.7*	2.6	2.0*
West Germany	1.6	1.1*	2.2	1.7*
Yugoslavia	2.5	2.3*	2.8	2.6*

23. Please indicate the relative importance you believe the U.S. should attach, in general, to the following policy objectives in its involvement with under-developed countries. If a choice must be made, which ones should be considered most important? *Use the Numbers 1–7* with a *1* being the *highest* rank. (Please do not assign equal ranks to objectives; assume there must be a choice):

	Business	*Military*
		Means
a. A stable government capable of preserving in-ternal order	2.3	*1.9**
b. A government which is neutral or pro-American in its foreign policy	4.0	*3.6**
c. Rapid economic development	4.4	*4.8**
d. A government which maintains civil liberties	3.7	*3.8*
e. A government which retains the free enterprise system	4.5	*5.1**
f. A government which will not engage in unpro-voked aggression against other nations	3.3	*3.0**
g. A government which allows broad opportunities for American business investment	5.7	*5.7*

24. Which of these positions best describe your views about military and economic commitments abroad? Please check each question.

	Business	*Military*
a. Economic aid appropriations (includes economic advisors, credits, commodities, etc.)		*
1) Increase	12.6	*27.8*
2) Keep at present level	33.8	*49.3*
3) Decrease	53.6	*22.9*
b. Military aid appropriations (military advisors and equipment)		*
1) Increase	1.8	*21.0*
2) Keep at present level	27.3	*48.8*
3) Decrease	70.9	*30.2*
c. U.S. troops in Europe		*
1) Increase	1.1	*1.4*
2) Keep at present level	8.0	*20.0*
3) Decrease unilaterally	20.4	*9.0*
4) Decrease if Mutual Balanced Force Reduc-tion accord is reached	58.8	*68.3*
5) Total withdrawal	11.7	*1.3*
d. U.S. troops in Asia		
1) Increase	1.1	*1.3*
2) Keep at present level	49.5	*41.0*
3) Total withdrawal	46.8	*3.4*
4) Decrease [omitted by error in business questionnaire]	2.7	*54.4*

	Business	*Military*
25. In the next 5 years should the level of U.S. defense spending be:		*
a. Raised substantially, by 25% or more	2.3	*3.4*
b. Raised somewhat, less than 25%	17.6	*39.3*
c. Kept about the same	26.7	*42.8*
d. Reduced somewhat, less than 25%	35.3	*10.6*
e. Reduced substantially, by 25% or more	15.2	*1.6*
f. Other	2.8	*2.3*

26. Do you think a 25% reduction in defense spending would have an adverse effect on American security vis-à-vis other nations?		*
a. Yes	52.3	*92.9*
b. No	36.0	*6.3*
c. Don't know	11.7	*0.8*

27. Do you think a 25% reduction in defense spending would have an adverse effect upon the American economy?		*
a. Yes	33.2	*62.1*
b. No	59.4	*31.1*
c. Don't know	7.4	*6.8*

28. Which of the following do you think the government should do to protect the investments of American businesses in less developed countries? Check *as many* (if any) *as appropriate.*		
a. Government insurance	44.7	*23.2**
b. Diplomatic or economic action to prevent expropriation or ensure just compensation	78.3	*85.7**
c. Military action to prevent expropriation or ensure just compensation	4.1	*6.3*
d. Nothing	9.2	*9.8*

29. Do you think a retrenchment of U.S. foreign policy commitments would have a negative effect on U.S. economic expansion abroad?		*
a. Yes	38.3	*61.9*
b. No	47.0	*29.3*
c. Don't know	14.7	*8.8*

30. Do you personally think it was correct for the U.S. to send ground combat troops to Vietnam?		*
a. Yes	37.2	*70.1*
b. No	52.7	*27.6*
c. Don't know	10.1	*2.3*

	Business	Military
31. Can you recollect approximately how long you have held this view? Since:		
a. The beginning of the war	52.1	58.3
b. 1965	10.9	15.9
c. 1966	4.7	6.5
d. 1967	7.3	4.2
e. 1968	6.7	6.0
f. 1969	5.1	3.1
g. 1970	7.5	2.8
h. 1971	4.2	1.6
i. 1972 or later	1.5	1.8

32. Which *one* of the following considerations do you regard as most important in the formulation of your opinion given in question #30 above?

	Business	Military
a. Consequences for the U.S. economy	4.8	2.1
b. Consequences for U.S. social and political institutions	30.0	14.5*
c. Consequences for you personally	0.2	0.2
d. Consequences for the Vietnamese people	15.7	26.9*
e. Consequences for U.S. image as an ally	20.1	36.9*
f. Poor prospects of victory	9.7	10.1
g. Poor prospects of victory without a still larger commitment	12.4	7.6*
Other and no answer	7.1	1.8

(Asked of Businessmen Only)

33. Do you think on the whole the Vietnam war was good or bad for the *economy* in general?

a. Good	8.9
b. Bad	77.1
c. No substantial effect	14.0

34. If you answered "bad" to #33, would your answer be the same if inflation had been controlled?

a. Yes	42.4
b. No	27.9
c. Don't know and not applicable	29.7

35. Do you think that on the whole the Vietnam war was good or bad for American *social and political institutions?*

a. Good	5.8

b. Bad   87.4
c. No substantial effect   6.7

36. Do you think that on the whole *you* are better or
    worse off as a result of the Vietnam war?
    a. Better   8.8
    b. Worse   50.1
    c. Same   41.1

37. Why? [*Open-ended for responses*]

38. Do you think American business involvement in
    foreign markets and foreign investment will in-
    crease substantially in the next decade?
    a. Yes   83.4
    b. No   12.6
    c. Don't know   3.9

39. Do you think that American sales and investments
    in less developed countries will increase or de-
    crease relative to American sales and investments
    in developed countries?
    a. Increase   61.8
    b. Decrease   19.2
    c. Don't know   19.0

40. Do you think that American business transactions
    with Russia and/or China will increase substan-
    tially over the next decade?
    a. Increase   97.7
    b. Decrease   0
    c. Don't know   2.3

41. Do you anticipate that *your own firm* will increase
    the proportion of its activities abroad in the next
    decade?
    a. Yes   72.8
    b. No   23.8
    c. Don't know   3.4

42. Do you anticipate that *your own firm's* activities in
    less developed countries will increase relative to
    its activities in developed countries?
    a. Yes   37.0
    b. No or Don't know   63.0

43. Do you think that *your own firm's* activities with Russia and/or China will increase substantially over the next decade?
    a. Yes   43.7
    b. No   42.5
    c. Don't know   13.8

44. Did foreign business (*excluding* Canada) account for more than 25%, 10–25%, or less than 10% of *your own firm's* sales (or assets, if more appropriate)?
    a. More than 25%   17.5
    b. 10–25%   20.8
    c. Less than 10%   61.7

45. What is your age?
    a. 20–29   0.9
    b. 30–39   5.7
    c. 40–49   29.7
    d. 50–59   47.6
    e. 60–69   16.2

46. Have you ever served in the armed forces?
    a. Yes   73.5
    b. No   26.5

47. When? Check *first* service only.
    a. Since 1964   1.2
    b. Between 1954 and 1964   7.5
    c. Between 1950 and 1953   8.4
    d. Between 1946 and 1949   3.1
    e. Between 1940 and 1945   76.1
    f. Before 1940   3.6

48. Highest rank:
    a. As enlisted man only   16.2
    b. As a non-commissioned officer   17.6
    c. As a commissioned officer below the rank of brigadier general or rear admiral   65.8
    d. As a general or fleet officer   0.4

49. Are you currently serving in a reserve unit?
    a. Yes   1.7
    b. No   98.3

Thank you for your help. If you wish to clarify or amplify any of your answers, please use the space below or on the back.

(Asked of Military Officers Only)

33. Statement a. and statement b. below represent two different ways of viewing violent conflict. With which view are you in closest agreement?
    a. Man is selfish, and his selfishness inevitably leads to violent conflict.
    b. Violent conflict is the product of social conditions and hence is not inevitable.

    1) Strongly agree with a. rather than b.   *9.9*
    2) Agree with a. rather than b. with qualifications   *34.3*
    3) Agree with b. rather than a. with qualifications   *46.1*
    4) Strongly agree with b. rather than a.   *9.7*

34. What should the Armed Forces involvement in nonmilitary tasks be? Choose one of the six levels of involvement listed below for each task.

    Extensive involvement   6
    Major involvement   5
    Some involvement   4
    Minor involvement   3
    Minimal involvement   2
    No involvement   1

    a. Participate directly with troops and equipment in the solution of the nation's environmental problems such as pollution control, restoration of land destroyed by strip mining, and reforestation.

    b. Participate directly in the solution of social problems *within the army* through such programs as drug abuse rehabilitation, race relations programs.

    c. Participate directly in the solution of social problems *within the civilian community* through such programs as drug abuse rehabilitation, race relations programs.

    d. Participate directly in the solution of the nation's educational problems by direct involvement in existing civilian educational programs.

Means

3.0

5.2

2.7

2.4

e. Participate directly by providing assistance in the solution of the nation's law and order problems by working directly with local law enforcement agencies in riot control and related matters.   *2.8*

35. Do you think that the military will be permitted to develop and buy the new weapons they may need to protect U.S. security over the next decade?
    a. Yes   *58.2*
    b. No   *9.7*
    c. Don't know   *32.1*

36. The role of U.S. officers as advisors to their counterparts in foreign nations should be strictly limited to technical matters.
    a. Agree strongly   *7.6*
    b. Agree with qualifications   *37.2*
    c. Disagree with qualifications   *39.3*
    d. Disagree strongly   *15.9*

37. There is only one way to wear the uniform. When any deviations in dress are condoned within the services, the way is open to the destruction of all uniformity and unity.
    a. Agree strongly   *29.3*
    b. Agree with qualifications   *48.5*
    c. Disagree with qualifications   *17.7*
    d. Disagree strongly   *4.5*

38. The Armed Forces are becoming so permissive that discipline is seriously threatened.
    a. Agree strongly   *14.5*
    b. Agree with qualifications   *37.7*
    c. Disagree with qualifications   *38.5*
    d. Disagree strongly   *9.2*

39. What is the highest level of civilian education that you have *completed*?
    a. Grade school   ——
    b. Some high school   ——
    c. High school graduate   ——
    d. Some college   *2.6*
    e. College graduate   *28.9*
    f. Master's Degree   *63.5*
    g. Doctorate   *5.0*

40. What is your age?
    a. 20–29   ———
    b. 30–39   *23.3*
    c. 40–49   *76.3*
    d. 50–59   *0.3*
    e. 60–69   ———

41. Using the following choices, classify yourself with regard to your *primary* military specialty.
    a. *Executives*—Includes all commanders, directors, and planners not elsewhere classified.   *68.9* (incl. g. & h.)

    b. *Tactical Operations Officers*—Includes pilots and crews and operations staff officers.   *19.7*
    c. *Intelligence Officers*—Includes strategic, general, communications, and counterintelligence officers.
    d. *Engineering and Maintenance Officers*—Includes design, development, production, and maintenance engineering officers.   *11.3*
    e. *Scientists and Professionals*—Includes physical, biological, and social scientists, and lawyers, chaplains, and other professionals.
    f. *Medical Officers*—Includes medical doctors, dentists, nurses, veterinarians, and closely allied professional medical service officers.
    g. *Administrators*—Includes general and specialized administration and management officers.   ———
    h. *Supply, Procurement, and Allied Officers*—Includes officers in supply, procurement, and production, transportation, food service and related logistic activities not elsewhere classified.   ———

42. Military service
    Check branch and what your principal duties have been:

Army: Combat arms	*30.2*	Other	*12.6*
Navy: Line	*17.4*	Other	*3.2*
Marines: Combat arms	*6.1*	Other	*0.2*
Air Force: Rated	*23.1*	Other	*7.1*

43. What is your current grade or rank?
    a. General/Flag Officer   ———
    b. Colonel/Captain   *31.6*
    c. Lieutenant Colonel/Commander   *67.8*
    d. Major/Lieutenant Commander   *0.6*

  e. Captain/Lieutenant   ——

  f. First Lieutenant/Lieutenant (j.g.)   ——

  g. Second Lieutenant/Ensign   ——

44. Total years of active service

  a. Under 2   ——

  b. Over 2 but 5 or less   *0.5*

  c. Over 5 but 10 or less   *1.0*

  d. Over 10 but 20 or less   *57.2*

  e. Over 20   *41.4*

45. What was the source of your commission?

  a. Academy   *23.3*

  b. ROTC   *39.0*

  c. Officer Candidate School, OTS

  d. Direct   *37.7*

  e. Other

46. Have you ever served in OSD, JCS, NATO Staff, or a combined staff in the past ten years? (If more than one list the latest assignment)

  a. OSD

  b. JCS

  c. NATO Staff   *29.6*

  d. Combined Staff—Europe

  e. Combined Staff—Far East

  f. No   *70.4*

Coding Sheet for Content Analysis

Column

 1–2 Year

 3–4 Month

 5–6 Day

  7 1 Business
     2 Military

  8 If Business: periodical
     1 *Business Week*
     2 *Wall Street Journal*
     3 *Kiplinger Washington Letter*
     4 *Fortune*
     5 *Barrons*

Regarding which kind or kinds of intervention does the article express opinion?

9   Military (Scale: 0–3 code highest item *favored* only)
0 Nothing
1 Military assistance: equipment, training, advisers (including field involvement), covert operations
2 Passive troop deployment: protection of American personnel and installations; symbolic show of force; blockade; combat support action of advisers
3 Active American air, naval, or ground combat support or combat action

10   Economic sanctions (0, 1) [The numbers 0, 1 indicate absence or presence]
Withdrawal or reduction of economic aid, trade (or trade concession), investment

11   Political/diplomatic action (0, 1)
Change in official diplomatic representation
Change in level of support in regional or international organization
Alteration of treaty commitment
Executive censure or support
Any positive action by official U.S. representatives to alter composition or performance of local government
Any positive effort to negotiate between contending sides
Use of propaganda campaign to alter perceptions of the crisis
Warnings
Efforts to organize collective action

12   Unspecified (0, 1)

13   Military intervention preference (and intensity) (Scale: 1–5, favor–oppose)

Categories 1 and 5:
a. Intervention favored (1) or opposed (5) emphatically
b. Intervention favored or opposed with substantiated arguments

Categories 2 and 4:
a. Intervention favored or opposed without emphasis or without substantiated argument
b. Intervention favored or opposed with reservations in the opposite direction
c. Intervention favored by absence of contradictory arguments

Category 3:
a. Pro-con: arguments given favoring and opposing intervention with equal emphasis
b. Neutral: no opinion expressed

14   Economic intervention preference (Scale: 1–5, as col. 13)

15   Diplomatic intervention preference (Scale: 1–5, as col. 13)

16   Unspecified intervention preference (Scale: 1–5, as col. 13)

What are the writer's reasons for favoring intervention?

17   Ideological (0, 1, 2)
To prevent the spread of communism as a system of ideas
To protect or promote democracy, American ideals and way of life, values of Western civilization

Key Symbols
Communism, Bolshevism, Marxism
Communist movement, ideology, creed, system of ideas
World revolution, wars of liberation, Red tide, Red banner, and so on
Democracy, freedom, free world, liberty, popular sovereignty, self-determination
Tyranny, barbarism, totalitarianism

18   Strategic/political (0, 1)
To contain an expanding power, halt aggression or use of force
To protect or promote the national interest, power, or security of the United States or an ally of the United States
To secure regional or international stability, order, peace, balance of power
To fulfill American commitment to party to conflict, region, ally, or international organization
To maintain or improve American image or credibility

Key Symbols
Power, balance of power (United States hegemony)
Prestige, image, credibility
Commitment, responsibility
National interest
Balance of power, equilibrium, stability, order, peace
Aggression, expansion, conquest, imperialism

19   Economic (0, 1)
Domestic United States economy
United States investments, trade, raw-material sources
Economy or economic interests of ally
Defense of free enterprise, private property generally, capitalism

20   Other Reasons—nationalism, self-determination, general moral reasons (without reference to above specifics) (0, 1)

21   Does one rationale predominate? If so, indicate. Code even if only one
      rationale given
      1 Ideological
      2 Strategic
      3 Economic
      4 Other

What are the writer's reasons for opposing intervention?

22   Ideological (0, 1, 2) [*Numbers indicate absence, possible presence,
      definite presence*]
      Same as for col. 17

23   Strategic (0, 1)
      Same as for col. 18 but include also pragmatic cost-benefit calcu-
      lations:
          Unlikelihood of success, achieving policy goals, impractical, un-
          feasible
          Disadvantages, difficulties, uncertainties, problems, poor cost/gain
          ratio, high cost, dangers such as risk of greater war
          Government to be protected or supported unable or unwilling to
          make use of support
          Unlikelihood of allied support
          Intervention will make matters worse or create more problems than
          it solves, damage United States interests

24   Economic (0, 1)
      Same as for col. 19

25   Nationalism, self-determination, internal matter, general moral rea-
      sons (without reference to specific considerations as in preceding
      columns or in col. 26). (0, 1)

26   Absence of reason to intervene, not necessary, not sufficiently im-
      portant to United States, does not endanger United States security.
      A clear statement of disinterest, more than simply cost/benefit calcu-
      lations as in col. 23. (0, 1)

27   Does one rationale predominate? If so, indicate. Code even if only one
      rationale given
      1 Ideological
      2 Strategic
      3 Economic
      4 Nationalism, internal matter
      5 Disinterest, absence of reason

28   How is revolt or attack characterized?
1 External attack
2 Internal revolt substantially fomented or aided from the outside
3 Primarily internal revolt with only slight or no outside aid

29   How are rebels or attackers (i.e., the party who is or might be intervened against) characterized?
1 Communist, communist-dominated
2 Procommunist, "tools" of communists, fellow travelers, noncommunists but tools of communists. (A Nasserite rebellion would be
coded here if rebels were characterized as tools of Nasser, and
Nasser were considered a tool of Moscow.)
3 Nationalist, neutralist; communist-anticommunist dimension essentially irrelevant
4 Anticommunist, pro-United States, pro-West

30   Case
1 Greece, Turkey
2 Korea
3 Indochina (1950–1954)
4 Lebanon
5 Cuba
6 Congo
7 Vietnam
8 Dominican Republic
9 Guatemala
0 Other

List of Military Journals with Coded Articles

Air Force and Space Digest
Airman
Air University Quarterly Review
All Hands
Armed Forces Management
Armor
Army
Army Digest (formerly *Army Information Digest*)
Army, Navy and Air Force Journal and Register
For Commanders: This Changing World
Marine Corps Gazette
Naval War College Review
Navy
Officer
Ordnance
Proceedings of the U.S. Naval Institute

INDEX